A JOURNAL

OF THE

LIFE, TRAVELS, AND RELIGIOUS LABORS

OF

WILLIAM SAVERY,

A MINISTER OF THE GOSPEL OF CHRIST, OF THE SOCIETY OF FRIENDS, LATE OF PHILADELPHIA.

COMPILED FROM HIS ORIGINAL MEMORANDA,

BY JONATHAN EVANS.

STEREOTYPE EDITION.

PHILADELPHIA:
FOR SALE AT FRIENDS' BOOK-STORE,
No. 304 ARCH STREET.
1873.

PREFACE.

In perusing so interesting a narrative as is presented in the account of the Christian labors of this worthy minister of the gospel, the inquiry may arise, why it has been permitted to lie so long unprepared for the public eye? In reply to this, it may be remarked that some of his papers were for a long time mislaid, and when collected, they were placed in the hands of several persons to examine and arrange, neither of whom made an essay for accomplishing the task. They were voluminous, and a variety of engagements arising out of the peculiar state into which the religious Society of Friends here has been thrown within the last fifteen years, seemed then to preclude the practicability of undertaking the work. But from the conviction that there was much in the papers to interest and instruct the seeking, religious mind,

I was induced to transcribe those parts, and to endeavor to arrange the whole so as to form a regular account of his life and labors, so far as materials could be obtained. In the course of his travels, he was much more particular in the memoranda he made than has been customary for Friends in his station; giving a cursory description of the country, its produce, the value of it, and the habits of the people where he travelled. This peculiarity is accounted for by the fact, that his notes were made for the information and gratification of his near connections; and it would seem, without any prospect of their publication. Some of those details, which may be found in other works, have been abridged, though there is more of this description still retained than is common in most journals of Friends, but which will probably be interesting to many readers, and render the work more acceptable to them.

I was intimately acquainted with William Savery, and esteemed him as a brother beloved. His affable disposition, his catholic spirit, and his truly Christian principles, endeared him to those who knew him, and peculiarly qualified him as an instrument in the Divine hand to draw others into the love of truth, and into an obedience to the convictions of the Holy Spirit. His ministry was generally more of a doctrinal nature than that of many other Friends, accompanied with a fervent engagement that his audience might be brought to an heartfelt experience of the unspeakable love of God, in sending his dear Son, our Lord Jesus Christ, into the world to save sinners; of the efficacy of his propitiatory sacrifice and the sanctifying power of his Holy Spirit, who hath by his own blood obtained eternal redemption for all that come unto Him in true faith: at times declaring with much solemnity and reverence, that he would rather lose all he had in the world, than be robbed of his faith in the divinity of Christ.

His submission to the power of Divine love in his own heart, by which he was brought out of sin and corruption, and his indefatigable devotion to the cause of Christ, present an instructive example, calculated to invite old and young to diligence and faithfulness in the path of manifested duty, that they may become lights in the world, and through Divine mercy, be partakers of that salvation which is only obtained through our Lord Jesus Christ.

JONATHAN EVANS.

PHILADELPHIA, *Seventh month,* 1837.

TESTIMONY

Of the Monthly Meeting of Friends of Philadelphia for the Northern District, concerning WILLIAM SAVERY.

It appears that he was born in the city of Philadelphia, in the year 1750, and educated in the principles of the Christian religion as professed by us; and was placed with a Friend in the country, to learn the trade of a tanner. On his return to the city in 1771, being naturally of a lively and social disposition, he soon joined with those who, being themselves the votaries of folly and vanity, encouraged him in a departure from the simplicity of truth; which, aided by his own propensities, drew him into many deviations from the religious principles of his education. In this situation he was arrested by the powerfully convictive evidence of the Spirit of Truth; and in the year 1778, at a meeting held at Merion after an interment, was much affected, and lasting impressions were made on his mind by that solemn scene, and the testimonies then delivered.

In the autumn of that year he married in Chester county, and settled within the limits of our Monthly

Meeting—spent much of his time in retirement at home, and in the thirtieth year of his age, first opened his mouth in a public testimony; and dwelling inward with those gifts and qualifications with which he was favored, he became an able advocate for the cause in which he had embarked; and by faithful attention thereto, his labors were blessed to the benefit of numbers, especially amongst the youth, to many of whom he was an eminent instrument of good.

He was engaged to travel much on this Continent in the service of Truth, being several months in each year, from 1789 to 1795 inclusive, absent from home on Gospel errands; and by accounts received, his labors of love were to the satisfaction of those among whom his lot was cast.

Having had his mind drawn into near sympathy with the Friends at Pyrmont in Germany—with the entire unity of his brethren at home, on the 18th of the Fifth month, 1796, he embarked for Liverpool, and thence soon proceeded to London, and then to Pyrmont. After paying an acceptable visit to the comfort and strengthening of Friends there, and in some other parts of Germany, he went to Nismes in the south of France, visiting a small company of such as professed with us, in that neighborhood, much to his own comfort and peace.—Then returning to England, he visited many of the principal towns and places in that nation, Ireland and Scotland, and had large public meetings with those not of our Society. Having thus discharged his religious duty in those parts, he returned to his family and friends in the Tenth month, 1798.

He labored diligently in his temporal business for the support of his family, as well as for the relief of the poor and distressed, to whose wants his liberal mind was ever ready to administer according to his ability; yet this did not interrupt his steady attention to other religious duties, being diligent in the attendance of meetings, and in various services to which he was called and appointed, for the benefit of society and the promotion of the cause of truth and righteousness.

In 1802, the neighborhood in which he lived was visited with a pestilential disease, which carried many off in a short time. Not being easy to leave this scene of woe and misery, he voluntarily resigned himself to visit those in distress, both Friends and others, with advice and counsel, in the love of the Gospel, to the great consolation and comfort of many. A like affliction befalling that and other parts of the city and neighborhood, in the following year he was again engaged in the same manner, freely devoting himself, both night and day, to relieve the distresses of others, with which his feeling mind was deeply affected.

In the early part of his sickness he was borne up above complaining, or admitting that he was much out of health, until the disease, which proved to be a dropsy, had made such progress, that it was visible to his friends. He continued to attend to his outward concerns and religious duties; and in some of the meetings which he last attended, was led to open a prospect that his time here would not be long; but, in an animating view of a blessed immortality, signified it was no matter how short, provided this were attained.

He was remarkable for punctuality and uprightness in his dealings; and not long before his decease, said to a friend who often visited him, "It is necessary to look to our outward concerns, there are so many reproachful failures;" and appeared desirous once more to get to meeting, that he might have an opportunity to warn such of the elderly part of society who had got into the earth, and of the youth who had got into the air. "I thought," said he, "I was once strong for the work, but now I am a child, brought back to my horn-book, and have nothing to trust to but the mercy of God through Christ my Saviour." Thus reverently depending, he was preserved to the last in great resignation and composure of mind.

He was mostly confined from the 26th of the Third month, except frequently riding out for the benefit of air and exercise, till the 18th day of the Sixth month, 1804, in the evening of which he was considerably worse, continuing ill through the night, and on the 19th in the morning, about six o'clock, closed his useful life in the fifty-fourth year of his age. On the following day, his corpse, attended by a great number of his friends and neighbors, was interred in Friends' burial-ground in this city.

THE JOURNAL

OF

WILLIAM SAVERY.

CHAPTER I.

Early religious visitations—Reflections made in after life—Marriage — Renewed exercises and their effects — First appearance in the ministry—Religious visits from 1781 to 1789—Visit to S. Carolina and Georgia—Deputation to the Indians of the N. West—Address by Friends to the Indians—Journey to meet the Indians—Voyage up Niagara River and Lake Erie — Drunken Indians — Detroit — Religious Meetings—Kindness of the Officers to Friends—Gathering and appearance of the Indians — Interview with a Wyandot Chief — Great heat of weather — Horrors of Indian Wars — Repeated Disappointments — Indian Slaves — Leaves Detroit—Joins the Commissioners in Camp—Continued detention—Dangers from the Indians — Meetings on the Frontiers — Sickness — Indians decline receiving the Commissioners—Address from Friends sent to the Council — Indians refuse the terms offered by Government —Start for home—Party divides—Voyage down the St. Lawrence — Terrible Storm and suffering Night — Montreal -- St. Johns — Voyage down Lake Champlain — Sickness and Suffering—Whitehall — Journey through N. York State—Albany—Yellow Fever in Philadelphia—Voyage down the Hudson—Arrival in Philadelphia — Reward for the Sacrifices made — Interest of Friends in the Indians.

William Savery was born in the city of Philadelphia, in the year 1750; received an education in the principles of the Christian religion, and was placed with a Friend in the country to learn the tanning business. Returning to the city after the expiration of his apprenticeship, he associated with those, who, like himself, were much inclined to vanity and folly; and seeking the enjoyment of ease and pleasure in a course of life far remote from true happiness, he became less susceptible of tender impressions, and gradually much estranged to the voice and heavenly care of the great Shepherd of the sheep. In this situation it pleased Divine Goodness, by the powerful reproofs of his Spirit, so to break in upon his wandering mind, as frequently to bring him to an awful sense of the bondage of corruption wherein he was held, to some glimpse of the peace and comfort consequent upon a life of piety and virtue, and the necessity of laboring to become a participant in that redemption, which, through our Lord and Saviour Jesus Christ, is graciously extended to the sincere penitent of every name and nation.

In a review of the benighted condition in which he had been involved, and of the extension of Divine mercy in plucking him as a brand out of the burning, he says,—

"I may acknowledge, that notwithstanding my revolt and turning aside from the paths of purity and peace, the Lord has been graciously near me all my life long, and has watched over me as a tender Father for good, smitten me by his Spirit when I have been rebelling against his holy law written in my heart, making merry over the Divine witness there; and has reached to me and tendered me in the midst of mirth and jollity. He often followed me to my chamber, and upon my pillow has drawn tears of sorrow and contrition from me, when none have been privy to it but his All-seeing Eye: so that my days of joy and laughter have often produced nights of sorrow and weeping. Still I continued sinning and repenting and turning the grace of God into wantonness for a number of years, being at times favored to see, in part, the beauty there is in holiness, but fearful of incurring the scoff and scorn of the world's deluded votaries should I turn my back upon it. Activity of spirits, loose discourse and noisy mirth, were my sad refuge to drown serious reflection: yet the worm that never dieth, a wounded conscience, often embittered my sweetest draughts of pleasure. In this state I was inclined sometimes in a serious hour to read a pious author, which, I think, by the assistance of the gracious Helper, was made serviceable to me, being roused to more serious thought than ever before.

"I now saw the iniquity of mispending my precious time, and refrained from frequenting taverns and places of diversion. I struggled hard to break myself off from my fondness for much company, seeing the snare there was in it; being apt to relate adventures and tales to provoke mirth, and often for the embellishment of them to strain beyond the truth—I was much concerned to watch over myself in this, which is both dishonorable and sinful. Oh the folly of thus mispending our precious time! how watchful! how careful ought we to be of our words and actions; always remembering, that the sacred eye of an all-seeing God pervades the most secret chambers we can retire to, and his ear is ever open to hear both the evil and the good. Yea, many of the present day have known, when the terrors of the Lord have overtaken them for sin, and they have had to taste of the spirit of judgment and of burning, that every secret thing has been brought to light, and all the hidden works of darkness have been made manifest; that even for idle words they have had to render an account.

"When we have long wandered, and got far and wide from the pure path, in which the Lord's ransomed children have to walk, though it may seem to have been in small things, yet they make close trying work for us; and many deep baptisms we have to pass through, before we can witness our sins to be wiped away and cast, as it were, into the depth of the sea. When this is experienced, such have indeed cause to acknowledge with great humility of soul, that it is of the mere mercy of Him whose mercies are, (blessed be his great name,) over all his works. Some, who with myself, have been rescued as from the very jaws of the devourer, can praise his holy name with songs of gratitude and joy, knowing, that in the midst of judgment he does still remember mercy."

In the year 1778, attending a meeting at Merion, held after an interment, he was on that solemn occasion, deeply impressed with serious thoughtfulness. Being married that year, he settled in business in Philadelphia. The state of his mind about this time is described by himself nearly as follows:

"I had been employed in bringing myself to a more circumspect life, being pretty careful in my conduct and conversation, and just in my dealings among men, and was willing to believe I had attained to great matters, and that I might now take up my rest; for by my own strength, abilities and contrivance, I could not only keep up a fair upright character among men, and make my life happy and myself respected; but also, (Oh, the deceitful workings of Satan! Oh, the mystery of iniquity!) that it would, at the close of time here, gain me an inheritance in the regions of purity and peace, among all those that are sanctified. But, how can I sufficiently adore my great and good Master, for his continued regard and care over me, in that he did not suffer me to remain long in this state of delusion and error. He disturbed my false rest, and made me at times exceedingly uneasy with it, and gave me at length to see, that notwithstanding my regularity of behavior and all my boasted attainments, I fell far short of that purity, which all the vessels in the Lord's house must come to; and that I was yet under the law, which cannot make the comers thereunto perfect, not having passed under the flaming sword, nor felt the day of the Lord to be come, which burns as an oven.

"This brought great distress and anxiety of mind over me, and sometimes I was ready to doubt the truth of these divine revelations; and was exceedingly desirous to find, if possible, an easier way to peace and happiness, than by submitting myself to the cross, of which I had as yet experienced but little. I was much tossed and distressed, as one who was in a dark and howling wilderness, where I could see no way out, either to the right hand or to the left. But at length, the Lord, who indeed watched over me continually for good, blessed and praised for ever be his name, brought me into some degree of composure. The strong impression then made on my mind, its application to the state I was in, and the instruction it conveyed to me, left me no room to doubt its being divinely intended for my good. My eyes became more clearly opened to discern where I was, and that all the righteousness of my own putting on, was as filthy rags, of which I must be stript, before I could experience a putting on of that purity and righteousness, which is the fine linen of the saints. In great distress and anxiety I saw nothing for me to lean upon, but to dwell alone and keep my eye open and my spiritual ear attentive to Him, who is the unchangeable High-Priest of his people, and with whom are all the treasures of wisdom and knowledge, who knows the states of all his children, and when and where He leads them, graciously affords ability to follow, to the praise of his ever adorable name.

"It pleased Him to lead me as into the wilderness, and to give me a sight of my former disobedience and folly. Oh! the bitterness and distress that covered me when I was alone or in meetings. I experienced but few pleasant draughts of his love, my meat was gall and wormwood, and my drink of the bitter waters of Marah. This was not unfelt by some sympathizing

Friends, who were anxious that I might know an establishment upon the Rock immoveable. Thus I continued, but was still preserved desirous to know the Master's will, and in measure made willing to obey, though under the cross; yet the way to the kingdom was for some months much darkened, and a sense of my sinful conduct often brought me almost to despair of ever finding forgiveness with an offended God: and my burden in meetings was almost insupportable.

"Oh! these were times of baptism never to be forgotten in mutability. One evening, sitting in my house alone, great horror and trouble seized me—I wept aloud, and after a short time went to bed; but my distress was so great, that it almost overcame me, and I thought I tasted of the misery of fallen spirits. Not being able to contain myself, I arose and walked the room. My spirits at length being nearly exhausted, I threw myself on the bed again, but had not lain long, before I grew cold like one near death, a clammy sweat covered me, and I was to appearance stupid. In this state I was, through adorable mercy, released from the horror that before surrounded me, and was comforted with a sight and feeling of a state of inexpressible happiness and joy; and when so far come to myself as to have utterance given me, I cried aloud on this wise, Oh! now I know that my Redeemer liveth.

"Oh! the sweetness I then felt, in being favored with such an evidence of the goodness and mercy of God! It far surpassed everything I had ever before experienced, and was such that I hope to bear it in remembrance as long as I have a being here. Tears of joy ran freely down my cheeks, insomuch that I could not restrain them nor scarcely utter a word for a considerable time; and my dear partner, who shared with me in my affliction, was also made a partaker with me in my exceeding great joy. Blessed for ever be the name of the Lord, though He sees meet for our refinement to try us even to an hair's breadth, yet in our utmost extremity his all-powerful arm is made bare for our deliverance."

Being thus, in infinite mercy, brought to a living experience of the unfathomable love of God towards his poor fallen, helpless creatures, and the extension of his power for their redemption, through our Lord Jesus Christ; he was concerned to abide under his purifying baptism, that he might really know the communion of saints, and have fellowship with the Father and with his Son Jesus Christ. Having felt the terrors of the Lord for sin, it led to close watchfulness and fear, lest the enemy, through his subtlety, should draw his mind away from a steady subjection to the cross; and when disengaged from his outward avocations, he spent much of his time at home in retirement.

In the year 1779, he accompanied a Friend on a visit to the meetings of Friends in Virginia and Carolina, and as far as appears, it was about this time that he was engaged to speak a few words in meetings, by way of Gospel ministry. To a mind sincerely desirous of advancing in the way and work of salvation, this journey must have furnished many instructive lessons, which, carefully treasured up, would be lastingly beneficial. Some circumstances seem to have made such deep impression on his feelings, as occasioned him to notice them with much concern. A Friend had been drafted to serve in the army, but being conscientiously scrupulous against bearing arms, could not comply with the requisition. He was therefore tried by a court-martial, sentenced to be whipt, and received forty lashes on his bare back with a whip of nine cords. Although he had no friend to sympathize with or to encourage him in a faithful testimony to the peaceable kingdom and government of Christ, he meekly and patiently suffered his flesh to be thus barbarously mangled in the presence of some thousands of persons. William says, "Great endeavors were afterwards used, both by threats and persuasions, to induce him to comply with some service in the military establishment, such as waiting upon the sick, or in some other employ that they might take hold of, so as to answer their purpose: but remaining steadily fixed, he could have no freedom to countenance their measures, let the consequence be what it might. I think it is worthy of remark. that his prudent wife appeared to be more concerned on account of an evil report that her husband had been brought to a compliance, than for all his suffering, or all they were worth in the world. After the time had expired, for which he had been drafted, he returned home. Here, I may mention the reasons offered by a certain Major Roberts in the American army, why the Friends ought not to suffer; he said, the Quakers had not deceived them, they had borne their testimony from the beginning, and were never known to bear arms on any occasion; they also paid taxes, which were three-fold more than their proportion; those treble taxes were in consequence of their not uniting in warlike measures. It may also not be improper to take notice of a remark made by a great woman of the church of England, that she observed some of the Quakers' children had departed from the plainness of their profession and got about half-way into the fashions of the world, which rendered them ridiculous in the eyes of others and a reproach to their own Society."

His appearances in the ministry being approved, he was acknowledged as a minister in the year 1781; and in 1785, with the concurrence of his Monthly Meeting visited the Yearly Meeting held in Baltimore, and some other meetings in Maryland. In 1787, he attended the Yearly Meetings of New York and Rhode Island, and visited several other meetings within the states of New York and New England; and in 1789, was again engaged in paying a religious visit to some meetings in Maryland and Pennsylvania.

In 1791, the Monthly Meeting uniting with his prospect of religious duty to visit the city of Charleston, South Carolina, and other places of the Southern States, he took his passage in a vessel bound for Charleston in the fourth month, and arrived there on the 22d.

He says, "24th being First-day, was at two meetings: they were attended by more people not professing with us, than Friends, who do not appear to be more than fifteen members in the place; but the meeting-house was too small to answer my concern of seeing the inhabitants. Second-day being a time generally allotted for recreation and amusement, the negroes appeared in their best trim and many of them cheerful, yet the great numbers of them, and the reflections consequent on their abject condition, gave everything a melancholy tinge with me. Appointed a meeting to be held in the Methodist meeting-house in the evening of the 26th. The house was filled, and it was said that several hundreds could not get in. Some fundamental truths were opened, showing that the work of righteousness is peace, and the effect thereof, quietness and assurance for ever. The Lord was pleased to favor with ability to my humbling admiration; the meeting was still and solid, and I went to my lodgings in peace.

"Colonel Laurens having obtained the privilege of the Baptist meeting-house, I agreed to have a meeting there in the evening of the first of fifth month. It being First-day, I was at Friends' meeting in the morning, which was large; that in the evening was also large and satisfactory. Left the city and got to T. Lewis's the 5th, about fifty-four miles. Here are about seven families, who have built a small meeting-house, being convinced mostly without instrumental means; they meet in the manner of Friends, twice a week, and appear to be an innocent people. Our landlord has freed ten negroes, several of whom cost fifty guineas each; he and his wife are united in this, that they never found peace of mind until they had so done. On our road we met between thirty and forty negroes, of both sexes, almost naked, some of them lame and decrepit, travelling to Ashley bridge, a considerable distance off; there to be put up and sold at vendue. This made our hearts sad, and caused the reflection; certainly there is a righteous and omniscient Judge that commiserates the poor and oppressed, and takes cognizance of the actions of hard-hearted and merciless oppressors, and by terrible things in righteousness will sooner or later plead the cause of the afflicted. It is sorrowful, that because judgment against an evil work is not speedily executed, the hearts of men are set to do evil.

"Rode upwards of one hundred miles, and got to Bush-river meeting the 8th; appointed one to be held at four o'clock in the afternoon, which was large, being attended by many professors.

"The 9th, had a meeting at Rocky Spring; many Baptists and others attending, it was very large, and through mercy strength was given to labor, but I fear little good was done. Proceeded to Cane creek and had a meeting; though the people appeared very raw, yet it was to pretty good satisfaction. The next meeting was at Paget's creek: a variety of religious professors were present, and near the close the people were much tendered. Had meetings at Raybor's creek, Mud-lick, and Allwood, and on the 15th was at Cambridge or Ninety-six. Had a meeting in the Courthouse, with a mixed multitude: it was large, and thought to be open and satisfactory. In the afternoon had another meeting in a large unfinished building; many attended, and we thought it was well we were there. Got to Wrightsborough, in Georgia, and attended their week-day meeting on the 18th. The neighbors being invited, it was a large gathering, and ended well.

"The 19th, had a meeting at Mendenhall's: a large number of Methodists and Baptists attended. Two women fell on their knees, and trembled, and shook, and prayed, and exhorted. I could scarcely account for such an extraordinary appearance, as they continued in these agitations some time after meeting broke up. Several wept, and most of the people appeared serious. I stept in among them again, and advised the women to stillness; and then thought I had a more favorable opportunity to speak to the people than before; upon the whole I felt easy when it was over. As we were riding through the woods on the 20th, the road being narrow, the iron of the swingletree breaking, it fell on the mare's legs and set her to running and kicking in a frightful manner. I expected nothing but to be dashed against the trees every moment, for I had not power to stop her, nor any possibility of jumping out, without imminent danger; but through the singular interposition of divine Providence, who has watched over me with the tenderness of a father all my life, the creature suddenly stopped and trembled exceedingly, when all my efforts were in vain.

A few yards further might, in all probability, have terminated the scene, and I was accordingly endeavoring to be collected in my mind. Such a marvellous escape was greatly to my humiliation, and presented an impressive lesson to me. What shall I render to thee, O Lord, for all thy unmerited mercies, and to what end hast thou so often been gracious to me, but that I might more fervently seek and serve thee, the remainder of my days. Lord grant me strength so to do!

"The 22d being first-day, had a meeting at Wrightsborough: the people of different professions and ranks came in great numbers; it was thought to be a solid, tendering time; but not feeling quite easy, I appointed another at four o'clock in the afternoon, the people continuing in the woods. This was truly a relieving time, and we thought we had never witnessed so much brokenness throughout: they were loath to part with us, and many tears were shed on both sides. I endeavored as soon as possible to retreat, but they stopped the sulkey frequently, and seemed reluctant to let us go. Accompanied by several Friends, we passed on to Augusta, and proposed a meeting at four o'clock in the afternoon of next day; but the people being thoughtless and dissipated, were so taken up with their diversion, that we did not obtain the company of more than twenty. We proposed another at ten o'clock, in the forenoon of the following day. As they can scarcely tolerate us on account of our abhorrence of slavery, this was truly a trying place to lodge in another night.

Near the time appointed, the bell was rung, and about one hundred collected; many of them appeared to be people of some note, and being favored with utterance, I cleared my mind, and before we parted, gave them a charge to be more cautious of discouraging disinterested religious visits in future.

"On the 28th we got to Savannah. The next day being First-day, the parson came and offered his meeting-house for a meeting at five o'clock in the evening, which was large; several of the clergy, and many people of note, attended; they appeared to be total strangers to us, and were at first light and airy, but became more serious, and were mostly very attentive. The Lord was near, and I trust was mouth and wisdom. I left them easy and comforted in mind, being glad I gave up to go there, though in the cross. Crossed Savannah river, and lodged at —— Blunt's, who is a hard hearted slave-holder. One of his lads, about fourteen, coming in from the field at dark, was ordered to go and milk the cows; and falling asleep through weariness, the master called out and ordered him a flogging. I asked him what he meant by a flogging. He replied, the way we serve them here is, we cut their backs till they are raw all over, and then salt them. Upon this, my feelings were roused, I told him that was too bad, and queried if it were possible; he replied it was, with many curses upon the blacks. It disturbed us much, but I hoped his orders would not be obeyed. We went to supper, and this unfeeling wretch craved a blessing, which I considered to be equally abhorrent to the Divine Being as his curses.

"31st. Rose in the morning, and whilst at the door musing, I heard some one begging for mercy, and also the lashes of a whip. Not knowing whence the sound came, I ran, and presently found the poor boy tied up to a post, his toes scarcely touching the ground, and a negro whipper, with five or six hazel rods lying by him. He had already cut him in an unmerciful manner, and the blood ran to his heels. I stepped in between them, and ordered him untied immediately, which with some reluctance and astonishment was done. Returning to the house, I saw the landlord, who then showed himself in his true colors, the most abominably wicked man I ever met with, full of horrid execrations and threatenings upon all the Northern people; but I did not spare him, which occasioned a by-stander to express with an oath that I should be 'popped over.'

"We left them, distressed in mind, and having a lonesome wood of twelve miles to pass through, were in full expectation of their waylaying or coming after us, to put their wicked threats in execution; but the Lord restrained them. This was a day of heaviness and sorrowful reflection, and the next house we stopped at we found the same wicked spirit. We rode through many rice swamps, where the blacks are very numerous, great droves of these poor slaves working up to the middle in water, men and women nearly naked: a peck of corn is their miserable subsistence for a week. A gloomy sadness covered them, so as scarcely to admit of the interchange of a sentiment. O Christianity and humanity, how are ye disgraced! Where will such astonishing horrible conduct end?

"Sixth month, 2d, got to Charleston. On First-day, the 5th, attended Friends' meeting in the morning, and had a public meeting in the evening at the Baptist meeting-house, which was large and a relieving time to my mind.*

"The 23d was at Cane creek, North Carolina; it being their week-day meeting. It was pretty large, many came to it directly out of their harvest fields, and our good Master was with us. Had meetings at several places to a good degree of satisfaction, and got to Petersburg, in Virginia, the 2d of Seventh month. On First-day, the 3d, had a public meeting at four o'clock in the afternoon, which was very large, the people of other religious denominations attending, the house could not contain them all; but it ended well." *

In the year 1792 he visited the meetings of Friends in Virginia, attended their Yearly Meeting, and appears to have been favored with strength to fulfil the service required of him, with peace to his own mind.

The condition of the Indian natives in this country had for some years engaged the attention of the Yearly Meeting of Philadelphia, and its representative body, the Meeting for Sufferings; and in the recollection of

---

* The reader will observe that there is a considerable interval between these dates; no memoranda appear to have been made, and the information requisite to fill the chasms which are left by the writer cannot now be obtained.

the kindness shown by those original proprietors of the soil to the Friends who first landed on these shores, and the friendship which subsisted between them, the Society had endeavored to cherish that bond of union, and to evince their gratitude and love by such aid as it was in their power to bestow.

These acts of benevolence, however, had been interrupted by war, devastating the frontier settlements, and staining the land with blood. Deeply affected with the horrors attendant on this cruel contest, the Meeting for Sufferings, in the Eleventh month, 1792, was engaged to prepare a respectful memorial to the President and Congress of the United States, recommending the adoption of such pacific and just measures toward the natives as might arrest this savage warfare, and establish peace upon a firm basis. In the Second month following, the meeting was informed that a treaty was likely to be held at Sandusky (now in the State of Ohio), and by messages received through Captain Hendricks and his brothers, two Indian messengers recently from the Western country, and also a letter from Hopackon, a sachem of the Delaware nation, it appeared that the Indians were very solicitious some Friends should attend it, and as a confirmation of the message and a token of their continued friendship, they sent three strings of white wampum.

Several Friends, of whom William Savery was one, feeling their minds religiously engaged to visit the Indian country about the time the treaty was to be held, and producing to the Meeting for Sufforings in the Fourth month, 1793, minutes, expressing the unity of their respective Monthly Meetings, and the approbation of President Washington having been obtained, they were deputed in its behalf to attend the said treaty, and present to the natives the following address, viz:

"*To the Indians living on the North-Western and Western borders of the United States, and all others whom this writing may concern:*

"BROTHERS,

"Hearken to the speech which your friends called Quakers, assembled in Philadelphia, from several parts of Pennsylvania, New Jersey, &c., now send to you by their brethren, John Parrish, William Savery, John Elliott, Jacob Lindley, Joseph Moore, and William Hartshorne.

"Brothers,—When our grandfathers came with Onas over the great waters to settle in this land, more than one hundred years ago, they kindled a large council fire with your grandfathers, and sat together around it in much good-will and friendship, smoking the calumet pipe together; and they told your grandfathers that they were men of peace, and desired to live among you in peace and love, and that their children might also be careful always to live in the same love one with another, as brothers of the same family.

"This council fire was kept burning with a clear flame many years, which gave a good light to all around the country, and the chain of friendship which was made at the same time, was kept clean from rust by our fathers and your fathers; until about forty years ago, an evil spirit whispered bad stories in the ears of some of your people and of some of the white people, so that the light of the ancient council fire was almost put out, and the old chain of friendship was made dull and rusty.

"Brothers, — Our grandfathers told your grandfathers, that the Great and Good Spirit who made them and all people, with a design that they might live on this earth for a few years, in love and good-will one toward another, had placed his law in the hearts of all men, and if they carefully attended to its inward voice, it would keep them in love and friendship, and teach them to shun everything that would occasion them to trouble and hurt one another.

"Brothers, — Do you not find that after you have been angry and quarrelsome, or done any bad action, you are made uneasy and sorrowful; and that when you are sober and serious, and do good actions, your minds feel pleasant, easy, and comfortable? It is the law from the Good Spirit, who is all love, and who placed it in your hearts, which gives you such peace and comfort when you do well, but when you do evil things, it reproves you and makes you feel uneasy and sad.

"Brothers,—We wish you to consider and remember, that the Great Spirit sees and knows all the thoughts of your hearts, and of the hearts of all mankind, and all their actions. And when their bodies die, such men of all colors and all nations, who have loved, served and obeyed the holy law of the Good Spirit, placed in their hearts, He will receive their souls, which are never to die, and they will live with Him in joy and peace for ever: but the souls of bad men who have lived wickedly in this world, must live, after their bodies die, with the bad Spirit in a state of distress and misery.

"Brothers,—We make profession of the same principles with our grandfathers, which teach us to love you and all men; and in that love we feel our minds drawn to send you this speech, with a great desire for your good.—We were made glad when we heard that the sober, good people among you were disposed to promote peace and brighten the old chain of friendship, with the white people of the United States; and that many of you have a desire that you may be instructed in tilling the ground, and to live after the manner of the white people, which we believe you will find to be more comfortable for you and your families, than to live only by hunting; and we think it will also be good for your young people to be learned to read and write, and that sober, honest, good men should be sent among you for teachers.

"Brothers,—We have often told some of your chiefs when we have had the opportunity of taking them by the hand in this city, that we are not concerned in the management of the affairs of government, which are under the direction of the President of the United States, and his counsellors, but that we should, at all times, be willing to do anything in our power to promote love and peace.

"Brothers,—We greatly desire that the commissioners who are now sent by the President, and also your counsellors and chiefs, may look up to the Great Spirit for his wisdom and help, that you may all be made wise and strong to light up the council fire, and brighten the chain of old friendship, that all things may be settled to satisfaction, and a lasting peace established, so that there may be no more difference or war between your people and the inhabitants of these States.

"We desire you may receive our friends, by whom we send this writing, in love, as brothers who are disposed to encourage you in all good things.—And, in the ancient love which our grandfathers felt for each other, we salute you, wishing you happiness in this life, and that which is to come, and remain your friends and brothers.

"Signed by forty-four Friends.

"*Philadelphia, fourth month* 19*th*, 1793."

Of this journey, which proved to be one of great exposure and personal suffering, William Savery has preserved memorandums; from which it appears, that they left Philadelphia in the Fifth month, 1793, and on arriving at New York, met with John Heckewelder, a Moravian missionary, who had lived among the Indians, and was going to attend the treaty. On First-day, the 5th of the month, they attended two meetings in the city, and appointed one at seven o'clock in the evening, which was largely attended by professors of several denominations: it was solid, and ended to satisfaction. They left New York that evening, and got to Albany the 8th.

William says, "our stores having arrived with general Lincoln, they were nearly all put on board of eight batteaux, built for the purpose; two of these were covered in the centre with painted canvas, about nine feet in length, surrounded with curtains, and had each a table in the middle. Embarking the 9th, our little fleet attracted the attention of the inhabitants, who were civil, and I believe wished us well. It was truly a novel scene to most of the passengers. The Mohawk has a strong current, frequently rapid, and so shallow that the bottoms of our boats often rubbed the bed of the river; this made hard work for the boatmen.

"The 13th, all our boats and baggage being transported to the landing, above the falls, we went on board, and arrived at fort Herkimer, making only seven miles to-day.

"14th. J. Heckewelder, Jacob Lindley, and myself, being with general Lincoln, we became engaged in religious conversation with much kindness and charity; the General expressed many just and valuable sentiments on the weighty subjects under discussion. Arrived at fort Schuyler in the evening.

"17th. The boats and stores being yesterday taken over from fort Stanwix to Wood creek landing, we sat off about eight o'clock in the morning, but as the creek was only about six inches deep, were obliged to take about two tons out of our large boats and carry it in wagons, to the junction of Canada creek; after this, having the aid of the waters of a mill-dam at the head of the creek, the boats readily floated. Most of the passengers walked this distance, which was about seven miles. At three o'clock we embarked again, and made about sixteen miles to-day; here we encamped, and next day got to the mouth of Oneida lake. About three o'clock got through the lake to fort Brewington, at the mouth of Onondaga river.

"19th. After breakfast sailed down a beautiful stream twelve miles, to Oswego falls. Some Onondaga Indians followed us in a bark canoe, and caught some fine salmon and other fish for us. We encamped and lodged comfortably, being about eighty in company.

"20th. After drawing our boats by hand on rollers, about one hundred yards, we launched them below the main falls, and again embarking, went down a rapid rocky current to Oswego fort, twelve miles. It is a strong British garrison, commanded by Captain Wickham, who sent his servant to invite us to his quarters, and treated us respectfully. After being hospitably entertained, we left the fort and embarked on lake Ontario; rowed hard to a harbor fifteen miles, which we reached about nine o'clock in the evening, and encamped. Made twenty-nine miles on the 21st. As the wind was high next day, we lay at the harbor until afternoon, then sailed seven miles, and encamped on the beach.

"The 25th, got to Niagara fort, and staid until about four o'clock; then crossed the river, which is about half a mile wide, and took possession of two rooms in an unfinished house, which the commissioners had prepared for us, having our own provisions and mattresses.

"26th. Waited on the governor at his request, and were treated respectfully; dined at our lodgings upon wild pigeons, which the Indians shot flying, with their bows and arrows. The town consists of about fifty houses: it is laid out in half-acre lots, and is likely, from the extensive navigation and increase of population, to be a place of considerable trade in a few years.

"27th. Packed up our bedding and proceeded with all the batteaux and stores to the landing-place, seven miles up the river; pitched our tents on the bank of a green meadow, and at the invitation of Captain Smith and other officers, several of us dined with them at the mess-house. Here are large barracks, with three or four hundred men, in a low unhealthy spot, many of them very sickly, and a number die almost daily.

"30th. Were visited by the governor, Timothy Pickering, and others. The governor offered his house, at this place, for our accommodation; but its low situation occasioned us to decline accepting it.

"31st. Several of us went down in our boat to Navy Hall, and spent several hours with the commissioners: we got passes from Governor Simcoe, to go on to Detroit, by the first king's vessel from Fort Erie.

"First-day, 2d of Sixth month, a meeting being appointed to be held in a barn, about four miles from our encampment; Friends, and some people from the landing, attended. It was larger than we expected, being composed of a variety of professors, among whom were eight or ten Friends, who are settled in the neighborhood. No regular place of worship being kept up for many miles, the opportunity of assembling for that purpose appeared to be very acceptable; the meeting was solid, and we hope may be useful.

"3d. Struck our tents, and packed up as many stores as were thought necessary—a wagon being prepared to take them, and one of our large boats mounted on a carriage, we set off for Chippeway, the landing place above the falls, where we lodged at a tolerably good house.

"4th. Proceeded early up Niagara river, against a strong current, which was rather unpleasant, for had we been driven down half a mile, every effort must have been unavailing to rescue us from descending the tremendous cataract. Arrived at a farm-house, where being supplied with milk and butter, we breakfasted; dined at a tavern four miles below Fort Erie, where we found a large number of farmers convened from a considerable distance, in order to render an account of their improvements and property; several of whom were Friends and Menonists from Pennsylvania. Reached Fort Erie about four o'clock, and finding three British vessels, we took our passage, but the wind being unfavorable, could not sail.

"Fourth-day, the 5th, the wind still unfavorable. The land between Niagara and this place, is generally rich and well timbered, and is settling fast by people who are mostly from the United States, and among them a greater number of members of our Society, than I had expected to find. While at dinner the wind becoming fair, a gun was fired to hasten the Indians and other passengers on board. We sailed pleasantly, at the rate of about four miles an hour, having on board about ninety persons, forty-five of whom were Mohawks, Messasauges, Stockbridge, and Cayuga Indians.

"Fifth-day, the wind pretty fair; sailed pleasantly in much harmony, the time spent agreeably and usefully. We conversed with the Indians and made them some small presents, with which they were much pleased. Towards evening the wind abating, the vessel rolled so much as to cause many of the passengers to be sick, myself among the number. A storm of rain, with thunder and lightning, coming on in the night, some of us got but little rest, and having a large quantity of powder on board, our situation was awful, but Divine Goodness preserved us through it, for which I desire to remain thankful, and increasingly studious in my inquiry, 'What shall I render Him for all his mercies?'

"Sixth-day, the wind unfavorable. Seventh-day, sailed perhaps thirty or forty miles.

"First-day, the 9th, about noon came in sight of the Bass islands, near which are abundance of fine fish; — continued heaving the lead from about eleven o'clock to three — the water near those islands being shoal. Held a meeting in the cabin, at which were present our cabin passengers, and some of those in the steerage, Captain Hendricks and his Indians, Captain John, and as many of his as could find room — they all behaved soberly, and it was satisfactory to us. Several of the Indians expressed the same; and Captain John informed the captain of the vessel, he should be glad if he could have had what was said in writing, and was more familiar and friendly ever after. Arrived at nine o'clock at the mouth of the river Detroit.

"Second-day, weighed anchor with a fair wind, but a strong current against us; the morning being fine, it afforded us a beautiful prospect of continued houses, farms, wind-mills, luxuriant meadows and orchards, which had a very pleasing effect, having seen nothing like it since we left the Mohawk river. Arrived at Detroit about eight o'clock, and after breakfasting on board, went on shore to procure lodgings, but finding the rent of two rooms to be four dollars per day, we gave up the idea of finding our own provisions, and took up our boarding at a house where we have a good table, and sleep upon our own mattresses: all kinds of foreign articles are about three-fold more than in Philadelphia. Veal, one shilling, beef, fifteen pence per pound, fowls, four shillings a couple, butter, two shillings and sixpence, &c.

"Third-day, the 11th, the weather was very warm: walked round the town and found the number of houses and inhabitants to exceed my expectation. We computed the houses, exclusive of the barracks, at two hundred; some of them good, especially along the bank of the river. There is only one place of worship, which is a Romish chapel. Lieutenant-colonel England commands the regiment quartered in this place; he is a very respectable man: the officers are civil and polite, and possess a good opinion of Friends.

"Fourth-day, the 12th, many Indians came to see us, but most of them being intoxicated, we had little conversation with them. The people seemed astonished to see Quakers; and some of the officers calling to visit us, treated us respectfully.

"Fifth-day, had a serious conference with Captain John, and other chiefs of the Mohawks, to our satisfaction; they expressed themselves friendly, and much approved of our attending the treaty.

"14th. Almost wearied out with the importunities of the Indians for rum, we however put them off. Some of the Chippeways having arrived last evening from Michillimachinack, and encamped outside the picquets, we paid them a visit, but they had drunk much rum before we went, were very rude, called us ill names, and appeared very angry. All the Indians I had ever seen were far short of these in their extraordinary terrifying painting, and the appendages of their dress; any description I am capable of giving, must afford a very faint idea of the ferocious appearance of this nation. On leaving them, one followed and took hold of the arm of one of us, crying very harshly, 'come back, come back.' A ship-carpenter who was near, and understood their language, said he believed if we had returned to them, they would certainly have killed us, which most likely they would; this made us more cautious of going into their company afterwards, especially when heated with strong drink. A number of Indians frightfully painted, passed through the town. dancing the war dance, some of whom having knowledge of us, came to our lodging to pay us a compliment; but I wish to be excused from a compliment of the like kind in future. The frightful painting of their faces and bodies, which are almost naked on such occasions, their terrifying whoops and yells, their ferocious countenances and actions, together with the tomahawks and scalping knives in their hands, form so horrid a scene, that every truly Christian mind must recoil from it with disgust and sadness. Sorrowful indeed it is to reflect, that such is the depravity of many, under the dignified character of Christians, whose conduct towards these poor creatures ought to have been marked with a pacific desire of inspiring them with the mild and blessed doctrines of the Gospel, that they are, alas! taking delight in encouraging them to this exercise, and stimulate them with large potations of strong liquor, until they become frantic.

"Dined by invitation at the officers' mess-house; their respectful, polite behavior to Friends, marked their character as gentlemen, and merited our acknowledgment; they permitted us to use great freedom with them, and I hope we kept our places.

"Seventh-day, after informing the colonel of our

intention to hold a meeting here to-morrow, to which he cordially assented, we viewed two places which were offered for the purpose; but they being somewhat inconvenient, the king's ship-builder offered his boat-house, which being large, and in a fine airy place on the side of the river, we accepted it. Being much troubled with the continual visits of the Indians, begging for rum and other things, we were obliged to retire up stairs to avoid them.

"First-day, 16th of Sixth month, attended the meeting at ten o'clock forenoon. The colonel having dispensed with the accustomed military exercise, which is practised at that hour, a large number of soldiers and most of the officers were present, besides a considerable collection of the inhabitants of the place of both sexes; and as the house was in a large open lot, great numbers stood out of doors. This being doubtless the first meeting of our Society at Detroit, curiosity was greatly excited; their behavior at first, as might be expected, was a little restless, talking, taking snuff, &c., but upon one of our company endeavoring to set before them the nature of our mode of worship, with a request they would join in our manner, they were very attentive and became still; some of them, especially among the poor soldiers, were reverent and thoughtful. The service, which was considerable, appeared to be received with openness, and I believe the opportunity ended to mutual satisfaction. There is no Protestant place of worship, that I can hear of, within a long way from this place: all that has the shadow of worship, except the Roman Catholic, is the reading of prayers and church service by an officer, sometimes on First-days, at which the Protestant inhabitants attend. After dinner the colonel's boat being prepared, about twelve or fifteen of us proceeded down the river to attend a meeting appointed at four o'clock, six miles off. Several other boats set off in company, but the wind being high, one of them put back—there were a number of Menonists with long beards present, some French people, and the farmers in the neighborhood:—I hope the meeting ended well. Returned to Detroit, thankful to the Author of mercies for his unmerited kindness during the day.

"Second-day, 17th. We have need to ask for both faith and patience to support us under our long detention, and the continual alarming reports of the disposition of the Indians, who are collecting for the treaty. Most of those who pass this place are said to go prepared for war, if the commissioners do not comply with their wishes: they are in a haughty spirit, being elated with their successes. There are many among the inhabitants here kindly disposed towards us, who appear to be very doubtful for our personal safety at Sandusky, and seem rather to desire we would not venture. We are thankful in being preserved so far in quietness and confidence, trusting in the Omnipotent arm for preservation. We cannot admit a doubt of the propriety of our coming, nor of the motives which led to it; yet I may say, it is the most trying situation I was ever brought into. May the Lord preserve the little band, 'wise as serpents and harmless as doves.' At four o'clock several of our company dined at Colonel England's. The state of my mind made me wish to be excused, but thought it improper to slight so respectful an invitation to us poor strangers. The colonel is a man of great openness of manners, quite a soldier, and his wife an amiable woman. Five of the officers of the regiment being present, we sat down to a table spread in all the elegance of a populous city. After travelling several hundred miles of wilderness, and encamping on the ground like poor pilgrims, it was really marvellous to find plenty and elegance, at least equal to the most fashionable houses in our city. He did everything to make our visit agreeable, which has also been the disposition of all the officers since we arrived.

"Fourth-day, a boat coming for us from the neighborhood of the Menonists, which arrangement had been made on the First-day preceding, all the Friends, except myself, went down in it. Having a pain in my head and bones, and being apprehensive it was the prelude of a fever, I took some medicine and confined myself all day. Towards evening was much relieved, but the prospect of a fit of sickness so far from home put my resignation to the will of an all-wise Providence to the proof, and I found, as I have often before, that it is one of the highest degrees of attainment, to say with sincerity, 'Thy will be done.' Fifth-day evening, at the request of the officers, I spent an hour or two with four of them, and conversed on the nature of our business with the Indians. They expressed a belief that much respect would be paid to the sentiments of Friends, and assured me that the discouraging sentiments we had heard respecting our personal safety at the treaty need not occasion us a moment's concern, for it was not strange that such insinuations should drop from those who were interested in the continuance of hostilities. Some remarks on the difference of our pursuits and profession produced the expression of a prospect which some of them had, that before very long they would exchange the sword for the ploughshare.

"Sixth-day, 21st, a number of Indians arrived from many hundred miles to the North-west. They were frightfully painted; their dress more singular than any I have yet seen, and generally large muscular men. It is amazing to reflect on the vast distance they travel in their canoes along the continued chain of lakes and rivers in this part of America. We are now fourteen or fifteen hundred miles by the water communication from the sea at Louisboùrg, and the trade is carried on, it is said, for two thousand miles beyond this, from whence none but the costliest furs, as beaver, marten, &c., are worth bringing. Schooners go about six hundred miles beyond Detroit; thus the trade in furs is brought to this place far beyond what I could ever have imagined. A vast country, which may in time become an extensive empire, remains unsettled in the British territories, in which are large bodies of excellent land: that which lies along the river Le French, about fifty or sixty miles above this, is fast settling, and two hundred acres to a family are given gratis. Good fish are plenty in these waters, but no eels have ever been found above the falls of Niagara, nor rats on the land.

"First-day, 23d, we held a meeting in a large sail-loft, but not having given notice to the colonel of our intention, the soldiers were out on parade. The gathering was pretty large, many coming in from the country; and the doctrine appeared to be closer than some present could bear. A serious call was sounded, to examine the foundation of a hope of salvation through Christ, while men remain under the dominion of a long catalogue of sinful indulgences and profanity; and inculcating the necessity of having our conversation such as becometh the Gospel of Christ, in order to obtain an inheritance in his kingdom. The labor was painful, and tended to our mortification, but this is good for us; indeed it would be a vain expectation for us to think to reign, where Truth so evidently suffers: may we be favored with an increase of resignation to the Divine will. In the afternoon I had some painful reflections on the state of the people, and the prospect of some weeks longer continuance among them. The upright intention of our hearts in coming on this fatiguing and exercising journey being recurred to, I went to bed somewhat revived, in humble confidence in the Divine arm for support; and remembering the gracious promise, 'Lo! I am with you always.'

"Second-day, 24th, Joseph Moore and myself went down to the river La Rouge, and proceeded five miles up it to a new grist-mill, where we dined. The people settled on the sides of the river are mostly French and Germans; the land flat and wet. We had conversation with several Germans, who appeared to have a great desire for us to hold a meeting; one man kindly offering to send horses for us whenever we gave them notice.

"25th. J. Heckewelder returned yesterday from the Moravian town, on the river Le French, and brought with him Gabriel Senseman, a missionary, and six or seven Indians, among whom was John Killbuck, and his son, who had been educated at Princeton College, but has again resumed Indian habits and manners. These poor Indians, who do not go to war, have been driven about, from place to place, and much distressed. Governor Simcoe has now granted them ten miles square of land, which they are beginning to cultivate; but at present their situation was represented to be very distressing, for want of provisions, having scarcely anything to subsist on, but roots, until their corn grows. Heckewelder and Senseman requesting our attention to them, Friends took it into consideration, and no other resources appearing, we thought it right to procure corn and flour for them, to the amount of one hundred dollars; part of which they immediately took off in their canoes. Dined at William Forsythe's, on the river side, and wrote an epistle to the Moravian Indians.

"27th. Spent most of the day at our lodgings; a Shawnese chief, who, we were informed, had come from the council at the Miami Rapids, desiring to see us, we had some conversation with him through an interpreter, but could not obtain his sentiments respecting the issue of the treaty: he appeared to be a quiet, cautious man, and thought the treaty would not be over before frost. We are almost ready, at times, to apprehend that our patience will be exhausted, yet cannot doubt but our unforeseen detention in this remote and libertine place, will have its use. I am thankful that our little band is preserved in good health, and favored with unity of prospect and concern; and hope our conversation has in good measure been such as becometh our profession. It has, however, been peculiarly trying to me to-day, to look forward to so long a separation from my precious home and dear friends, which, with the sentiments we daily hear expressed, of the danger of losing our lives at the treaty, if the Indians should not be gratified in their demands, causes us to be serious and thoughtful, and to search for that foundation where we may stand unshaken in every trial that yet awaits us. Some evenings past, two Indians being intoxicated, quarrelled outside the garrison, and one killed the other; of which I do not hear that any notice has been taken; but probably the survivor will ere long be killed by some friend or relative of the deceased, according to Indian custom. No Indian is suffered to stay inside the gates of the garrison, after the drum beats; nor more than thirty to be within at once in the day-time; and these all disarmed.

"28th. Visited Captain Labourne, who granted us the use of his library, and we spent most of the forenoon in reading. Captain Drake giving us his company, related many curious observations he had made during four years' employment on these lakes, having arrived a few days past from Michillimachinack, about one hundred and thirty leagues distant, at the further end of lake Huron. He informed us that many hundred men are employed by the North-West company, who are constantly travelling to a very great distance, trading with the Northern Indians for the richest peltry, which is mostly brought from high Northern latitudes. They are generally French Canadians, and continue a number of years without coming into the settlements of the whites; living principally on fish and game without salt—they are remarkably healthy. All accounts agree that the most distant Indians yet discovered are peaceable and harmless. Many of those here are, on the contrary, fierce, artful, and much prejudiced against the inhabitants of the United States. This we experienced, before they knew anything of us, by their angry looks and drawing away their hands when we offered ours — calling us Shomochoman or long knives, by which they distinguish all who are citizens of the United States. Yet when we have an opportunity of informing who we are, and our motives in coming here, they become kind, and do not use those epithets. Much, I conceive, may be done with these poor people, by persuasion, kindness, and honest dealing; but little by compulsion.

"29th. Visited by a Wyandot chief, who said he remembered some long and broad belts that were given to Friends in former treaties, which were intended to bind us together by the hands and arms, so that no small accident in future should be able to make a separation; and notwithstanding all that had happened, the Wyandots felt some of the old affection to remain. We assured him, we had the same love and friendship for them that our forefathers had, and that our principles had always restrained us from war; but believing our government was disposed to make peace with them on principles of justice, we were made willing to leave our families and take this long journey, to endeavor to promote it, and to be present at the conclusion of so good a work. He replied, he knew long ago that our Society did not fight, that he was glad to see us here on so good a work; and that as we had come a long journey, and were all preserved in health, as he saw us, it was evident the Great Spirit was pleased with our journey, and he hoped some good would be done, and that the Great Spirit would bring us home in health and safety.

"30th. A blind chief, of the Wyandot nation, visited us with some of his relations. The meeting for worship in the sail-loft was large and solid, considering the company; held another at five o'clock in the afternoon, which was large, as before, and to good satisfaction; the citizens, officers and soldiers, all quiet, though a very warm day.

"Seventh month, 3d. Very warm. The Ottaway having arrived from Fort Erie, we fully expected the commissioners, or at least some letters from home, but were disappointed of both; a fresh occasion for the exercise of patience and resignation was thus afforded. Eighteen Oneida Indians came in the Ottaway, with sixty of other nations, intending for the Grand Council at the Rapids, where the vessel touched, and all but these were landed with Colonel Butler; but these Indians being esteemed in the American interest, and the chief unpopular with the war chiefs of other tribes, the colonel was of opinion their lives would be in danger, and therefore he sent them here to go forward with us to Sandusky. This day the thermometer was at ninety-six.

"Fifth-day, 4th of the month, were informed the thermometer was at one hundred degrees in the shade, and one hundred and twenty in the sun. 5th of the month. We desire to be preserved from murmuring at our confinement in this place, but many considerations conspire to prompt the wish to be released. Our ears are constantly assailed with multiplied instances of Indian perfidy and cruelty in their wars; several fresh cases related this morning by one, who, with her husband and some others now in this place, were prisoners. About three hundred and ninety-five of them had fled into forts, for protection, near the close of the war with Great Britain, consisting of men, women, and children, inhabitants of Kentucky. They capitulated to a body of British troops and Indians, on the condition that their lives were to be spared; but after a march of a day or two, a number being aged and infirm, they were tomahawked; after which each nation of Indians claiming a proportion of the prisoners; husband and wife, parents and children, were separated, and thus involved in the deepest distress. The family of our informant, with many others, were brought to this place. After some time, receiving intelligence that one of their children was with the Shawnese, about two days' journey hence, and that a day was appointed to burn him, the father went off immediately, and with the interest of some traders. and at the expense of one hundred pounds, obtained his child. They were now in a thriving way, but had not yet fully discharged the debt. Numerous well-authenticated instances equally distressing, we daily hear, showing the horrors of Indian war — burning prisoners in a slow fire of one or two days' duration, with shocking tortures of different kinds, too much even to relate without the most painful feelings to every mind not callous to the sensibilities of humanity. O ye professors of the benign and heavenly doctrines of the Gospel, that breathes nothing but peace and good-will to men, how will ye appear in the awful day of retribution, when our Divine Master shall come to judge the world in righteousness, if any of you have been promoters of the great devastation, wretchedness, and misery, which mark the footsteps of war? In justice to the humane and generous officers of this garrison, we may say, that their efforts have been numerous, and mostly successful, in alleviating the miseries of the poor captives, many of whom they have purchased at a great price; some have cost near one hundred pounds; and they have also relieved and clothed many who have escaped, besides furnishing them with provisions to return home. This, however, they are instructed by government to do; yet their acts of private benevolence are very extensive, this post being a door of communication to all the Indian country, objects are continually offering.

"Intelligence from the council, at the Rapids, informs us, that two chiefs, from every nation there assembled, had embarked for Niagara to inquire of the commissioners the extent of their powers; and if they should find that they may lead to a reconciliation, they are requested to abide till all the Indians are collected at Sandusky, being determined, that unless the commissioners agree to give up all the lands west of the Ohio, they will not make peace; and if any terms short of this should be offered, it is the opinion here, that the Indians will sacrifice all the Americans on the spot. One of the two Shawnese that arrived here, says he was daily an ear-witness to their counsels, and assures us we may depend on his words as truth. He says they want neither presents nor purchase-money, but their hunting-grounds; without which they cannot subsist; and for their recovery they will risk their lives. He further added, what he had at times heard from old men concerning the first coming of the white people. The wise men among the Indians, at that time, foresaw what has now happened, and warned their brothers not to countenance each other in receiving gifts from the white people; saying, that the Great Spirit had made the land over the great lake for white people, and this island for the yellow people. They then refused to drink rum, and told the whites, the Indians did not want the bitter water; that it was only drink for white people, and that the Great Spirit had given the brooks and springs to the Indians for their drink; and foretold the consequence of Indians receiving that, and knives and hatchets, which would be the ruin of them. He remarked, that now several of those original tribes were extinct, and yet the Indians had not adverted to the advice, but had continued parting with their lands for these things, until they were almost driven to where the sun set. Happy would it have been if these poor Indians had continued to refuse the bitter water to this day. This day the thermometer was one hundred and two in the shade.

"6th. Not quite so hot as yesterday: spent the morning in reading and conversing with some visitors. A vessel arriving, confirms the account of deputies having gone down to the commissioners; if their motives are such as we have heard, probably we may be at the end of our journey.

"First-day, the 7th; meeting in the morning, in the sail-loft. A large number of the officers and soldiers attended, and it was a solid meeting. In the afternoon went six miles to the river Rouge, and had a meeting in a mill, among the new settlers on the river; it was as large as we expected, being composed of Germans, French, and English, and was a satisfactory time: the people attend with gladness, being willing to go far in these back countries where opportunities seldom offer.

Here are no places for worship established but Roman Catholic. One woman told us, she would be glad to attend our meetings diligently, even though she might have thirty miles to come, and did not understand much English. O happy Philadelphia, what privileges thy inhabitants enjoy! Mercies unthankfully received or unimproved, will increase condemnation.

"Second-day, 8th. Received a letter from Captain Hendricks, an Indian, at the Rapids, complaining of short allowance of provisions. We sent them a barrel of flour, some pork, five dollars in money, tobacco, &c., and wrote an answer. He appears to have some hopes of peace being accomplished; but if we attend to the various opinions and sentiments we hear, we are likely to be kept in continual fluctuation. Persons who appear very friendly, and men of information, advise us by no means to attend the treaty, that our lives are in the utmost danger. It is grateful to find the people at large solicitous for our welfare; but our principal business in this time of suffering and exercise, is to labor to experience that 'quiet habitation,' where we may be preserved from being tossed off the foundation by the many voices we hear. I endeavor after the resignation of all, even my life, to the Divine disposal; yet hope we shall be conducted by prudence in our movements, not rushing hastily or presumptuously into danger. Saw a burial procession, in the pageantry and superstition of the Roman Catholic Church; the deceased was said to be one hundred and fifteen years old.

"Third-day, 9th, had an interview with the famous war chief Blue Jacket, a Shawnese; he was reserved, saying he had given his sentiments at the council.

"10th. Had a fuller opportunity with Blue Jacket, who appears to be a man of understanding, but still reserved. Reports state, that the Chippeways and Sioux of the Woods, who are near Lake Superior, have had a battle, wherein many of the latter were killed, at which some people rejoice. Visited by several Indians, some of whom understand a little English, and appeared pleased with our views in coming here. The Shawnese, Wyandots, and Delawares, all appear to have more or less knowledge of Friends, and acknowledge that they have confidence in the Society, because we are peaceable and just. We have seen some of almost every nation, which are collected at the council, and have been more or less conversant with them every day since we arrived. A vessel arriving this afternoon, we were in great expectation of receiving letters from home, and some directions from the commissioners, but are proved with repeated disappointments, and must be longer exercised in the school of patience, yet dare not murmur. We were informed that the commissioners were coming on, and would encamp at the mouth of the river Detroit, until the treaty commenced; but we apprehend the deputed Indians would arrive in time to prevent their coming.

"11th. Dined at James Abbott's, who being much acquainted with Indian affairs for thirty years, expressed his opinion that no treaty would take place at present;

or if it did, no peace would be obtained; with which our two interpreters joined; all agreeing that the Indians must first be chastised and humbled. Friends urged their pacific sentiments towards the natives, and that kind, lenient measures, accompanied with justice, would prove more effectual than the sword; but without much effect. Men who are in the spirit of war, we have found in many instances in this place, cannot possibly see as we see. A long and truly afflicting recital of Indian cruelty and perfidy was brought into view, of which we have been obliged to hear enough before to fill a large volume. I could, several times, have been glad to have stopped my ears from hearing of blood, as I am confirmed in opinion that it has a tendency gradually to eradicate the tenderest feelings of humanity.

"12th. Embarked with all the family of our landlord, for his place, down the river; walked several miles below, and rested at a French-house; felt the want of the language, as I have often done before in this journey. A vessel arriving from Fort Erie, we were informed that the commissioners, after waiting five days for a fair wind, being met by the deputation of Indians, had returned back to the governor's. With this disappointment, and that of having no letter for us, our patience was almost exhausted.

"13th. A custom is still retained here, that whenever there is a sale of lands, it is to be public, and at the church door; and if a plantation is sold, even twice in a year, one-ninth of the purchase-money goes, by an old French law, to the church; this has enriched some parishes in Lower Canada to an almost incredible degree. By this great imposition they are enabled to support the superstitious ceremonies of that church, with great pomp and pageantry; but the people entertain a hope, that it will not continue long. Of all the land in Upper Canada, which is granted, and now granting, two-sevenths are reserved in every township, one for the king, and the other for the priests. The French interest in the legislature has hitherto overbalanced the English. The arrival of letters from our friends and relations, at home, was truly refreshing in our tried situation, and tended to animate us to patience and perseverance.

"First-day, 14th; meeting at ten o'clock; was large and satisfactory.

"15th. Our friend, Captain Elliott, arrived from the Rapids, and brings no additional information to encourage the hope of a treaty taking place; he says there are deputies from the Cherokee nation, who are at war.

"16th. On further conference with Captain Elliott, as to the best mode of promoting the concern of our Friends at home, with which we remain unitedly exercised, it terminated in this, that there was neither propriety nor safety in going to their council at the Rapids, and that if the result of the meeting of the commissioners and Indians at Niagara should prove unfavorable, and prevent the treaty, the Indians, on such intelligence, would immediately disperse. It was, therefore, deemed most advisable to write to Colonel M'Kee [a British officer], enclose him the address of Friends, and request him to deliver it to the Indians, if no treaty was likely to be held.

"17th. Wrote letters, one to Colonel M'Kee, at the Rapids, and one to the Indians assembled there in council; which, with the address of Friends, were enclosed, as before stated, and forwarded by Captain Elliott. Horrid instances of Indian barbarity related, and many of them too well authenticated to occasion a doubt of their foundation.

"18th. A false rumor of a vessel being arrived in the river, — our hope of release from this dark and wicked place is thus frequently baffled. Further information makes us almost despair of any treaty at this time, or if it should take place, that the desirable object of peace will be obtained; hence we feel our situation increasingly trying, yet hope we shall be preserved in patience to the end.

"19th. Being informed by a merchant, that the Indians had latterly mixed the sugar, of which they bring considerable quantities to this place, with sand — when told of it, they replied, You learned us by mixing water with your rum. Thus Christians, so called, are their instructors in many vices. An old Indian who paid a visit to the white people a few years past, and who, on account of his residence far in the North West, had seldom ever seen any before, being inquired of respecting the country in that remote region, which had been but little explored, replied, 'that he was old, but his sons had travelled very far, and told him some extraordinary things;' upon which he was asked, 'whether his sons had not told him lies?' 'Lies!' said he, in amazement! 'No, that is impossible, for they have never yet seen a European.' Friends retiring into the colonel's garden, spent the time in serious consideration of the present distressed circumstances of the poor Indians, and the various matters that have contributed to occasion it; which opened to us the great obligation laid upon rulers, in order to promote the general welfare of mankind, that they do justly, and love mercy; without which there can be no solid basis for a hope of enjoying peace, harmony, and concord: a blessing to nations, and individuals, infinitely more valuable than the most heroic conquests of war, the accumulation of riches, or the extension of territory.

"20th. Visited by Indians of different nations, daily — we thus become acquainted with their customs and dispositions, which we hope will some time turn to profit. Saw another Roman Catholic funeral, giving us a greater opportunity than heretofore, of being acquainted with their superstitious ceremonies and empty parade: we could not behold it without secret pity.— The Chippeway Indians being at continual war with the Pawnee nation, of whom they take many prisoners, men, women, and children, they bring them into this settlement, and sell them at from ten, to one hundred pounds, each; and it is computed that at present there are here about three hundred of these poor creatures in slavery. This trade commenced about twenty-five years ago, before which time, we are informed, the Chippeways put all their prisoners to death, being determined to extirpate the nation.

"First-day, 21st, had a large meeting in the sail-loft, which was thought to be a solid, favored time; that in the afternoon not quite so large. As this was likely to be a parting meeting with the people here, many of whom had constantly attended and shown themselves very affectionate to us, the congregation was unusually serious, and we were favored to take leave of them, under a solemn sense of Divine mercy and goodness being with us; which I believe will not soon be forgotten by them or us. Many took leave of us with expressions of gratitude that Divine Providence had permitted our being among them, and prayers for our return home in peace. Divers of the soldiers were tender.

"22d. A vessel arriving last evening, brought us intelligence that the commissioners, several interpreters, &c., had landed at the mouth of the river, eighteen miles from hence, where they wait the invitation from the Indians to go to Sandusky, and they request us to come to them when this vessel is ready to take us. This reanimated us with hope that a treaty would yet take place, and our long detention here would soon terminate. Every countenance expressed the relief it gave us. The interview between the commissioners and the Indian chiefs concluded more favorably than we expected. Such is our interest in the affections and good wishes of many of the people of this place, that I believe it would make them unhappy to hear of any injury being done to us.

"23d. The vessel not being likely to sail for some days, the commandant and Captain Robinson called on us, and consistent with his usual generosity and attention, desired to know our wishes respecting our departure, that he might order things accordingly; if we wished to go before the vessel sailed, his barge well manned should be at our command; for which, and for all his former favors, we thanked him, but concluded to stay for the vessel.

"25th. After taking an affectionate leave of many kind friends, who appeared much interested in our preservation and welfare, being accompanied by their good wishes, we went on board with Colonel England, Adjutant O'Brien, and Lieutenant Hendricks, and several women, who had been captives with the Indians, and were desirous of returning home with us. We sailed pleasantly for two hours, when the wind falling, the colonel, officers, and three of us Friends, got into a large covered barge, and were rowed down to the commissioners, at the mouth of the river. They and we were glad to see each other, after our long separation.

"26th. Having pitched our tents on a fine green, making a wing to a long row before erected, we slept comfortably. The commissioners were well accommodated in Captain Elliott's house, which is large and convenient. Fourteen tents, pitched on a beautiful green bank before the door, are occupied by Friends, the interpreters, two British officers, General Chapin, &c. A number of Indians encamped along side of us. The day was spent agreeably, and the colonel and officers from Detroit returned.

"27th. About one o'clock in the morning came on a tremendous thunder storm, which continued two hours, raining most of the time very hard, with continual flashes of lightning, and heavy peals of thunder. The ground of our encampment being very flat, we were soon deluged with water over our mattrasses, and retreating promiscuously into the house, we got no more sleep. It being necessary for some of us to return to Detroit, Joseph Moore and myself went off in a batteau about ten o'clock, being rowed by Indians. The day was hot, with the wind and current against us, which made the voyage tedious and unpleasant. Arrived at Detroit about sunset, where many of the inhabitants were glad to see us.

"28th. First-day morning I was unwell, probably the effect of our being so wet the night before last. Several of our acquaintances came to see us, and others sent to inquire whether there was to be a meeting at ten o'clock; but being poorly, and feeling weak without our friends, we declined it. Afternoon, not being satisfied at spending the day idly, we determined that it would be best to hold a meeting at five o'clock. Accordingly, upon our intention being known, many people assembled, and through renewed mercy, it proved a very tendering season, both to them and us — we thought more so than at any other time in Detroit.

The colonel, with his usual kindness, invited me to dine with him; but I desired to be excused from dining out on First-day.

"29th. Captain Freeman, Lieutenant Broadhead, and myself, breakfasted at Freeman's, at five o'clock in the morning; and the colonel's barge, manned by eight soldiers, took us down to our encampment, about twelve o'clock, where they dined, and spent the day with us. Joseph Moore stayed behind to finish some business at Detroit, and to come on to-morrow.

"30th. A deputation of twenty-five or thirty Indians, accompanied by Captain Elliott, Thomas M'Kee, Simon Girty, and one Smith, an interpreter, having arrived last evening from the Rapids, and encamped on an island opposite to us, delivered their message this morning to the commissioners. The purport of it was, that they had not fully delivered the message from the grand council to the commissioners at Niagara, and were now sent to be more explicit, and to put the question, Whether the United States were willing to make the Ohio the boundary line? This they now brought in writing, and required an explicit answer; and that if the United States agreed to this, it was expected they would immediately remove all the inhabitants off the land on the west side of the river. Our commissioners informed them, that they would take their message into consideration, and give them an answer when they were ready. After this they separated, and conversed with us. Among them were representatives of ten nations, and several of them great men among the Delawares and Shawnese.

"The Shawnese, Delawares, and Wyandots, as usual, said they knew Friends, and were acquainted with our motives in coming. I presented five of the principal men with neat tobacco-boxes filled with tobacco, which they said, when they looked upon, they should think of Friends. They departed in the afternoon, and slept upon the island. Their demand occasioned us to feel discouraged as to being able to effect a peace, and we retired to bed with heavy hearts. A number of Indians who were encamped very near us, joined by some white people, were dancing, singing, and yelling most of the night, accompanied with some Indian music, which, though not what they style the war-dance, was very disagreeable to us, and we got but little rest. This kind of disturbance we have before been, and no doubt shall continue to be, afflicted with. Our situation, at present, is very painful on several accounts; our family consists of about forty, including the servants, several of them very loose in their principles; and we are sorry to find that open debauchery is too generally practised on the frontiers; and so common has it become, that white men of the first rank do not appear ashamed of it. Three young women, Indian captives, designing to go home with us, went in the vessel to Fort Erie, to wait our coming.

"31st. The Indians came over to us after breakfast, and staid smoking their pipes and conversing with us until five o'clock in the evening, when the council-fire was again kindled, and the commissioners requested their patient attention to their answer, which, as the subject was of the highest importance, they could not comprise in a few words. It occupied several sheets of paper, to explain the reasons why they thought it impossible to make the Ohio the boundary line; but were still desirous of meeting them in full council, where, they could not doubt, from the amplitude of their powers, and the disposition of the United States to do them strict justice, and settle large annual payments upon the Indians for such lands as should be agreed to be confirmed to us at the general council, that the business would yet end in peace, to the satisfaction of both parties. The speech was then delivered to them in writing, and they withdrew to the island, with their interpreters and agents, saying they would give us an answer to-morrow. Three British officers from Detroit, who visited and dined with us to-day, were present.

"Eighth month, 1st. At nine o'clock in the morning the Indians returned; and after the fire was kindled, and they and we had smoked our pipes on the benches under the trees, as before, they delivered an answer; and remarked principally on that part of the speech which mentioned the impossibility of removing the white inhabitants off the lands which had cost so much to improve them, and said, it was equally hard for them to give up their land; that they should now return and inform their warriors what we had said, and that we might also return and tell our chief Washington. This last sentence was not approved by Captain Elliott; and some of the Indians, after the council had risen, taking the speaker aside, informed him that what he had said, was not intended to have been offered — upon which they returned, and told us they would now go to the great council, and lay our speech before them, and would send us an account of their result, and requested us to continue here till we heard from them.

"The business now appeared to most of us to be near a conclusion; and not knowing whether we might ever see them together, we sent our address, and a letter from ourselves, to the care and attention of Colonel M'Kee and Captain Elliott to deliver, and have interpreted to them. Friends consulted together on the propriety of some of our number going with these chiefs to the council. The concern and fervent engagement of our minds that the poor Indians might be wisely directed in the present juncture, produced a resignation in my mind to be one, though it appeared to me there would be some risk of our lives; but upon laying it before the commissioners, Captain Bunbury and Thomas M'Kee, they were not easy we should attempt it, as the Indians had positively forbid any American citizen to come on the ground, while the grand-council held; we therefore declined it.

"Eighth month, 2d. The morning passed in reading and conversation upon the trying situation we were in, and the necessity of asking for fresh supplies of wisdom and patience to enable us to answer, as much as in us lay, the objects of our journey. In the evening had conversation with the most libertine part of the company, who glory in their debaucheries; but it was like casting pearls before swine, they turn again and rend you.

"3d. The vessel called Detroit, bound to Fort Erie, appearing in sight, I wrote a hasty letter home.—Appointed a meeting to be held at Simon Girty's, tomorrow, at ten o'clock.

"4th. First-day morning. Very rainy, and much wet in my tent; rose about three o'clock, bundled up my mattress, and tied it in a painted cloth, and sat upon it till sunrise. The rain continuing, three of us went to Simon Girty's, but finding none met, except the family, returned. Captain Hamilton, an amiable man, and an officer in the fifth regiment, dined with us. The Chippeway, a vessel bound from Fort Erie to Detroit, brought one hundred and eighty Indians, and landed them at the Miami river. The afternoon being pleasant, had a meeting at Simon Girty's, about one and a half miles from our camp, at which a number of Indians were present, and behaved soberly. General Lincoln, General Chapin, Captain Hamilton, Lieutenant Gwans, and several seamen, also attended; I believe it was to satisfaction. The few scattered white people in this Indian country, many of whom have been prisoners of war, have no opportunity of public worship; yet some of them are glad of our meetings; among whom was the wife of Simon Girty, who also had been a prisoner among the Indians. Several of the Indians who were encamped near us, having got too much drink, were very abusive and unruly, and some serious consequences were apprehended; but they were restrained.

"5th. Spent the morning in serious conference with Friends, and with some Wyandot Indians; they think it unsafe for us to pay them a visit in the present state of things. This night was very uncomfortable, owing to swarms of mosquitoes; and notwithstanding every effort to avoid them, I did not sleep one hour, and many of our company walked the green most of the night.

"6th. Were afflicted with disagreeable conversation after dinner, which we are subject to have imposed upon us daily by the libertine part of our company. One of Captain Elliott's Pawnee slaves, who has been unwell since our first arrival, died while we were at dinner, and was buried the same evening; many of our company attended, and a number of Indians, &c. Joseph Moore spoke at the grave, which appeared satisfactory.

"8th. Twelve Indians called on us, being on their way home from the council, which they left with impressions that a peace would be made; but they said there still remained an opposition, principally from the Shawnese, Delawares, and Pottawattomies; and also a few of several other nations. They said the council had held too long for them, being tired, and their clothes worn out, but they had left the principal chiefs of their nations, Chippeway, and Munceys, at the

Rapids. In the evening, two Indian canoes having come down from Detroit, each having a keg of rum, some of our new visitors (Indians) got drunk, and came into our camp, just as we were going to bed, making a great noise, and going from tent to tent. Much persuasion being used, I at length prevailed on the worst one to let me lead him away some distance: he frequently called me brother, and seemed pleased with my attention; but after I returned, it appeared to me to have been a very dangerous undertaking, as he had a long knife at his side, which he had before drawn out and brandished in our camp; but Providence preserved me. They still kept at the distance of about a quarter of a mile from us, yelling and whooping; several of our company offered to be watchmen, which we thought prudent; and an uneasy night it was, as they passed frequently backward and forward by our camp; but no mischief was done to any. Early in the morning I was awakened by one of them, who had gotten into the middle of our encampment almost naked, very frantic and noisy, with his knife drawn, which he vapored in the air, and beat on his breast. Some of the servants and others would have seized him, but this would have been imprudent. After troubling us about half an hour, an old Indian, who was sober, came and led him away.

"9th. Most of the day, at intervals, we looked with anxiety towards a point of land in the lake, expecting a deputation from the Indians to invite us from this place, of which we are all weary, to the council; but no boats appearing, we must be longer trained in the school of patience.

"10th. Complaints were re-echoed from side to side of the camp against the dilatory proceedings of the Indians, and their squandering away the whole summer without coming to treaty: indeed it has been the most trying situation I ever experienced. — We were fully supplied to-day with poultry, butter, eggs, sheep, and pork, from Gross Isle, but at a very high rate; yet it is a mercy we can have such a plentiful supply at any rate.

"11th. First-day. The Ottaway from Fort Erie passed us; a number of passengers were on board, some of whom landed; among them was Jasper Parrish, an interpreter, who brought letters for us from Philadelphia, which was agreeable. The commissioners also received papers and other intelligence. Took an early dinner, and being accommodated with a boat and four hands, all the Friends but W. H. attended a meeting at Gross Isle at three o'clock, where I believe several received us gladly, and all heard patiently. Although the weather was hot, and we had nearly four miles to walk from the place where the boat landed us, yet I was glad I attended. These poor frontier people have very seldom any opportunity of assembling for religious worship; and though many of them in their dress and manners, as well as their information, are very little above the Indians; yet they esteem it a favor to have the benefit of a free ministry, travelling far on foot to attend meetings. Some are rude and restless at times, but others appear like thirsty ground, which I trust the great Lord of the harvest will in his own time water. Returned to our camp, and passed a painful night with the tooth-ache and swelled face, from which, with the addition of swarms of mosquitoes, I slept very little.

"12th. At break of day was seized with a chill. I arose, and, as well as I could, put on my clothes. Joseph Moore rising at the same time, we went to the house and knocked them up, being advised to take something by way of medicine. I continued very sick, with shivering and chill. After some time a fever succeeded, which continued very hot for about six hours, with pain in my head and limbs. Towards evening, with the doctor's advice I took an emetic, which operated violently; and being much fatigued, and falling asleep for a few minutes, I awoke in such a profuse perspiration, that by day-break my clothes and the blankets were wet, and I left extremely weak. This was a very trying scene to me, so far from my dearest connections and beloved relations; not knowing but it might be the Lord's will now to put a period to my stay on earth. I labored earnestly to be enabled to say, 'Thy will be done,' and did not perceive much cloud in the way, but saw it to be an awful thing to die. — It is a very sickly time among the inhabitants here, and many of the Indians have been carried off with a few days' illness; some of whom I knew. — I had my mattress removed into the shade of the tents of Friends, and laid there most of the day, taking little nourishment. My friends the commissioners and their companions were kind and attentive: at the same time several of our retinue were unwell; Jasper Parrish was thought to be dangerously ill.

"13th. Very languid and weak, with pain in my head and face. Captain Wilbank, who came with the Cherokee Indians to council, and eight other white people from Detroit and parts adjacent, dined with the commissioners. A gloomy depressing day with me, my mind frequently turned towards home, yet dare not wish to be there, believing we are in our right allotment, whatever may be the issue. Towards evening I was somewhat better, and a hope revived of being favored to see my dear wife and friends again. The Lord grant I may be preserved without a stain on my profession.

"14th. The servants and others sat up most of the night and were noisy, with music and dancing, which, with the abundance of mosquitoes, caused me to sleep very little until day-light; after which I got some quiet rest, and rose much refreshed and thankful, and was enabled to go and sit with Jasper Parrish, who remains in a high fever, is low in his spirits, and doubtful of recovery. I walked a little about and felt myself mending, yet my face continued much swelled. About noon, three Indians came from the Wyandot town with intelligence, that an Indian who had left the council had arrived there yesterday morning, and says that a deputation was agreed to be sent, inviting us to the treaty; but that the wind being unfair, they could not be expected suddenly. He also says, that disputes have run high among themselves, whether we should be sent for or not, as the commissioners had declared they could not make the Ohio the boundary line; but at length it was agreed to hear what the commissioners had to offer. All this appeared not to be so fully authenticated as we could wish. We are, however, often looking towards the point, twenty miles distance, with a spy-glass, desirous of discovering a boat, but are baffled by the canoes of the neighboring Indians, who are daily fishing along the opposite shore. Our commissioners, becoming almost impatient at the delay, despatched two swift Indian runners to the Rapids, about forty miles by land, for information. I felt much recovered, and slept tolerably.

"15th. My stock of patience was somewhat renewed, and we sat down with the company to breakfast, where we were obliged to explain many things respecting our principles, which were but little understood; this has indeed been our almost daily employment to one or another, and frequently to many at once. I hope nothing has ever suffered by our defence, though we often feel ourselves weak, especially as there are among us several men of consideration and understanding, as well as others, who make light of almost all religion. The weather being fine in the afternoon, our company spent much of the time in walking up or down the river. As our camp was thus rendered quiet, I passed the time in reading.

"16th. Colonel Pickering being desirous of giving

me more information than I had yet received, of the treaties held by the United States with the Indians, and the nature of their uneasiness, I cheerfully sat with him in his room till breakfast, and was pleased with the knowledge obtained; being also sensible of the confidence he reposed in me, by showing me the commissioners' books and papers. About four o'clock in the afternoon a canoe was discovered coming from a point a few miles distant, manned by two Indians, who proved to be deputies from the council; they brought a definite. message in writing, importing that the council had considered the answer of the commissioners to the former deputies, and objected to several parts of it, viz.:

"'They did not acknowledge the right of pre-emption to their lands as vested in the United States; but that they (the Indians) had a right to sell them to whom they pleased.

"That all the lands west of the Ohio were theirs; and that as we had told them of a large sum of money which we would give them to confirm the sale of those lands to us, they advised the commissioners to give it to the poor people who occupied them, and remove them away; and that unless this was acceded to, a meeting was unnecessary.'

"As these terms were inadmissible, the commissioners answered by a line or two, and immediately began to strike some of the tents, and to take part of the baggage aboard. About nine o'clock at night our two runners arrived, bringing no intelligence, as they said the Six Nations were not admitted into the private councils, and they knew not but that the message of the two Wyandots had been to ask us to council. As the Six Nations are in the interest of the United States, the other nations did not condescend to transmit any answer. Passed a painful night, under the prospect that the desirable end of our embassy would not be answered, and that great devastation and bloodshed would be the consequence. The writing was signed by the Creeks, Cherokees, and all the nations present, except the Six Nations.

"17th. Struck the remainder of the tents, and got all our baggage, sheep, fowls, ducks, &c., on board the Dunmore, by eleven o'clock. We were about sixty souls on board, including the commissioners' retinue, sailors, marines, prisoners returning home, &c. The wind not being fair, we waited some time, when it became rather more favorable — we sailed easily away, and reached the Bass islands, forty miles, by seven in the morning.

"18th. First-day, judging it proper to hold a meeting, we sat down in the cabin, being joined by General Lincoln, and several others; the remainder were above, round the cabin door. It was a solid time, several testimonies were borne, and the meeting concluded in supplication and thanksgiving to the Father of mercies, who had preserved and sustained us in the present arduous journey.

"19th. The servants and seamen having quarrelled, one of the marines was ordered to walk the deck with his sword, and to be relieved by the others, alternately, during the voyage.

"22d. The wind being high and fair, we sailed rapidly, and arrived at Fort Erie about twelve o'clock at night.

"23d. Wind so high all day, that it appeared imprudent to attempt landing; but in the afternoon, Captain Bunbury left us for Niagara, to engage a vessel going to Kingston, for our accommodation, when we should arrive.

"24th. In the afternoon, Jacob Lindley being furnished with a spare horse by the commissioners, and John Parrish, John Elliott, and Joseph Moore, having their horses sent to them, they took leave of us, intending to spend a day or two with a few Friends in the neighborhood, and wait the recovery of Parrish, the interpreter, who lay sick at a house a few miles off, as he was to be their guide through the wilderness. I felt heavy at parting with them; but seeing no alternative, wrote by Jacob Lindley, informing my wife of my intention to return by Montreal. Colonel Pickering, Governor Randolph, and their servants, with all the interpreters, also left us, with intention to proceed on different routes, and to spread information of the issue of the treaty, as it was apprehended that the Indians were already dispersed and doing mischief. Five women, who had been prisoners, also went off with General Chapin. Our company having now become small, we felt lonesome at parting with those who had been the companions of our trials. Five o'clock in the afternoon, a number of Canada Indians, accompanied by J. Launier, a Frenchman and interpreter, came on board to see us, conversed pleasantly with us, and invited our company on shore to a dance; many from on board accordingly went; but I had no inclination to behold what I had already seen too much of.

"25th. Captain Pratt sent us two batteaux, one of them large, for our baggage, the other for the passengers. Taking breakfast once more on board the Dunmore, we left her about nine o'clock, the sailors and marines parting from us with many good wishes. The boats being well manned with soldiers, we got on, and put in at Winternut's tavern, where Jasper Parrish, the interpreter, was confined, and still very weak. Here we again met with our friend, John Elliott, and soon after arrived at Chippeway. Captain Hamilton being the commandant of the fort, he met us at the shore, and took us to his apartment, where we were entertained with great frankness and generosity. About four o'clock in the afternoon, the general, doctor, secretary, Lieutenant Gwanz, and myself, proceeded in a wagon for Queenstown, stopping a few minutes on our way at the falls of Niagara; and got to our inn about seven o'clock in the evening. The farmers who live near the falls, would be subject to the loss of their geese and ducks, by their being carried down with the rapidity of the current, and dashed over this mighty cataract, were it not for an expedient which they have discovered as a preventive. They pluck the feathers entirely off their breasts, about the size of a dollar, and keep it constantly bare. The water so affects them in this part, that they stay in it but a few minutes; otherwise they would continue in their favorite element, and be destroyed, as many hundreds have already been. We were informed, that some years past, a sergeant and four men attempting to cross the river too near the falls, were all carried down and perished; those on shore not being able to render them any relief.

"28th. Got to Navy Hall, where we lodged.

"30th. Sailed about three o'clock in the morning, in a small sloop, and having a fine wind, made about one hundred and thirty miles; and as there were several islands ahead, the captain concluded to stand off and on all night.

"31st. Arrived at Kingston, a garrison formerly built by the French; now occupied by the British. A batteau being ready to receive us, we embarked for Lachine, and got on about twenty-five miles before dark. No houses appearing, the general orders were to lap ourselves in our blankets, and sleep in the boat; which we did as well as we could, having nine passengers and four Frenchmen on board, one or other of whom steered the boat all night.

"First-day, the 1st of Ninth month, sailed down the river St. Lawrence, and passed a fort on the American side, and also two Indian towns, one of them on an island. In the evening, after passing through the greatest number of islands I ever saw in a river, which are called the Thousand Islands, and also through a long rapid, we arrived at lake St. Francis. The wind being fresh, it was doubtful whether we could cross it or not in the night; but our Canadians concluding to venture on, we all laid down as in the preceding night. The lake is about fifteen miles long and six broad. I slept none; the clouds appeared wild and threatening for a night voyage. About ten o'clock, the helmsman seeing a gust rising, roused all up; and in a few minutes a terrible hurricane came on, with tremendous lightning and thunder, and very dark; but by the flashes of the lightning, we judged we were about a mile or a mile and a half from shore. The rain poured down in torrents, and it appeared almost a hopeless attempt to reach the shore; but some of our company, possessing considerable fortitude and skill, were active in directing and encouraging the men to persevere in rowing—notwithstanding all which, such was the impetuosity of the waves and violence of the winds, added to a deluge of rain and perpetual thunder and lightning, that one of our best hands threw down his oar, and cried out in French, 'We shall all perish,—we shall all perish!' But Providence, whose tender mercies were over us, had more gracious designs concerning us, and at length brought us safe to shore, which happily proved to be sandy, or we might still have been dashed to pieces. Having a piece of painted cloth on board, as many of us as could got under it, as it continued to rain very hard. About twelve o'clock it cleared away, and, being very cold, we concluded to go on shore, and walk about to warm ourselves, being thoroughly wet, and shivering with the cold. It was thought impossible to kindle a fire, as everything was so wet; but one of our Friends striking to light our pipes, we were enabled to kindle one, which was a great relief to us, and, sitting round it till daylight, were enabled to prepare something for breakfast, and set sail again. I believe all of us were thankful for our deliverance. The man who was most intimidated had a consecrated wafer about his neck to preserve him from drowning, but his faith failed him in the hour of trial.

"Ninth month, 2d, with a fair breeze we soon reached the far end of the lake, and got to a large new tavern, with a view of warming ourselves and procuring some refreshment; but there being no other fire than a little in an out-shed, we departed and sailed down the rapids, nine miles in thirty-five minutes; and a little further on came to another rapid, also said to be several miles long, which we passed in about four minutes, and arrived at Lachine about three o'clock in the afternoon. Feeling myself very unwell, I went to bed early, and had a restless night.

"3d. Having provided carts for our baggage, and each pair of us a calash (a kind of open carriage), and a French driver, we set off for Montreal, which, though unwell, and a great part of the road extremely bad, we reached about ten o'clock. This town is populous, and carries on a great trade. The chapels are open all day, and seldom without persons in them paying their devotions. Some we saw on their knees; and as we did not interrupt them, they continued thus engaged, and retired as they got through their performances. Here are several nunneries richly endowed; the sisters employ themselves in acts of benevolence, visiting the sick, relieving the poor, and at times in needle-work and in making images: several of them were passing to and fro in the streets, clothed in long black robes and hoods. The law which gives the church one-ninth of the purchase-money of all lands sold by public sale at the church door, has enriched this church to a degree that is almost incredible. The market, which is said to be one of the cheapest in America, is attended by a number of little cars about twice the size of a wheel-barrow, in which they bring vegetables, fruit, &c., and are drawn by two large dogs, which appear to be well kept and in comfortable condition.

"4th. The commanding officer at Montreal having sent orders to the farmers to find us two carts for our baggage, and four calashes for ourselves to convey us to St. Johns, they attended about six o'clock in the morning, being obliged to submit to such arbitrary commands, however much engaged in their husbandry, which was the case at this time, it being their harvest of oats and flax. Such are the effects of military government.—Breakfasting at Chambly, and riding through a beautiful country about twenty-seven miles, we arrived at St. Johns. I continued unwell, having a high fever on me, which was also the case with Captain Scott, and several others of our company. Fifteen of us embarked after dinner-time in a small boat, but there being scarcely any wind, and no current, we had to put in at a very undesirable place, the character of which was bad, and, we had reason to believe, in part at least, justly so. I retired to obtain some rest, but a company of rude people, who had got to the house before us, made such a continual noise, that I was kept awake until towards morning, when I got a little sleep.

"6th. Passed several garrisons, and proceeding with a fair wind, stopped at an American custom-house on the New York side: here we were obliged to leave the master of our boat, who was so ill he could go on no further. We had now none to steer or manage the boat, but a boy of about sixteen, who knew the lake; but the wind being fine and we anxious to proceed, William Hartshorne took command of the vessel, and we sailed pleasantly till evening. We aimed to harbor at Gillis's creek, where we might go on shore and sleep; but it being after dark before we arrived there, and none of us being acquainted with the entrance, we ran upon shoals and rocks, and the sea and winds being high, our little bark thumped as though the bottom would have been beaten out. In great danger we continued on the shoals near an hour; at length, with much difficulty, we got off, and anchoring in sufficient depth of water, were obliged to lay here the remainder of the night, and a painful one it was to me; it being rainy and a high wind, and no light to find our blankets. I laid down on some casks and trunks, but slept none, and my disorder returned upon me with double force in the morning.

"7th. Sailed about eight miles to a pretty good

house to breakfast; but I ate none and could scarcely walk from the vessel, in order to get upon a bed until the company were ready to depart. Went on all day without stopping again, and arrived at a small house with poor accommodations. I wanted nothing but a bed, and although there was but one, and our company consisted of the passengers of three vessels, yet they kindly gave that up to me, and I got a little sleep the fore part of the night.

"First-day, the 8th, arrived at Skeensborough or Whitehall, about ten in the forenoon, where I soon went to bed, as did likewise Captain Scott and others. In the evening I walked out a little, but had a very poor night, with high fever and much parched with thirst. My indisposition was now so serious, as to induce the fear that I must be left behind; yet I had a great desire to reach home, if practicable.

"9th. Friends encouraged me to proceed, though in great suffering, and we got to Fort Ann, after riding about eight miles over an exceedingly rough road. Here I took a little nourishment and laid down to rest; from thence we went to Fort Edward, and in the evening arrived at Saratoga: though the roads were somewhat better this afternoon, yet it was a very trying day to me.

"10th. After a tolerable night's rest, we put on and breakfasted at Still-water, having passed through a beautiful country, though at one time the seat of war, where General Burgoyne was captured. General Lincoln having been on the spot at the time, informed us of many particulars connected with that memorable event. We rode through a very pleasant country, and reached Albany in the evening.

"11th. Remained here all day, had a very poor night, and my fever coming on about three o'clock in the morning, I seemed almost ready to die with thirst.

"12th. Went on board a sloop for New York.—I was still very unwell, and my spirits increasingly depressed by receiving a confirmation of a report which we had heard at Saratoga, that my beloved city, (Philadelphia,) was in an alarming condition, from the prevalence of a very contagious and mortal fever—that the stages and all other means of communication between New York and it were stopped—that the vast numbers which died daily occasioned the common rites of burial to be intermitted, and a variety of other affecting accounts. After sailing about three miles, the vessel being heavily loaded, got aground, and though great exertions were made in the night, at high water, to set us afloat, they were without effect. Our passengers kindly gave me a berth, but my fit of illness coming on as usual about one o'clock in the morning, I passed a distressing time.

"13th. The Captain ordered a considerable part of our deck-load, which consisted of boards, to be rafted and to meet us a few miles below; this lightened the vessel, and she was with much labor got off; but the wind having left us, we made little way. In the morning, before day-light, I was attacked with the most violent chill I had ever experienced, followed by fever.

"14th, 15th and 16th, the wind being unfavorable, we made slow progress."

He gradually recovered from the chills and fever, and was able, in a short time, to return to his family, who were in the vicinity of Philadelphia. The yellow fever then prevailing in the city, his sympathetic mind was deeply affected with the great affliction and sufferings under which the inhabitants were laboring, in consequence of the awful pestilence then permitted to overspread that place.

Although Friends had not the satisfaction of seeing a general treaty of amity concluded, owing as was apprehended, to the interference of some evilly disposed and interested persons, yet the opportunities afforded for amicable intercourse with the Indians, for religious service among the frontier inhabitants, and for mingling with the families of Friends then newly settled in the parts they visited, together with the peaceful evidence that they were in the way of their duty, sustained them under the trials and privations they met with, and compensated for the sacrifices which they made in leaving home.

In rendering to the Meeting for Sufferings an account of the engagement, they remarked: that notwithstanding the desirable object of peace was not obtained, they had not a doubt of the rectitude of submitting to go on the arduous and exercising journey, believing that their company had tended to renew the ancient friendship with the Indian natives; many of whom, particularly the Wyandots, Shawnese, and Delawares, appeared to appreciate their motives in going, and some of those nations travelled sixty or seventy miles, in order to have the company of Friends —that they had been favored to travel together in much unity and harmony, and to return in peace.

The Society continued to feel a deep interest in the welfare of the natives, and to cherish toward them the obligations of justice and Christian benevolence. They commiserated their situation as an untutored race, liable from their ignorance to be easily imposed upon, and subject to the dominion of ferocious passions when excited. In their intercourse with them, therefore, they endeavored not only to satisfy the claims of justice to the fullest extent, but by kind and liberal treatment, to convince them of the sincerity of their friendship, and that they were actuated by the desire to promote their comfort and happiness. This course of procedure had procured for the Society a place in their confidence and affections, and an influence over them, which was often beneficially exerted in their councils, when deliberating on the most important subjects. When treaties were about to be negotiated, the Indians generally solicited the attendance of some Friends to advise and assist them; and after consulting the President of the United States, and obtaining his consent, which was always cheerfully accorded, the Society mostly deputed a few of its members to be present on such occasions, in the hope that they might be instrumental in calming the minds of the natives, and inducing both parties to accede to such reasonable propositions as might facilitate the settlement of the subjects in dispute, stay the effusion of blood, and restore those amicable relations, which it was so desirable should subsist between the United States and the aboriginal proprietors of our country.

CHAPTER II.

Joins another Deputation to an Indian Treaty—Address from Friends to the Indians — Journey from Philadelphia to the western part of N. York — Hard fare in the Wilderness—Canandaigua—Interview with Oneidas—Jemima Wilkinson and her followers—Oneida Council—Col. Pickering—Council of the Six Nations — Speeches of Indian Chiefs — Red Jacket — Cornplanter — Interference of British Agent — Number and Possessions of the Six Nations — Speech of Col. Pickering — Remarkable Spring — Speech of Red Jacket to the Friends — Red Jacket's reply to Col. Pickering — Another Speech by the Commissioner — Reply by Red Jacket — Interruptions to closing the Treaty — Efforts of Friends to compensate the Indians formerly owning the land about Hopewell, Va. — Speech of Cornplanter — Reply of Commissioner — Treaty signed—Address of the Indians to the Friends—Start for Home—Difficulties of the Journey—Arrival in Philadelphia — Reflections respecting the Indians — Visit to Virginia Yearly Meeting — Remarkable Service in Richmond—Return Home.

In the Eighth month, 1794, the Meeting for Sufferings was informed through the officers of government, that a treaty was shortly to be held at Canandaigua, in the State of New York, between commissioners appointed on behalf of the United States, and the chiefs of the Six Nations; and that they were particularly solicitous Friends should attend it — the government also encouraging their doing so.

After seriously deliberating on this important movement, four Friends, viz: David Bacon, John Parrish,

William Savery, and James Emlen, under an apprehension that it was their religious duty, offered themselves for the service, and being approved by the meeting, were furnished with a number of articles, as presents for the Indians, and with the following address, viz:

"*The people called Quakers, in Pennsylvania, New Jersey, &c., by their representatives assembled at Philadelphia, the 9th of Ninth month,* 1794:

"To our brothers, the Indians of the Six Nations, who have appointed to meet at Canandaigua, in order for the promotion of lasting peace;

"BROTHERS,

"We are always glad when we have an opportunity of hearing from you, our old friends, and using our endeavors in promoting the good work of peace.

"Brothers,—We understand the President of the United States has proposed holding a treaty with you, by his commissioners. Our religious profession has always led us to promote so good a work; and having been informed that the President of the United States, as also your nations, are willing and desirous we should be at the treaty, we have therefore authorized our beloved friends, David Bacon, John Parrish, William Savery, and James Emlen, to attend the said treaty for us; on whose behalf we make known to you, that they are our friends, whom we greatly love, being true men, whose love is so great to their Indian brethren, the old inhabitants of this land of America, that they are willing to come to see you, with desires to do you good.

"Brothers, — We meddle not with the affairs of government; but we desire to do all we can to preserve and promote peace and good-will among all men.

"Brothers, — Our grandfathers and friend Onas, were careful in their day to preserve peace and love with their brothers, the Indians: — We, their children and successors, endeavor to do the same, and are happy when we can prevail on the people to be kind, and do good and not evil to one another.

"Brothers, — We pity the Indians, as well as the white people, when they are brought into suffering and distress, and would do them all the good in our power. — We hope the Great and Good Spirit will put it into the hearts of the great men of the United States and your great men, to adjust and compromise all their differences.

"Brothers, — We hope you will receive kindly our friends and brothers, David Bacon, John Parrish, William Savery and James Emlen. We have put under their care a small token of love for you, as the descendants of the first inhabitants of this land of North America, whom our forefathers found here after they had crossed the great water. Desiring that the chain of our friendship may be kept bright, we bid you farewell.

"Signed by forty-four Friends."

The benevolent and sympathetic mind of our beloved friend, was so deeply interested for this injured people, that though he had endured so much in the late painful and hazardous journey to Detroit, yet he could not withhold his aid, when another attempt was to be made for adjusting the many grievances of his red brethren, and, if possible, settling the terms of a lasting peace. He has left the following narrative of the undertaking, viz:

"Left Philadelphia in company with my friends, David Bacon, John Parrish, and James Emlen, the 15th of ninth month, 1794; being accompanied by several Friends to Germantown, where we took an affectionate leave of them. Nothing from without affords so great consolation and strength in undertaking such arduous journies, as a sense that we are favored with the precious unity and affectionate concern of our near connections and brethren. This, to me, has been a comfortable reflection, and softens the trials I have felt at leaving my home at this time, especially as the Yearly Meeting is near at hand.

"Having got on the Blue mountains the 18th, we proceeded a short distance when it began to rain, and increased till our clothes were wet through; but after riding several miles, we stopt at a house, got some refreshment, dried our clothes and rode to Cattawissa. Neither the land nor the appearance of the country round this place appears very attractive.

"19th. Riding through a better country on the west side of the Susquehanna, we stopped at a place where they at times entertain travellers, and expected to dine; but they having neither feed for our horses, bread nor meat, we rode two miles further and dined upon bread, the people having neither meat nor milk.

"20th. Got to the house of a Friend at Loyalsock. Before I alighted from my horse I felt unwell, and immediately went to lie down. A fever coming on, I was very sick until evening, and began to doubt the propriety of going on, yet was glad that my indisposition was not the cause of detaining my friends, for it rained too hard to travel, until near night.

"21st. Being much recruited I went on, and after crossing the Lycoming eight times, proceeded over an exceedingly stony and miry path through the woods; we thought the road very long and tiresome, both to ourselves and the horses. At dark we heard the barking of a dog, which rejoiced us; but it proved to be at a place called the Block-house, a poor shelter indeed. We were now convinced of our neglect in not providing ourselves with necessary stores when we had the opportunity; such as sugar, tea, meat, bread, &c., for this family had nothing for us but a little flour, which the woman in a very dirty manner kneaded up in the fat of an elk, shot some days before. Our lodging and fare were truly uncomfortable. I could but admire how very few, even of what are called the necessaries of life, supported this family; the children, however, have a far more healthy appearance than is common in luxurious and populous cities; and having near thirty miles to send for salt, sugar, flour and other necessaries, a girl about fourteen, and a boy about thirteen years of age, generally performed the journey alone, sometimes lying all night in the woods. We had to lie on the floor, with the house open on all sides; yet were content, though we slept but little.

"22nd. Our horses being tied up all night without either hay or pasture, we fed them with some oats and rode about ten miles over an exceedingly bad path, the most difficult we had yet seen. Stopping a short time on the banks of the Tioga at the house of a new settler, we procured some feed for our horses, and a small piece of meat for ourselves. The country so abounds with wild game, bears, deer, elk, foxes and wolves, that it is difficult to keep hogs or sheep.—There being no taverns, all the farm-houses take in travellers and charge very high for poor fare.

"24th. We got to an Indian cabin on the bank of the river which runs by the town of Bath, and twelve miles further reached a sort of public house, having rode the whole of this day through the woods.

"On the 25th, we arrived at Canandaigua, in the afternoon, where Colonel Pickering and General Chapin were holding a conference with the Oneida Indians. Having welcomed us, they directed us to the lodgings prepared for us.

"26th. Attended a second conference with the Oneidas, which chiefly consisted in a relation of what had befallen them since the last treaty. They informed us, that as we were now met again, they hoped we should discuss all the necessary objects of the treaty with candor and freedom, and for that purpose they now unstopped our ears that we might hear, and opened our throats that we might speak freely. To this Colonel Pickering expressed his wish to conduct the business with the unreserved candor they desired, and that he also opened their ears and unstopped their throats.

"27th. Seeing some persons in the garb of Friends, they informed us they lived about five miles beyond this, and being glad to see us, invited us to their houses.

"28th. First-day, having appointed a meeting, to begin at eleven o'clock, it was largely attended by the people, and a considerable number of Indians, so that the house could not contain the whole. Appointed another at four o'clock in the afternoon, both of which were to satisfaction, and we believe to the people generally. There is no public worship maintained within many miles of this place.

"30th. Abraham Lapham came to our lodgings, and conducted us to his house, where we were kindly received, and spent a pleasant day. This country has two great disadvantages attending it, the scarcity of springs and rivulets, and the unhealthiness of the climate in its present uncultivated state, yet it is settling very fast, the land being very fertile; but as the Indians are all round, and the settlements of the whites very thin, there still is some danger to be apprehended. The first settlers have passed through great difficulties, having near one hundred miles to go to mill, and struggling under many privations to procure a living for their large families; some have staid for many weeks under the shelter of bark and bushes before they could erect a hut.

"Tenth month, 2d, fifth-day. Six of the Indians, each of them brought in a deer, and one of them made us a present of a piece, signifying that he gave it to us for Jesus Christ's sake, who had made us brethren.

"First-day, 5th of the month. The weather not being very favorable, the meeting was not so large as last First-day, nor so satisfactory. The Indians were remarkably sober, making but little noise; the Oneidas pay some regard to the First-day of the week.

"7th of the month. Went to Judge Potter's, and being kindly received stayed all night. The Judge is a respectable man, but having some years back been induced to entertain a favorable opinion of Jemima Wilkinson and her doctriues, he and several others came with her into this country, and took up forty-one thousand acres of excellent land near the west side of Seneca lake, at four pence per acre. But the good understanding of the Judge not suffering him to remain a dupe to the delusions of an assuming, presumptuous woman, he has for some time past thrown off the shackles, and is now no more accounted one of her fraternity. He said he believed her whole scheme was for self-interest and aggrandizement; he himself having suffered by her in a pecuniary point of view, but had now asserted his right to a part of the land occupied by these people, and forbade their making use of it. After breakfast we went to see Jemima, and found her about three miles from Potter's, in a sequestered, romantic place, suited to her genius. The family appeared to consist of ten or twelve persons, one of whom being acquainted with us, welcomed us in; another was a man far gone in a consumption, who had left his wife at some miles distance and brought so much of his little property with him, as to reduce her to great difficulty in getting a subsistence. His design appears to be to spend his last breath under Jemima's benediction, assuring us he was very easy about his soul. O, wretched infatuation! that can break the most solemn ties of God and nature, and yet flatter its votaries that they are the favorites of heaven.

"Here are several hovels adjacent, which are the residences of women who have forsaken husband and children; and also of men who have left their families, to become what they now literally are, hewers of wood and drawers of water to an artful and designing woman. One young woman who had been with them several years, told me the women frequently washed Jemima's feet and wiped them with the hair of their heads. Asking for the rest of the family, Rachel Malin stepped into Jemima's room and invited her out. She was attired in a loose gown or rather a surplice of calico, and some parts of her dress were quite masculine; she accosted us with a look of importance, and called me by name. The conversation becoming of a religious nature, she said much in a kind of prophetic manner. So great was her volubility, that we were obliged to interrupt her in order to express our disapprobation of the exalted character she gave to her own mission, and that it savored strongly of pride and ambition to distinguish herself from the rest of mankind by the appellation of the Universal Friend. Some other remarks were made to check her rhapsodies, but her assurance, and artful manner of leading off from a subject which she did not relish, rendered our efforts abortive. We were, however, not disappointed, for it cannot be expected that any power but that which is Divine, can bring her to a state of reason or of Christianity. This people have a meeting-house, and some of the scattered neighbors meet with them on First-days, but it appears they are declining fast; and both reason and religion inform us, that their fall is at no great distance, and perhaps the last days of this deluded woman may be spent in contempt, unless her heart becomes humbled and contrite, and the mercy of the Lord be eminently manifest to pity and spare her. Some credible persons resident in the neighborhood informed us, that Jemima had asserted, and it was believed by her credulous disciples, that the prophet Elijah had taken possession of the body of one James Parker and spoke through his organs; and that the prophet Daniel, in like manner, inhabited the body of Sarah Richards, another of her followers; but the prophet Elijah, (James Parker,) and she having afterward disagreed and separated, and Sarah Richards having died, they are now deprived of their counsel.

"9th. The Senecas are very slow in coming to attend the treaty, and the lesson of last year is to be learned over again; this is patience, which will always be needed by those who attend Indian treaties.

"11th. Colonel Pickering having called on David Bacon and myself, we attended him to the Oneida camp, where an interesting council was held, in which Captain John, an Indian sachem, and Peter the chief warrior, were the speakers. Colonel Pickering made a very suitable speech, informing them that he had heard of divisions among them, and if they would inform him of the cause of them he should be happy in using his endeavors to settle them. Captain John then informed us in a long speech of many things which had occasioned uneasiness in their nation, principally in relation to the manner wherein they had several times suffered in the sale of their lands; and lately by leasing to Peter Smith one-third of the land they had reserved, being a tract of four miles wide and twenty-four miles long, which they had leased to him for twenty-one years, at two hundred dollars per annum. This had occasioned great dissatisfaction between the sachems and the warriors, the warriors protesting against the lease; that the two parties, whilst the land was surveying, faced each other in arms, and had not the surveyors desisted, it might have proved destructive to the nation, and they were yet divided into parties. He began by observing, that we were all in the presence of the Great Spirit, and he knew that he could not conceal anything from Him, and as he was now surrounded by his brethren, he should speak uprightly and withhold nothing. He spoke nearly an hour, and delivered to Peter, the chief warrior, five strings of wampum, which Colonel Pickering gave into his hand as he closed his speech. He then desired, if the warriors had heard anything that was not true, they would point it out. Peter, after reminding Colonel Pickering of the advice which he gave them at Newtown in the last treaty, said he found no fault with what the sachems had said, but desired that if they had gone out of the path they were recommended to walk in when at Newtown, which he suspected they had, the colonel would put them right again.

"Colonel Pickering told them he believed they had, but as it was a matter of great importance, he desired to consider it until the day after to-morrow, that he might prepare an answer. The conference held three hours, after which Colonel Pickering acknowledged that both private persons and the governor of New York had given great occasion for their complaints. Smith's lease contained sixty-one thousand four hundred and forty acres. In the evening John Parrish and James Emlen returned from the encampment of the Senecas at Gennessee river, about twenty-six miles distant, bringing an account that there were about five hundred of them at that place.

"12th. Understanding a person expected to occupy our former place of meeting, we concluded to prepare the house where we lodge for holding a meeting. Friends who are settled in the neighborhood, and several others, with a number of the Indians coming in, we had a solid favored opportunity. Some who had expected us at the school-house as usual, came after that meeting was over, and said that they had been disappointed in not finding us there, but thought that for the future they should come to our lodgings on a First-day morning to know where the meeting was to be held. In the afternoon we went at four o'clock to the Oneida camp, having previously informed the chiefs of our intention of a meeting there, the interpreter being with us. We found some collected in the woods where many trees were felled, which served as seats, and one of the chiefs went round the camp, vociferating a certain sound used as a signal for them to assemble, which they did in large numbers. The curiosity of the white people being raised, and some coming from other motives, we had a large and good meeting, which held till near sunset; both whites and Indians were quiet and behaved decently; as many of the Indians had received some notion of the Christian religion from missionaries, and were desirous to begin the service with singing of hymns or psalms, and we not thinking it would be best to object to their wishes, they appeared very devout, and I thought that the melody and softness of their voices in the Indian language, and the sweetness and harmony that attended, exceeded by far anything of the kind I had ever heard among the white people. Being in the midst of the woods, the satisfaction of hearing these poor untutored people sing, with every appearance of devotion, their Maker's praise, and the serious attention they paid to what was delivered to them, conspired to make it a solemn meeting, long to be remembered by me. We left them in much love and sympathy, rejoicing in the midst of the wilderness that the Lord is indeed everywhere.

"13th. Ruminating on the state of the Oneida Indians, who are said to be more civilized and better instructed in religion than any others, it is natural to inquire what influence it has had on their manners and morals, which, from anything I can discover, has yet been very small. It is true, they generally cultivate a small portion of land, and for that reason are less exposed to absolute want than other Indians: they have also heard of Jesus Christ through their missionary, and have been taught to sing psalms and hymns in their own soft and engaging language; but it appears to me that the great body of the nation have received the Gospel in word only, and not in power. It has therefore had but little influence on their conduct; and a few excepted, they appear to remain enslaved to all the vices common to the other Indians; yet I think the way is gradually preparing when some more enlightened and spiritual men than have yet been their teachers, men who will unite example with precept, may be sent among them with a good effect.

"Colonel Pickering having called on us again, we went with him to the camp, where the chiefs and warriors being assembled, he delivered a long written speech, containing suitable advice for reconciling the differences in the nation, and also as a rule for their conduct in future respecting their lands, which appeared well calculated to prevent the frauds and impositions of designing men. They heard all patiently, and then desired us to withdraw a few minutes while they consulted among themselves. Being again called in, Captain John said they were in hopes that Colonel Pickering would have informed them whether the sachems or warriors had been wrong, for it would not have hurt the sachems if they had been so told plainly. The advice to them had been very long, and he could not retain all parts of it, but he recollected they were told that Peter Smith, agreeably to our laws, was not only subject to have his bargain made void, but also liable to pay a fine of a thousand dollars and suffer a year's imprisonment; the two latter they hoped would not be inflicted, as it was not their wish. He also noticed what was said concerning our government and laws, saying, the Indians had also their mode of law, which had been handed down by their forefathers; and one of their customs was, for the sachems only to sit in council on civil affairs; but of late, their warriors appeared jealous of them, and had intruded into matters contrary to the ancient customs of Indians; hence we might see, that when they were about to answer the commissioner, Peter the chief warrior had gone off and took the warriors with him, which indicated his being displeased; and he thought he would show it either during the present council-fire, or afterwards. Indeed, he apprehended that Peter was aspiring to be something more than the nation was willing he should be, and aimed at being the chief sachem. He then told us in very drolling style, the manner of the white people persuading them out of their lands, even some who had not half the understanding naturally, that was possessed by some of their chiefs, but they were skilled in dissimulation and acquainted with the propensities of the Indians. They agreed to take the advice given them and wished it again repeated.

"Colonel Pickering told them, he would use his influence to have their lands, which Peter Smith had taken upon lease, restored to them, and that after they were restored, if that could be obtained, he wished them still to offer them upon lease, and to take the assistance of some judicious men that might be appointed by government; they might then lease them in three hundred separate farms, with certain stipulations that the land and timber should not be ruined, &c. The consequence of this would be, that in twenty-one years, there would be so many improved farms in their possession, which would result in a great accumulation of wealth to the Oneida nation. He concluded by promising to return by the Oneida castle, as he went home, where he would repeat his advice to them, that they might not forget it; and told them they had reason to rest peaceably and quietly, though it should not even be in the power of government to reclaim the lands which Smith had got upon lease; for they should consider that a great estate was still in their possession, if the best use was made of it: whereupon the council broke up.

"14th of Tenth month. The party of Senecas, headed by the Farmer's Brother, Little Billy, &c., having arrived, last evening, within four miles, were expected this forenoon; but having to paint and ornament themselves before their public entry, they did not arrive till three o'clock this afternoon. The Oneidas, Cayugas, and Onondagoes, were drawn up, dressed and painted, with their arms prepared for a salute before General Chapin's door. The men able to bear arms marched in, assuming a good deal of importance, and drew up in a line facing the Oneidas, &c.; Colonel Pickering, General Chapin, and many white people being present. The Indians fired three rounds, which the other Indians answered by a like number, making a long and loud echo through the woods. Their commanders then ordered them to form a circle around the commissioner and General Chapin; then sitting down on the ground, they delivered a speech through the Farmer's Brother, and returned the strings of wampum which were sent them, when they were requested to come to the treaty. Colonel Pickering answered them in the usual complimentary manner, and ordered several kettles of rum to be brought; after drinking which, they dispersed, and went to prepare their camp. Each chief delivered in a bundle of sticks, answerable to the number of persons, men, women, and children, under his command, which amounted to four hundred and seventy-two. They made a truly terrific and warlike appearance.

"16th. About three o'clock this afternoon, Cornplanter and his party of the Senecas arrived, amounting to about four hundred. They drew up in three sides of a square, the Oneidas, Onondagoes, &c., facing them; each fired three rounds, and performed some manœuvres; all in full Indian dress, and painted in an extraordinary manner. Then encircling the commissioners and us, they exchanged a short speech of congratulation, and as it rained, the rum was soon brought, and the company dispersed. There are now about sixteen hundred Indians assembled. Last night one Indian stabbed another, who, although not yet dead, is unlikely to continue long.

"17th. Sixteen hundred Indians are around us, many of them very noisy night and day, dancing, yelling, and constantly intruding upon us to beg for rum, &c., but we uniformly resist their importunities for strong drink. The attendance at Indian treaties is a painful task, wherein resignation is highly necessary. May it be granted. They kill plenty of venison, and sell it for three half-pence, or less, per pound. Whilst at our present place of abode, I sat in company with an Indian Queen, who had a small child in one of their kind of cradles, hung with about one hundred small brass bells, intended to soothe the child to rest.

"18th. This morning Cornplanter, Farmer's Brother, Red Jacket, Little Beard, and a number more of the Seneca chiefs, came to our lodgings to hold a conference, the interpreter being with them. Cornplanter congratulated us upon our safe arrival among them, and acknowledged the kindness of General Washington in informing Friends of the request of the Indians, that they should attend the treaty. He then opened the business, which more particularly occasioned their present visit. This was to answer a request made to them a year or two past by Friends at Philadelphia, that they might make inquiry after the Indians, or their descendants, who formerly lived about Hopewell, in Virginia.* He said that they had conferred together on the subject several times, and believed they had come to the knowledge of the original owners of that land, two of whom, ancient men, were now present, who said their people were once settled about Conestogo, and that they remembered well the state of matters respecting the land in question: they had no doubt those two ancient men could clear up the matter to our satisfaction, at a future opportunity, and would retire for the present.

"In the afternoon, Obeal, son of Cornplanter, came with a message from the Indians, inviting us to council. We found a large body of them collected, Colonel Pickering, General Chapin, and three interpreters being in the centre, and the surrounding assemblage presenting a very striking aspect; the chiefs appeared solid and thoughtful. Captain John, and another of

* Some members of the Society of Friends had purchased and settled upon lands about Hopewell, and there was reason to believe that the Indian title had not been extinguished by a fair and honorable purchase of the natives, by those occupants who had sold to Friends. The Society, consonant with its known principles, was desirous, that notwithstanding the Indians had left or been driven to remote parts, yet that if the original proprietors could be found, however feeble and insignificant they might now be, they should be fully compensated, in order that its members might hold those possessions on such a firm and justly acquired fee, as true Christian principles would dictate.

the Oneidas, spoke, addressing themselves to their brothers, the Senecas, Tuscaroras, and Delawares, who lived westward, holding in their hands, as they spoke, one after the other, several strings of wampum and belts; which they handed to the Seneca chiefs, one by one, at certain periods of their address, till they delivered all they had. As it was only an address to their brethren, the Indians of other nations, agreeably to their ancient custom, when they meet at a council fire, it was not publicly interpreted; but we understood it was in the way of condolence, on account of the loss of many chiefs of the Six Nations by death, since they last met at a council fire. They expressed their desire to wipe the tears from their brethren's eyes, to brighten their countenances, and to unstop their throats, that they might speak clearly in the present council fire. The Fish Carrier, Clear Sky, and Red Jacket, returned a brotherly salutation, handing the eastern Indians belts and strings of wampum, to unite each to the other, and thus to open the council as with the heart of one man. They then informed Colonel Pickering, that the Six Nations were now embodied in council. He made them a complimentary and congratulatory address, informing them that he should hold a council of condolence to-morrow at four o'clock in the afternoon, to wipe away the tears from the eyes of the Delawares, who had lost a young brother, murdered by a white man at Venango, last summer; he would then take the hatchet out of the head of the deceased, and bury it in the earth, preparatory to the treaty. Several kettles of rum and glasses were brought, and the conference closed.

"19th, First-day. Held a meeting for worship; a considerable number attended, who lived generally from two to ten miles distant. Many of them came on foot, there being but few horses in this country, and fewer wheel-carriages of any kind. One family came a considerable distance upon a sled drawn by four stout oxen. The people were solid, and through Divine favor it proved a good meeting, many were very tender and parted with us lovingly. It does our hearts good to see the gratitude some of the poor frontier people manifest, and the pains they take to be at a religious meeting. O Philadelphians, how abundant ought your gratitude to be for the enjoyment of your multiplied blessings.

"Tenth month, 20th. Attended a very large Indian council, at which the commissioner condoled with the Delawares for the loss of one of their people, and by his speech and gestures performed the ceremony of burying him after the Indian custom, and covering the grave with leaves, so that when they passed by they should not see it any more. He took the hatchet out of his head, and *in words* tore up a large pine tree and buried the hatchet in the hole, then covered it thick with stones and planted the pine tree on the top of it again, so that it should never more be taken up. He wiped the blood from their beds and the tears from their eyes, and opened the path of peace, which the Indians were requested to keep open at one end and the United States at the other, as long as the sun shone. Many other things of the like nature he said to them, after the figurative style of the natives, that all might be cleared out of the way before the business of the treaty commenced. In the course of his speaking on different subjects, he gave them as many strings of wampum as were thought to be worth near one hundred dollars.

"The Farmer's Brother then spoke with great energy to his Indian brethren, and they not being ready to answer Colonel Pickering's speech, the council fire was covered and the rum brought in as usual.

"Third-day, 21st. Jemima Wilkinson being come to this place last evening, sent a message by two of her flock to James Emlen and myself, desiring our company; but as it snowed very fast and was a stormy time, we did not immediately obey the summons. After an early dinner, David Bacon being with us, we went and found her at Thomas Morris's, by invitation of Colonel Pickering to dine with him; D. Waggoner, and Enoch and Rachel Malin were also there. The Colonel paid great attention to Jemima, and seemed to be glad of having an opportunity to gratify his curiosity, as he had never seen her before. She was placed at the head of the table, and the conversation being on a variety of subjects, she bore a considerable part therein. A message was received informing that the Indians were collected. We went to council, whither Jemima and her disciples followed us, and were placed in the centre. Fish Carrier spoke in answer to the commissioner's address yesterday, till he had passed through his hands one by one, all the strings that were given them, and made a full reply: then with assurances of the determination of the Six Nations to keep hold of the chain of friendship with the fifteen fires, he delivered fifteen strings of chequered wampum as a seal to it. Colonel Pickering introduced himself as sole commissioner on the part of the United States, whom the Six Nations had requested might be appointed on the present occasion; gave them assurances of his desire to promote the happiness and peace of their nations, and told them that they might depend upon one thing at least, which was, that he never would deceive them. He also introduced us, their old friends the Quakers, as having come forward at their (the Indians') request, and with the approbation of the President. We then read the address from Friends, Jasper Parrish interpreting, which they received with frequent expressions of *entaw* or approbation; and afterwards Clear Sky said, they were glad to see us among them, and thanked us for our speech. It is however expected that they will give us a more full answer before the treaty is over. Immediately after we had read our speech, Jemima and all her company kneeled down and she uttered something in the form of prayer, after which she desired to speak, and liberty not being refused, she used many texts of Scripture, without much similarity or connection. The Indians having prepared belts as records of the death of several of their noted chiefs, intended to preserve the memory of their usefulness to the nation; a short speech was made on each of them to their brethren, and they were then delivered to the care of an ancient chief, whereupon the council fire was covered.

"23d. Captain John, an Indian chief, visited us, and had much to say about the many deceptions which had been practised upon them by the white people; observing, that however good and honest white men might be in other matters, they were all deceivers when they wanted to buy Indian lands; and that the advantages of learning which they possessed, made them capable of doing much good and much evil.

"Colonel Pickering requesting our attendance at a council, we went about eleven o'clock. Nearly forty chiefs being assembled, Captain John, in a humorous manner, informed the commissioner of a council they were called to attend; but when the chiefs had collected, they were invited up stairs to take a dram before they began. Perceiving that Berry was to be the commissioner, they concluded it was no good council fire, so he came off and drew the rest of the Indians with him; it appearing that it was a design to get the chiefs to convey to him some Indian lands, after he should have filled them with liquor. The colonel highly approved of the Indians' conduct, and said he would have Berry removed off those lands. An account was brought to the council of the death of an ancient Oneida, upon which Captain John made a speech to their brothers of the other nations. They agreed that as the Great Spirit had brought them together to promote the work of peace, it could not be unacceptable to Him if they went on with the council, though it was contrary to their common custom. Being about to proceed to business, a request was made from three Indian women, to be admitted to the council, and deliver their sentiments, which being granted, they were introduced by Red Jacket. He addressed himself to the sachems and warriors, desiring their indulgence of the women, and also to the commissioner, enforcing their request by observing, that the other day one of our women had liberty to speak in council. He was then desired to act as orator for the women, and deliver to the council what they had to say. The substance of this was, that they felt a deep interest in the affairs of their nation, and having heard the opinions of their sachems, they fully concurred in them, that the white people had been the cause of all the Indians' distresses; that they had pressed and squeezed them together, until it gave them great pain at their hearts, and that the whites ought to give them back the lands they had taken from them. That one of the white women had yesterday told the Indians to repent; and they now called on the white people to repent, for they had as much need as the Indians, and that they should wrong the Indians no more.

"The colonel thanked them for the speech, and replied, that it was far from him to think meanly of women: he should always be willing to hear them when they had anything of importance to say, but as they had mentioned as a precedent, the woman who spoke the other day, he must assure them, that it was not with his approbation; she had forced herself into council contrary to his advice; but as she was a woman, he was tender of her.

"The commissioner gave us some information of the speech of the Indians yesterday, when we were not present. They said, when the white people first came on this island, they saw that they were men, and must have something to subsist upon, they therefore pitied them, and gave them some land, and when they complained that the land became too small for them, they gave them more, from time to time, for they pitied them. At length a great council fire was kindled at Albany, where a silver chain was made, which was kept bright for many years, till the United States and the great king over the water differed; then their brothers in Canada talked with them, and they let the chain fall out of their hands, yet it was not their fault, it was the white people's. They then repeated how things went at the end of the war, the substance of the treaty at Fort Stanwix, and several grievances which they had suffered. The commissioner spoke, perhaps two hours, respecting the ancient boundaries of the Six Nations' land, and inquired what was the extent of it. They told him, all the land from a point on Lake Erie to Muskingum was theirs, and that the council at the Miami, last summer, acknowledged it. This takes in a great part of what the Western Indians are fighting for. The commissioner told them, he did not approve of the conduct of the commissioners at Fort Stanwix — that they had just then become conquerors, and the Indians must make some allowances, if they spoke harshly and proudly to them. This council held five hours, and much was said on both sides.

"This morning, the 25th, snow was seven or eight inches deep, and having been out in it yesterday, I was unwell. Abundance of deer are killed by the Indians, perhaps not less than one hundred to-day, within a few miles of this place, some in sight; one man killed three in a short time. A man named Johnson, having arrived two days ago from Fort Erie, with a message from Captain Brandt, a Mohawk chief, to the Six Nations, assembled some chiefs yesterday and delivered it to them. Being in the character of a British interpreter, he appeared at the council with the Indians to-day, and seemed very intimate with them. Cornplanter rose to vindicate his coming, being privy to the great uneasiness it had given Colonel Pickering: he expressed his surprise, that ever since the conclusion of the peace with the British nation, such an antipathy had existed, that the United States and the British could not bear to sit side by side in treaties held with the Indians. He said, Johnson had the care of the Senecas at Buffalo-creek, and had brought a message to the Six Nations assembled at this council fire, from Brandt, whom he left with Governor Simcoe at Fort Erie; they having just returned together from Detroit: that when he went some time ago to see the Western Indians, he sat in council with the Delawares, Shawnese, Wyandots and Miamies, and the Western Indians expressed great joy at seeing the Six Nations represented by him among them; they told him he recollected that the business of the treaty last year did not go on, but the fault was not theirs, it was that of other people, and the Indians were led astray, for which they were sorry. The misfortunes that had fallen upon them were very heavy, and our brothers the British, who were sitting by, gave us no relief. We allow you who are listening to us, to be the greatest, we will therefore hear what you say. We desire a council fire may be kindled next spring at Sandusky, for all nations of Indians. Captain Brandt sends his compliments to the chiefs at Canandaigua, and says, you remember what we agreed on last year, and the line we then marked out: If this line is complied with, peace will take place; and he desires us to mention this at Canandaigua; after the council at Canada is over, it is my earnest desire you will immediately come to Buffalo-creek, and bring General Chapin with you—I will wait here till you return.

"Colonel Pickering rose and said, he was sorry that anything should happen to interrupt this council fire: but it is now interrupted by the coming of Johnson, whom he considered as a British spy, and that his being here was an insult to him, to their friends the Quakers, and to the fifteen fires. That the intrusion of this man into our councils, betrayed great impudence, and was a fresh proof of British insolence. It was perhaps as well that there was no council yesterday, for he could not say how far the first emotions of his mind at seeing this fellow here, might have carried him; he hoped he was now a little cool, and would endeavor to moderate his expressions as much as he was capable of. He begged their patience, for he must be obliged to say a great deal to inform them of many of the reasons of his indignation at this step of the British government, and why it was totally improper to go on with the business while a British spy was present. He then went into a very lengthy detail of the ill-treatment of that government to the United States, for several years past, and concluded with saying, that either this man must immediately be sent back to those who sent him, or he, Pickering, would cover up the council fire; for his instructions from General Washington were, to suffer no British agents at the present treaty.

"The Indians appeared in amazement at the warmth with which the commissioner delivered himself, and said, when he sat down, the council fire grows warm, the sparks of it fly about very thick. As to Johnson, he appeared like one that was condemned to die, and now rose and left us. The Indians requesting we would withdraw, counselled among themselves about half an hour, and sent for us again. Cornplanter rose and said, the reason why the council fire has not been uncovered to-day is, because of a British man being present. It was caused by us, we requested him to come here, it is true, but the fault is in the white people. I am very much surprised and deceived by what you told us at Fort Stanwix, when you laid before us a paper which contained the terms of peace agreed on between you and the English nation; and told us it was agreed on in the presence of the Great Spirit, and under his influence. We now discover what the commissioners then told us was a lie, when they said they had made the chain of friendship bright; but I now find there has been an antipathy to each other ever since. Now our sachems and warriors say, What shall we do? we will shove Johnson off: Yet this is not agreeable to my mind, for if I had kindled the council fire, I would suffer a very bad man to sit in it that he might be made better: but if the peace you made had been a good peace, all animosities would have been done away, and you could then have sat side by side in council. I have one request to make. which is, that you would furnish him with provisions to carry him home. The council having sat about five hours, adjourned till to-morrow. We dined by candle light, with the commissioner and about fifteen chiefs, among whom were Cornplanter, Red Jacket, Little Beard, Big Sky, Farmer's Brother, Fish Carrier, Little Billy, &c. Many repartees of the Indians, which Jones interpreted, manifested a high turn for wit and humor. Red Jacket has the most conspicuous talent that way; he is a man of a pleasing countenance, and one of the greatest orators amongst the Six Nations.

"26th. First-day, several of our friends from parts adjacent came in, expecting a meeting for worship, but the commissioner having called the council together, no meeting was held. The council being assembled, the first business was the presentation of a letter which the Indians having got prepared since yesterday; they thought proper for the commissioner to see it, as they intended to send it by Johnson to Captain Brandt. The contents of it were not altogether agreeable to the commissioner. They expressed their sorrow that Johnson could not be permitted to stay, the reasons for which, he would doubtless inform them when he got home. It assured Brandt, they were determined to insist on the line agreed to last year, and expressed the sense they now had, that they were a poor, despised, though independent people, and were brought into suffering by the two white nations striving who should be greatest. The Indians appeared pretty high to-day, and little was done but clearing up some misunderstanding respecting the cause why the treaty was not held at Buffalo-creek, agreeably to the Indians' request—the disposition of the Senecas appeared rather more uncompromising than heretofore.

"27th. Expecting a council, we went to the commissioner who was in private conference with some chiefs; but he informed us he is now preparing the way for a full and general council to-morrow, when he will cut the business short by decidedly opening the proposals of accommodation: this is agreeable news to us, who have been already much wearied with continual delays. Colonel Butler of Niagara, had despatched a runner, a Tuscarora, who brought intelligence of a late engagement between the Western Indians connected with some British soldiers, and General Wayne, fought near the forks of the Glaize, in which many on both sides were killed; and being weary, the combatants withdrew from the field of battle. The Indians appear cautious of letting out the particulars, probably from the fear that they may operate to their disadvantage at this critical juncture of the treaty; and the accounts being very various, nothing can be clearly ascertained. Sagareesa, chief of the Tuscoraras, and several others of his nation, spent most of the afternoon with us; a half-Indian who lives with them, interpreted, and the conference was to satisfaction. We endeavored to obtain a correct account of the numbers remaining in the Six Nations, and find as follows, viz: the Senecas number about nineteen hundred; the Tuscaroras, three hundred; the Oneidas, six hundred; the Cayugas, four hundred; the Onondagoes, five hundred; the Mohawks, eight hundred. A considerable part of the Cayugas and Onondagoes, have moved off their reservation and reside mostly with the Senecas and Tuscaroras, but some of them have gone over the lake to the Mohawks, within the British territories. By the best computation we can make, the number of acres that each nation still holds, is as follows, viz: The Senecas, about four millions of acres; the Oneidas, two hundred and fifty-six thousand; the Cayugas, sixty-four thousand; the Onondagoes, seventy thousand. The Tuscaroras have no land of their own, but are settled near the Senecas on their lands. The Stockbridge and Brotherton Indians, two small remnants, have some land which was granted to them by the Oneidas and confirmed by government, viz: Stockbridge, twenty-three thousand and forty acres; Brotherton, thirty-eight thousand and forty acres. The Brothertons are an assemblage of about one hundred and fifty Indians, of various tribes from New England, settled near Brotherton on the Mohawk river. The Mohawks are at the Grand river and the bay of Quinta, on the North sides of Lake Erie and Lake Ontario, in the British government.

"This evening Friends being quietly together, our minds were seriously turned to consider the present state of these Six Nations; and a lively prospect presented, that a mode could be adopted by which Friends and other humane people might be made useful to them in a greater degree than has ever yet been effected; at least for the cause of humanity and justice, and for the sake of this poor, declining people, we are induced to hope so. The prospect and feelings of our minds were such as will not be forgotten, if we are favored to return home. The happy effects of steady perseverance in the cause of the Africans, is an encouraging reflection, and may serve as an animating example in this. Our business here, though trying and tedious, is sometimes accompanied with an ample reward.

"28th. Red Jacket visited us with his wife and five children, whom he had brought to see us; they were exceedingly well clad in their manner, and the best behaved and prettiest Indian children I have ever met with: Jones came to interpret. Red Jacket informed us of the views which the Indians had in inviting us to the treaty; which Jones confirmed, being present at the council at Buffalo-creek; viz. Believing that the Quakers were an honest people and friends to them, they wished them to be present that they might see the Indians were not deceived or imposed upon.

Yesterday many of the chiefs and warriors were very uneasy at Cornplanter's frequent private interviews with the commissioner, and Little Billy spoke roughly to him, told him he should consider who he was, that he was only a war chief, and it did not become him to be so forward as he appeared to be; it was the business of the sachems, more than his, to conduct the treaty. He told them he had exerted himself for several years, and taken a great deal of pains for the good of the nation, but if they had no further occasion for him, he would return home; and he really intended it; but Colonel Pickering and General Chapin interested themselves to detain him. The dissatisfaction of the Senecas rose so high, that it was doubtful whether a council would be obtained to-day, but about three o'clock they met; Cornplanter not attending. The commissioner spoke, and told them of the several conferences that had been held with a number of the chiefs since last public council, and what the substance of their business was. He also told them he was sorry that they were made uneasy at the conduct of their war chief, but they ought not to blame him, for he, the commissioner, had invited Cornplanter to his quarters, and therefore if there was any impropriety, to blame him, for it was his fault. This pacifying them, he then said the business of the treaty had been retarded so long, that he was now determined to open to them, fully and candidly, the terms upon which the chain of friendship would be brightened, and the extent of what he intended to do towards it. He produced his commission, with full power to propose and adjust the accommodation of all differences between them and the United States; which he handed me to read.

"After many observations upon former treaties, and the grant made by their old father, the king, to William Penn, he opened the terms, which were as follows: but in the first place, perhaps, as this is an important matter, it will be most proper to take notice, that he acquainted the Indians now collected, both chiefs and warriors, being more than at any council we have yet had, that the chiefs had laid before him only two rusty places in the chain, one of which he had already brightened, the other was thought by their chief warrior to be very deep, though the sachems thought it not of so great moment; that in order to clean this rusty spot, their chief warrior had proposed a new line between them and the United States, to begin where the Alleghany crosses the north line of Pennsylvania, thence to French creek below the forks of ——— creek; thence to the forks of Muskingum; thence down the Muskingum to the Ohio. This, he apprehended, would remove every cloud of difficulty. He observed to them, that the sachems had acknowledged it was now four years since he had been brightening the chain of friendship between them and the United States, and that it had been even as in the days of Sir William Johnson, that the rusty part now alluded to had never before been complained of to him, except by their elder brother, the Mohawk. Colonel Pickering thought it was rather within the claim of the Western Indians; and as they had, from time to time, acquiesced in the treaty of Fort Stanwix, they might reasonably suppose that their conduct in relation to the affair at Presque Isle must have given surprise to the President, who, feeling a fatherly care for their nations, had required of the persons to desist, who were about to form a settlement at that place; and had appointed him to inquire into, and endeavor to adjust, the difference subsisting between them: since which he had examined all former treaties, and reminded them, that at the treaty of Fort Stanwix, they had ceded all the lands within the bounds of Pennsylvania — that many of them were acquainted with the charter granted by the king of Great Britain to William Penn; that at the last treaty held before the war, at Fort Stanwix, about twenty-six years ago, they had received ten thousand dollars from Pennsylvania, and had agreed that they would sell no lands within the said boundaries, but to the proprietors of that (then) province. That treaty at Fort Stanwix had been confirmed at Muskingum in 1786, which was also acknowledged by the chiefs at Tioga; at which last place complaint was made that Phelps had cheated them, yet not a word of the former treaties. He then had reference to the triangle on Lake Erie, which Pennsylvania has purchased of Congress, and showed them on the map that it was ceded by them to the United States at the treaty of Fort

Stanwix; and for which the State of Pennsylvania paid them two thousand dollars at the treaty of Muskingum, in confirmation of the title. Butler and Gibson, the commissioners at the last mentioned treaty, expected the east line of the triangle would have extended to Buffalo-creek; but that not being the case, he offered to cede back to them all the land between the triangle and a line running due south, from near the mouth of the said creek to the Pennsylvania line, which comprehends three or four times the quantity of land included in the triangle; and that the new line might run thus: to begin at Johnson's landing-place, about four miles distant from Niagara; thence along the inlet, including a strip of land four miles wide, till it comes within four miles of Buffalo-creek; thence to said creek at one mile distant from the mouth of it; thence along Lake Erie to the aforesaid triangle; bounded on the west by the said triangle, and on the south by the Pennsylvania line. The commissioner observed that the four mile path on the side of the inlet, between Lake Erie and Lake Ontario, was ceded to our predecessors, the British, in the days of Sir William Johnson; yet, that the Indians shall have the right of hunting on these lands, as well as on all those ceded at the treaty of Fort Stanwix; and on all other lands ceded by them since the peace; and their settlements thereon shall remain undisturbed: and also, that in addition to the annuity of fifteen hundred dollars which had heretofore been paid to them, the President had empowered him to add the sum of three thousand dollars more, amounting in all to four thousand five hundred dollars, to be paid to them annually, and to their posterity for ever; for the providing of clothing, encouragement of artificers, school-masters, &c., to settle among them. He had also goods at this place to the amount of ten thousand dollars to distribute among them, if the treaty should issue to mutual satisfaction. In consequence of the liberal offers now made, he hoped the Indians would cheerfully comply, and join him in digging a deep pit to bury all former differences, and take hold of the chain of friendship so fast, that nothing should ever be able to force it out of their hands. The Indians, after considering a few minutes what had been said, concluded to take it into further consideration, and return an answer.

"29th. Sagareesa, or the Sword-Carrier, visited us; he appears to be a thoughtful man, and mentioned a desire he had, that some of our young men might come among them as teachers; we supposed he meant as schoolmasters and artisans. Perhaps this intimation may be so made use of in a future day, that great good may accrue to the poor Indians, if some religious young men of our Society, could, from a sense of duty, be induced to spend some time among them, either as schoolmasters or mechanics. At eleven o'clock, Colonel Pickering called and gave us an invitation to dinner; Captain Hendricks, an Indian, and several strangers, dined with us; after which, Robert Nealy came in, who had been taken prisoner about forty years ago, being then about nine years old, and had continued with the

Indians ever since, without any desire of returning or making much inquiry after his parents. Being entirely reconciled to the Indian life, he had taken several wives among them, none of whom were dead; but whenever they grew dissatisfied with each other, they parted and took others more agreeable, which, he said, was the general custom; and when the Indians lost a near connection, they were inconsolable till some of their friends made up a belt of wampum, and gave it to the family of the deceased, in remembrance of their deceased relation; after which, they betrayed no sorrow — a scalp from an enemy answered the same purpose, if taken with that design. Many of the Indian chiefs being drunk, no council was held to-day.

"Fifth-day, 30th. A fine warm day, the Indians almost all turned out of their cabins; some of the young warriors having good horses, were running races all day with the white people; others engaged in different sports, dancing, &c., which is almost a daily exercise. They performed one which they call the brag-dance; when, whoever deposits a bottle of rum, has the liberty to make a brag of the feats he has performed in war, the number of scalps he has taken, &c. A sensible man being present, after he had deposited his bottle, and the others had boasted of many marvellous exploits, made his brag, which was, that he had been a man of peace all his days, in the profession of a physician; that he had been very industrious, and restored many who had been ready to die. He said, all that the others had bragged of, was nothing to this, for any child might kill a man, but it required the judgment and wisdom of a great man to save another's life. They all acknowledged the doctor's was the best of all. The sachems and chiefs were engaged in council, by themselves, and sat till near night, and inform that they will meet us in council to-morrow. The interpreter says, parties rise high against Cornplanter, that he is in a difficult situation with his nation, and they are not able to conceive what he has done with eight hundred dollars received in Philadelphia, from the Pennsylvania government, and what induced the government to give him fifteen hundred acres of land for a farm; these things have created jealousies unfavorable to him.

"There is a remarkable spring near this place, called the brimstone spring, which is so strong, as to have deposited in its course a large quantity of sulphur. Also, the salt springs of Onondago, which are said to be inexhaustible, and all this country is supplied with salt made from the waters.

"31st. Red Jacket, Clear Sky, Sagareesa, and a chief of the Cayugas, waited on us at our lodgings, being a deputation from the Indian council that has been deliberating several days upon the proposals of the commissioner, bringing with them the interpreter. Several Indians and some white people being in the room with us, they were desired to depart, as the business they came about would not admit of their presence. Apprehending that we should be interrupted in the house, we retired to a distance, and sat down upon some logs, when Red Jacket spoke nearly as follows:

"Brothers, — You see here four of us of the Six Nations, who are assembled at this place, in the will of the Great Spirit, to transact the business of the treaty. You have been waiting here a long time, and often visited by our chiefs, and as yet no marks of respect have been shown you.

"Brothers,—We are deputed by the council of chiefs assembled, to come and see you. We understand that you told Sagareesa, that you should not have come, but at our request, and that you stood ready to afford us any assistance in your power.

"Brothers, — We hope you will make your minds easy. We who are now here are but children; the ancients being deceased. We know that your fathers and ours transacted business together, and that you look up to the Great Spirit for his direction and assistance, and take no part in war. We expect you were all born on this island, and consider you as brethren. Your ancestors came over the great water, and ours were born here; this ought to be no impediment to our considering each other as brethren.

"Brothers,—You all know the proposals that have been made by Cunnitsutty (Colonel Pickering, the commissioner), as well as the offers made by us to him. We are all now in the presence of the Great Spirit, and we place more confidence in you, than in any other people. As you expressed your desire for peace, we now desire your help and assistance—we hope you will not deceive us; for if you should do so, we shall no more place any confidence in mankind.

"Brothers,—We wish, if you know the will of Congress, or the extent of the commissioner's powers, that you will candidly inform us.

"Brothers,—We desire that what we are now about communicating, may be kept secret. We are willing to give up the four-mile path, from Johnson's landing-place to Cayuga-creek, agreeably to our compact with Sir William Johnson, long ago. The other part proposed by Colonel Pickering to be relinquished by us; that is, from Cayuga to Buffalo-creek, we wish to reserve on account of the fisheries; that our women and children may have the use of it for that purpose. We desire to know if you can inform us, why the triangle on Lake Erie cannot be given up.

"Brothers,—Cornplanter and Captain Brandt, who were only war chiefs, were the persons who attended the treaty at Fort Stanwix, and they were to have sent forward the proposals for our more general consideration. At that time Old Smoke was alive, who was a man of great understanding; but they were threatened into a compliance, in consequence of which Captain Brandt went off to Canada, desiring Cornplanter to do the best he could."

"They delivered us seven strings of wampum, and we desired them to call on us about three o'clock for an answer. We felt it to be a weighty and delicate matter to answer their request in our situation. They returned about the time fixed, but finding us not entirely prepared to give them an answer, told us not to hurry ourselves, and they would come to-morrow morning; for they are never in haste.

"Eleventh month, 1st. Our house was full of Indians and others all the morning. About ten o'clock, the interpreter and the four chiefs came for our answer; we had endeavored to digest their request as well as we were capable of, desirous of dealing honestly with the poor Indians and of keeping a conscience void of offence. My friends laid it upon me to deliver the answer, which I did, holding the seven strings of wampum in my hand; and the reply being interpreted to them, I returned the strings at the end of our speech according to the Indian custom. Red Jacket went over the three points to which we had spoken, to know whether he had perfectly understood us, that he might deliver our sentiments to the great council. He thanked us for our advice, and said, though we might account it of small value, they did not consider it so, but thought it would afford them considerable strength.

"After dinner, John Parrish and myself rode to view the Farmer's Brother's encampment, which contained about five hundred Indians. They are located by the side of a brook, in the woods; having built about seventy or eighty huts, by far the most commodious and ingeniously made of any that I have seen; the principal materials are bark and boughs of trees, so nicely put together as to keep the family dry and warm. The women as well as the men, appeared to be mostly employed. In this camp, there are a large number of pretty children, who, in all the activity and buoyancy of health, were diverting themselves according to their fancy. The vast number of deer they have killed, since coming here, which they cut up and hang round their huts, inside and out, to dry, together with the rations of beef which they draw daily, give the appearance of plenty to supply the few wants to which they are subjected. The ease and cheerfulness of every countenance, and the delightfulness of the afternoon, which these inhabitants of the woods seemed to enjoy with a relish far superior to those who are pent up in crowded and populous cities, all combined to make this the most pleasant visit I have paid to Indians; and induced me to believe, that before they became acquainted with white people and were infected with their vices, they must have been as happy a people as any in the world. In returning to our quarters we passed by the Indian council, where Red Jacket was displaying his oratory to his brother chiefs, on the subject of Colonel Pickering's proposals.

"Eleventh month, 2d. Held a meeting for worship in the school-house; a number of Friends residing in this part of the country, came in; and a considerable body of Indians were in and about the house; several of whom, as well as the white people of other societies, behaved well, and it was thought to be a good meeting. We went immediately after meeting to the council which had just assembled, and was very numerously attended both by Indians and whites. The business was introduced by Clear Sky, an Onondaga chief, in the following manner: He expressed a hope that there would be no hard thoughts entertained, on account of their having been several days deliberating on an answer; the subject was of importance, and he wished his brethren to be preserved in unanimity. Then Red Jacket being principal speaker, said,

"Brothers,—We request that all the nations present will attend to what we are about to deliver. We are now convened on one of the days of the Great Spirit; Then addressing Colonel Pickering:—

"Brother,—You now represent the President of the United States, and when you spoke to us, we considered it as the voice of the fifteen fires. You desired that we would take the matter under our deliberate consideration and consult each other well, that where the chain was rusty, it might be brightened. We took General Washington by the hand, and desired this council-fire, that all the lines in dispute might be settled.

"Brothers,—We told you before of the two rusty places on the chain, which were also pointed out by the sachems. Instead of complying with our request, respecting the places where we told you the chain was rusty, you offered to relinquish the land on Lake Erie, eastward of the triangular piece sold by Congress to Pennsylvania, and to retain the four-mile path between Cayuga and Buffalo-creek, by which you expect to brighten the chain.

"Brothers,—We thought you had a sharp file to take off the rust, but we believe it must have been dull, or else you let it slip out of your hands. With respect to the four-mile path, we are in want of it on account of the fisheries; although we are but children, we are sharp-sighted, and we see that you want that strip of land for a road, that when you have vessels on the lakes, you may have harbors, &c. But we wish, that in respect to that land, the treaty at Fort Stanwix may be broken. You white people have increased very fast on this island, which was given to us Indians by the Great Spirit; we are now become a small people, and you are cutting off our lands, piece after piece — you are a very hard-hearted people, seeking your own advantages.

"Brothers, — We are tender-hearted, and desirous of peace—you told us what you would give us for our land, to brighten your end of the chain. If you will relinquish the piece of land we have mentioned, our friendship will be strong. You say you are not proud; neither are we. Congress expects we are now settling the business with regularity; we wish that both parties may have something to say in settling a peace. At the time we requested a conference, we also requested that our friends, the Quakers, should come forward, as they are promoters of peace, and we wanted them to be witnesses to what took place; we wish to do nothing in private. We have told you of the rusty part, which the file passed over without brightening it, and we wish you to take up the file again, and rub it very hard; you told us, if it would not do without, you would apply oil.

"Brothers,—We the sachems, warriors and others,

all depend on you; whatever is done, we regard as final and permanent; we wish you to take it under consideration, and give us an answer.

"Colonel Pickering replied, If I understand you right, your minds are easy excepting with respect to the strip of land between the two lakes. He then recapitulated what Red Jacket had expressed, which is the usual custom of the Indians in their answers; reminding them why they decreased, and the white people increased, and gave them advice in what manner they might increase also; observing, that he did it as their friend, for he wished to see them rise and become a great people. Here Red Jacket called out earnestly, in his language, 'keep straight.' The commissioner proceeded.

"Brothers,—You say you are anxious for peace; so are the people of the United States, anxious for peace with all the Indians on the whole island. We do not speak it with our lips only, it is the language of our hearts. You say, if we relinquish the four mile path from Cayuga to Buffalo-creek, a lasting peace will take place. The other day I gave you strong reasons why we could not give it up. I told you, if I could not rub out the rusty spots, I would cover them over, and I told you how I would cover this; alluding to the money offered as an equivalent. You seem to be sensible that the United States stand in need of a passage from lake to lake, by land. I therefore conclude, you would have no objection, if the land remains yours, to our cutting a road, and if we do so, it will be very inconvenient, unless we can have taverns to accommodate travellers, as the distance is great. You know they have a road and accommodations on the opposite side of the river, and as there can be no communication between the lakes, unless we have that privilege, the United States will have the same necessity for a road on this side.

"Brothers, — If you should travel it yourselves, you would like to have a house to get a walking-staff; you justly observe, the United States will want a harbor for their vessels on the lakes, but they can have no benefit from a harbor, unless they have the privilege of building houses and stores. If this is all the difficulty between us, I trust we shall not be long in coming to a conclusion.

"Brothers, — When I came from Philadelphia, it was not expected I would relinquish a hand's breadth of land; but finding your villages on that part which I have offered to cede back, I freely give it up. I am growing impatient to conclude the business, and would be glad to know, whether you will give me an answer, or take some time longer to consider of it." As the Indians did not appear ready to give a final answer, he told them, he observed it to be a tender point with them, and proposed their taking it into consideration until to-morrow, and that he wished to confer with some of the chiefs at his lodgings, previous to their coming to council, which he thought would expedite the business.

"It is a custom with the Indians, after the decease

of one of their brethren, to return to the donor any present which he had received in his life-time as a mark of respect. In conformity with this usage, Red Jacket now returned to the commissioner a silver gorget, belonging to one of their chiefs, who died last year, which had been presented to him by the United States. Farmer's Brother made a speech of condolence on the occasion, and presented some strings of black wampum to the family of the deceased. Clear Sky, then in a short speech, covered up the council fire.

"3d of the month. Big Beard, Sonochle, Canundach, Canatounty, and a John Whitestripe, all Oneidas, called at our lodgings. Big Beard mentioned, that some Friends whom they had seen at New York, requested them to make inquiry who were the original owners of the land about Hopewell, and that if it could be ascertained, it was probable a present would be made them by the Friends who reside in that neighborhood. He said, they had accordingly made the inquiry, and although, it was beyond a doubt, that the original proprietors were incorporated with the Six Nations, yet they were so mixed and intermarried among the different tribes, that it would be difficult to point them out; they therefore apprehended, it would be most equitable, to distribute it among the Six Nations at large. No council was held to-day; a number of the chiefs being much intoxicated. We were teased by them for liquor, and were, at last, obliged to flee from their persecutions.

"4th. Sagareesa and Captain William Printup, a

chief and warrior of the Tuscaroras, with an interpreter, visited us, to converse about the Hopewell lands, appearing to have no doubt that the Tuscaroras were the original proprietors. Colonel Pickering came to our lodgings, to read the proposed articles which were to conclude the treaty, the signing of which, as witnesses, if we were called upon to do it, had, for several days, been a subject of serious consideration with us. We told him, on hearing what was proposed, that we apprehended for reasons given, we could not be free to sign the treaty; which did not appear to be agreeable to him; but we have not now to begin to learn to suffer at Indian treaties. At two o'clock, an Indian messenger from the council, came to inform us they were assembled and waiting for us, the Indians not being disposed to proceed in our absence: a great number were assembled, and Red Jacket addressed the commissioner:

"Brothers,—We, the sachems of the Six Nations, will now tell you our minds. The business of the treaty is, to brighten the chain of friendship between us and the fifteen fires. We told you the other day, it was but a very small piece which was the occasion of the remaining rust in the chain of friendship.

"Brothers, —Now we are conversing together, in order to make the chain bright. When we told you what would give us satisfaction, you proposed reserving the piece of land, between Cayuga and Buffalo-creek, for building houses, &c., but we apprehend, you would not only build houses, but towns. You told us, these houses would be for the accommodation of travellers in winter, as they cannot go by water in that season, and that travellers would want a staff to help them along the road. We have taken these matters into serious consideration.

"Brothers,—We conclude that we do not understand this as the white people do; if we consent to your proposals, we know it will injure us. If these houses should be built, they will tend to scatter us and make us fall in the streets, meaning, by drinking to excess, instead of benefiting us: you want land to raise provisions, hay, &c.; but as soon as the white people settle there, they would think the land theirs, for this is the way of the white people. You mentioned, that when you got possession of the garrisons, you would want landing-places, stores, fields to plant on, &c.; but we wish to be the sole owners of this land ourselves; and when you settle with the British, the Great Spirit has made a road for you, you can pass and repass by water; what you want to reserve is entirely in your own favor.

"Brothers,—You told us, when you left Philadelphia, it was not expected by the President you would release a foot of land. We thank him for having left you at liberty to give up what you please.—You have waited with patience at this council fire, kindled by General Washington; it is but a very small thing that keeps the chain from being brightened; if you will consent to give up this small piece and have no houses on it, the chain will be made bright. As to harbors, the waters are between you and the British; you must talk to them, you are of the same color. I see there are many of your people now here, watching with their mouths open to take up this land: if you are a friend to us, then disappoint them, our patience is spent; comply with our request; dismiss us, and we will go home. The commissioner then replied:

"Brothers,—I wish your attention to a few words. —I thought you knew the necessity the United States had for a road from Fort Schlosser to Buffalo-creek. You appear sensible of it now, by referring to the road by water, made by the Great Spirit; you may see we can have no benefit of that without a passage by land. You have forgotten what I said the other day, respecting the treaty of Sir William Johnson, by which he obtained a right to pass and repass through your country. I then observed, that what was granted to the King was transferred to the United States by our treaty of peace with the British; now since so small a piece is between us, to convince you that I am not difficult, if you grant us but liberty to pass and repass, I will give up the rest. You know there is a path already from Buffalo-creek to Niagara; I only ask liberty to make a better path, to clear the stumps and logs out of the way. I am sure, that about so small a matter you can make no difficulty; I will sit down and wait your answer. After a short space, Colonel Pickering observed, he had forgot to inform them that the road should be opened under the direction of the superintendent of the Six Nations, Canadesago; who would take care to have it done so as to be as little injurious as possible to the Indians.

"The sachems having consulted together about half an hour, Red Jacket replied:

"General Washington, now listen; we are going to brighten the chain of friendship between the Six Nations and the Americans. We thank you for complying with our request, in giving up the particular spot in dispute. You mentioned that you wanted a road through our country; remember your old agreement, that you were to pass along the lake by water; we have made up our minds respecting your request to open a road.' Colonel Pickering writing what was said, Red Jacket would not proceed till he looked him in the face.

"Brothers,—It costs the white people a great deal to make roads, we wish not to put you to that great expense; we don't want you to spend your money for that purpose. We have a right understanding of your request, and have agreed to grant you a road from Fort Schlosser to Buffalo-creek, but not from Buffalo-creek down this way at all. We have given you an answer; if, on considering it, you have any reply to make, we will hear you.

"Commissioner.—I confess, brothers, I expected you would have agreed to my proposal; but as this is not the case, I will give it up, only reserving the road from Fort Schlosser to Buffalo. There has been a mutual condescension, which is the best way of settling business. There are yet several matters to be attended to before signing the articles of the treaty; which I can best communicate to some of your chiefs, as it would not be so convenient to discuss them among large numbers. One matter is, how the goods and annuity had best be appropriated; and as there are some bad people both amongst you and us, it would be well to fix some modes of settling disputes, when they arise between individuals of your nations and ours. As soon as we have digested a plan, we will introduce it into the public council. I therefore invite two sachems and two warriors of the Senecas, and a sachem and a warrior of each of the other nations, to take an early breakfast with me to-morrow morning. I now cover the council fire.

"5th of Eleventh month. No council to-day— Colonel Pickering and some chiefs busy in preparing the articles of treaty.

"6th. An interpreter, with four other Indians, came to have further conversation about the Hopewell land. It does not appear probable, that the Conestogoes were the original owners. We requested them to convene some sensible chiefs of each nation, and we would meet them at General Chapin's, with a map of the United States, and endeavor to settle the matter, if possible. General Chapin is of opinion, that the Tuscaroras are the original owners of the Virginia land. No council in public, Colonel Pickering being engaged all day, in conference on the articles of treaty; new objections and dissatisfaction were started by several principal chiefs, who are unwilling to relinquish Presque

Isle. They were surprised to find that Cornplanter, Little Billy, and others, had received two thousand dollars worth of goods from Pennsylvania at Muskingum, and two thousand dollars at Philadelphia. Their minds being much disturbed, they broke up the conference; this was a sad disappointment to us, who expected that all would be amicably settled, and we should set off to-morrow. General Chapin says, he hopes all will come right again, but the Indians must have time to cool. It is to no purpose to say you are tired of waiting, they will only tell you very calmly, Brother, you have your way of doing business, and we have ours; we desire you would sit easy on your seats. Patience then becomes our only remedy.

"7th. No business to-day; many of the chiefs being drunk. Colonel Pickering spent the afternoon with us. The idea he entertains respecting the lands ceded at Fort Stanwix, is, that as the Indians did the United States a great deal of injury by taking part with the British in the late war, it was strictly just that they should make compensation by giving up the lands which they relinquished at that time. He instanced the case of an individual who had committed a trespass on another; the law determines that the trespasser shall suffer either in person or property, and this law is just. Such is the reasoning of conquerors.

"8th. The Indians were sober to-day. General Chapin and the commissioner have determined to give them no more liquor, until the treaty is over. The chiefs and warriors were engaged till three o'clock with the commissioner, and agreed on all the articles of treaty to be engrossed on parchment, and signed to-morrow. At four o'clock, we met Cornplanter, Red Jacket, Scanadoe, Nicholas, a Tuscarora, Twenty Canoes, two ancient Conestogoes, Captain Printup, Sagareesa, Myers Paterson, a half white man who lives with the Tuscaroras, and several other chiefs at General Chapin's, to determine about the Hopewell land; examined maps and conversed with them on the subject, which resulted in the opinion, that the Conestogoes should quit claim to it; it appearing to those present, that the original right was in the Tuscaroras; one of whom, an ancient man, put his finger on the place in the map, saying, he had papers at home that would, as he thought, confirm their claim to it. We desired him to send them to General Chapin to examine, and if he thought they contained anything worth notice, he might forward them to us in Philadelphia.

"First-day, the 9th. Several Friends in this part of the country came to the meeting; one of them thirteen miles. A number of other white people attended, and a large number of Indians. It was a solid meeting; several, both of whites and Indians, were tender, and wept; and after it was over, one man in a particular manner, confessed to the truth, and prayed that the Lord might bless it to all who were present. On my part, it was an affectionate farewell to the people hereaway. We returned to our lodgings, and before we had finished our dinner, a messenger came to inform us that the council was gathered, and waiting, which we immediately attended. Two large parchments, with the articles of the treaty engrossed, being ready for signing, we were in hopes the business would now close; but to our surprise and disappointment, we soon discovered some dissatisfaction among the Indians, by their putting their heads down together and whispering. After waiting impatiently for about an hour, not knowing what it meant, Cornplanter rose and spoke, as follows:

"Brothers, — I request your attention, whilst I inform you of my own mind as an individual. I consider the conduct of the United States, since the war, to have been very bad. I conceive they do not do justice. I will mention what took place at New York at one particular time. After the treaty of Fort Stanwix, I went to New York under an apprehension, that the commissioners had not done right; and I laid before Congress our grievances on account of the loss of our lands at that treaty; but the thirteen fires approved of what the commissioners had done, and in confirmation of it, they held up the paper, with a piece of silver hanging to it; (the treaty with the British.) Now, Colonel Pickering, you have told us at this treaty, that what was given up by the British, was only the land around the forts. I am very much dissatisfied that this was not communicated to us before. There has already been too much blood spilt; if this had been known at the close of the war, it would have prevented any blood being shed. I have, therefore, told our warriors not to sign this treaty. The fifteen fires have deceived us; we are under the sachems, and will listen to what they do. Though we will not sign it, yet we shall abide by what they do, as long as they do right. The United States and the Six Nations are now making a firm peace, and we wish the fifteen fires may never deceive them, as they have done us warriors; if they once deceive the sachems, it will be bad. He then took his seat, and after a short pause, said, I will put a patch upon what I have spoken; I hope you will have no uneasiness at hearing the voice of the warriors; you know it is very hard to be once deceived, so you must not make your minds uneasy. Eel, the herald, then made a warm speech to the Indians, exhorting them to abide by the decision of the sachems, which was received with loud shouts of applause. Entaw! Entaw! Entaw!

"Colonel Pickering then addressed them as follows:

"Brothers of the Six Nations and your associates,— I confess I am greatly surprised at the speech of your head warrior, after all the pains I have taken to make the articles of the treaty easy. I endeavored to please both sachems and warriors, they were both present when the articles were agreed on, and there was not a word of objection.

"Brothers,—The design of this treaty is, to bury all differences; you know I candidly and explicitly disapproved of the conduct of the commissioners at Fort Stanwix, but as this treaty was to establish a firm friendship between the Six Nations and the United

States, I did not wish to bring former transactions into view, which was also the desire of your chief warrior; now he brings up the old matters to make a division in your councils.

"Brothers, — I wish for calmness and deliberation, as the subject is of importance to us, and of the utmost importance to you. He expresses his dissatisfaction that our treaty with the British was not explained before; but this was done last year to the Western Indians, when many of the Six Nations were present; I think many of the chiefs must remember it. I will explain it again to prevent mistakes. A certain line was drawn between the British and us; what the British had obtained of the Indians on our side of that line before the peace, was transferred by that treaty to the United States: it was agreed that the British should not interfere with the land on this side of that line, nor were we to interfere with the land on their side of the line.

"Brothers, — I am very sorry that these objections are made now when we are just about to sign the treaty. The chief warrior has called it the treaty of the sachems, and said, that they only were to sign it; but the warriors, as well as the sachems, were present when it was agreed on, and made no objection to it. He says, they will abide by what the sachems do, as long as they do right. Does he mean they will abide by them no longer than the warriors think them right? If this be the case, we may as well let things remain as they are. He says also, the United States and the sachems are now making a firm peace, but I cannot consider it so, unless the sachems and warriors unite; for unless this is the case, it will cause divisions among yourselves; consider whether this will not be attended with dangerous consequences. He speaks of the United States deceiving the sachems; as I represent the United States, I have told you I will not deceive you; I can add nothing on that head to what I have told you already.

"Brothers,—I cannot consent to close the business in this manner, after so much care and pains have been taken to make all things easy; but wish you to consider of it until to-morrow, and give me an answer. If the warriors expect to live in peace with the United States, as well as the sachems; if they desire to brighten the chain of friendship; if they wish to act for the advantage of themselves and their children, I am sure they will sign this treaty." Cornplanter then addressed the warriors in a short speech, desiring they might be firm and steady to what they had agreed on.

"10th. The warriors of the Six Nations met in council in the forenoon, to consult respecting signing the articles, and came to a judgment. In the afternoon they met again, expecting the commissioner and the sachems; but several of the principal sachems being intoxicated, did not come, so nothing was done. A number of the chiefs and warriors of the Tuscaroras came to pay us a visit respecting the Hopewell land. Captain Printup spoke for them as follows, viz:

"Brothers,—We believe it was from motives of

benevolence and good-will to us, that you were induced to make inquiry after the original owners of some land in Virginia.

"Brothers,—You have now found them, and as you are a people that look up to the Great Spirit for direction, we hope you will now make us some compensation: we are in hopes the business may be accomplished at this time.

"Brothers,—As the Friends on the land have long received the benefit of its produce, and live at so great a distance, it would be much more convenient to receive what they please to give, at one time, than to have a small sum paid yearly. We have been given to understand, that whenever the former owners of the land could be discovered, Friends stood ready to make them some compensation; as we apprehend this has been sufficiently ascertained, we are thankful to the Great Spirit, that there is now a probability of receiving something for the inheritance of our ancestors.

"By the above speech, we found they had still some mistaken ideas, which we endeavored to remove, by again stating to them the true reason of the inquiry, and informing them we should represent to our brethren at home, what now appeared to us to be the state of the case, as soon as we conveniently could. This satisfied them, and they requested to sign their names to General Chapin's testimony, which most of them did in their usual manner.*

* Some time after, a number of these Indians came to Philadelphia, for the purpose of examining more fully into the

"11th. Had much conversation with several of the Indian chiefs. In the afternoon, at two o'clock, we were sent for to council, where a great number were assembled. The Eel, an Onondaga chief, spoke to the Indians in a pathetic manner; which we understood to be an exhortation to unanimity among the chiefs and warriors in closing the business. Colonel Pickering then held up the two parchments containing the articles of the treaty, and asked if we should proceed, which they assenting to, he told them he would give one of the parchments to one of their friends to examine, while he read the other. I accordingly examined one, and informed them they were word for word alike. They then agreed to sign, and pointed out the two head warriors, who, though they were young men, were by some custom in their nation, the persons who were to stand foremost in ratifying contracts; they signed, and then the chiefs and warriors, some of the most eminent in each nation, being in all upwards of fifty.

---

validity of their claims to be the original proprietors of these lands. Friends were very desirous of making a full compensation to the natives for any lands on which they had settled; and accordingly great pains were taken to adjust this business. But, after a close investigation of all the circumstances, and an examination of ancient maps and documents, by both Friends and Indians jointly, it did not appear that the Tuscaroras had ever been the possessors of the soil in question. Yet as they had entertained strong expectations of receiving a donation, rather than disappoint them, Friends raised a considerable sum of money, and gave it as a present to them, with which they were highly gratified.

"After the articles were signed, we desired Farmer's Brother and Cornplanter, to collect as many chiefs of the different nations as they thought proper, to go down to our lodgings; the interpreter was also requested to come with them: accordingly, about forty came. We smoked and conversed with them freely, on several subjects relating to their welfare, gave them further information of our principles, and expressed our good wishes for their prosperity. We then had our presents brought and spread upon two tables. They did not choose to divide them themselves, but left it to the interpreter; which being done, they were much pleased and satisfied with the division, and the articles were very agreeable to them. They soon after retired, informing us of their desire to see us to-morrow morning, as they had something further to communicate.

"12th. About thirty or forty of the sachems and chief warriors met at our lodgings, and delivered the following speech, by Farmer's Brother, the chief sachem.

"Brothers, the Quakers from Philadelphia! I wish you would attend to what we who are now present are about to say. We speak as one.

"Brothers, — Yesterday, after receiving your invitation to come and partake of your presents, we agreed to meet here this morning to speak a few words, which we will now do.

"Brothers,—We are very glad you have lengthened out your patience to see the end of the business which is now brought to a close. We thank the Great Spirit that he has preserved you in health, from the time you left your seats [homes], until you arrived here, and has continued to preserve you to this time. We put you under the protection of the same Good Spirit on your return, and shall be very happy to hear that you get safe home; and hope you may find your friends and families well on your return: it would be very acceptable to be informed of this, by letter to the chiefs now present.

"Brothers,—We give hearty thanks to the descendants of Onas, that you so willingly rose from your seats to attend this council fire according to our request; here are the articles of treaty for you to look over, in order to impress them on your minds, that you may tell them to your brothers who are sitting on their seats at home.

"Brothers, — You have attended this treaty a long time; the articles which we have now signed, we hope you fully understand. Now, as we have shown them to you, we would wish to know your opinion, whether we have made a good peace or not; as we cannot read, we are liable to be deceived; you have no doubt considered them; we want to know your minds, whether there is any flaw or catch in them, which may hereafter occasion uneasiness.

"Brothers,— If you think that peace is now established on a good foundation, we wish you would come forward and sign the articles: as you are a people who are desirous of promoting peace, and these writings are for that purpose, we hope you will have no objection, but all come forward and put your names to them, and this would be a great satisfaction to us."

Immediately after this speech, the treaty being concluded, and the council having broken up, our friends took their leave and set out for home. The following memorandum is the first which occurs respecting the journey, viz:

"13th. Rose at three o'clock in the morning, after a very poor night's rest in a cold open hut, where it snowed in upon us as we laid. The weather was very cold and the roads exceedingly bad; we had an uncomfortable ride of four hours, during which John Parrish had his face bruised by a fall; and such was the difficulty in part of the road, that it appeared as though we travelled at the risk of our lives. We at length arrived at a public house at the head of Canandaigua lake, thirteen miles, where we got breakfast and refitted. We then rode on seven miles, and put up for the night, there being no stage ahead for twenty-two miles.

"14th. Rose early and pursued our journey through bushes, swamps, and deep mud-holes; the road so bad that, with hard pushing, we could make but three miles an hour. In about three and a half hours, we found the remains of a fire where some travellers had fed yesterday, which was a pleasant sight; and having some oats with us, we fed our horses and breakfasted upon hoe-cake, dried meat, and cheese. We felt like poor, forlorn pilgrims, and mounted our horses again, the path being as bad as it could be; and the snow falling on us continually in passing among the bushes, it made the travelling truly hard. As it continued snowing very fast, and there being but one house to stop at between Bath and the Painted Post, we accepted the kind invitation of Captain Williamson to lodge with him at the former place. He is a very polite man, had been many years in the British service, and entertained us elegantly; a great contrast to our last night's fare.

"15th. By daylight we left Bath, it still continuing to snow very fast. A most trying time it was to us, but in about two hours we reached a house where they were able to give us some breakfast, which was refreshing. We arrived at the Painted Post about one o'clock, got some corn for our horses, and eat our bread and cheese; after which we rode eleven miles, crossing the Tioga several times, and arrived at the widow Lindley's, who kindly invited us to stay at her house, where we were entertained very hospitably.

"16th. After breakfast went for our horses, but the family were so friendly they would not receive any pay for their keeping. We crossed the Tioga twice more, and found the road so exceedingly fatiguing and the day unpleasant, that we rode only about two and a half miles an hour, and arrived at an ordinary about three o'clock in the afternoon. There being no house for about twenty-four miles ahead, we were under the necessity of lodging in a poor hovel, where there were already a man, his wife, and seven children. We laid our blankets on a bark floor, and endeavored to get some rest, but the cold pinched us to such a degree, that we had but little repose. We were all affected with an addition to our colds; this is hard travelling and living, and it is a mercy that we are preserved as well as we are.

"17th. Rose between two and three o'clock, intending to make forty-two miles, as there is but one miserable house in the intermediate distance, which we desired not to lodge at, but disappointments and vexations are to be ours, and no doubt they are good for us. The depth of the snow, which was continually balling under our horses' feet, and the excessive badness of the path, it being little else but a continued succession of mud-holes, roots, and stones, rendered our hopes of getting through quite abortive; and from necessity we had to stop at the Block-house. Our horses had to stand out all night without hay, which gave us the most concern; as for ourselves, we procured a tolerable supper, and taking our lodging upon the floor, got some sleep. There being no chimney to the house, occasioned them to have but little roof, that the smoke might have sufficient vent to pass off, which gave us a pleasing view of the brilliancy of the stars, it being the first clear night since we left Canandaigua.

"18th. Rising very early, we rode over the Alleghany mountain, which was covered with snow about ten inches deep. There were abundance of tracks of deer, bear, wild cats, white rabbits, &c. Near the top, a great bear raised up from the side of a log and frightened our horses. We fed our horses, and after eating some biscuit and dried beef at the foot of the mountain, proceeded on our journey, getting to the widow Harris's to lodge that night."

A few days after this, they were permitted to reach home in safety and good health. In closing the report of their proceedings, they remark in substance — that during a sojourn of seven weeks with the Indians, they had frequent opportunities of observing with sorrow the melancholy and demoralizing effects resulting from the supply of ardent spirits furnished them by the whites — that the difficulties and hardships to which those poor people, once a free and independent nation, are now subjected, appeared to them loudly to claim the sympathies of Friends and others, who have grown opulent in a land which was their former inheritance, and that they believed a mode might be devised of promoting their comfort, and rendering them more essential benefits than any which had yet been adopted. They likewise remark that the engagement was one involving trials of a peculiar and painful nature, yet they had reason to hope that the objects they had in view were in good degree answered, and that they were thankful in being permitted to return with the reward of peace.

As the articles of the treaty confirmed the right of the United States to large tracts of land which had been obtained by conquest, without making the Indians what Friends deemed an adequate and just compensation for it, they could not consent to the requests so frequently made to sign the treaty.

Soon after reaching home, this diligent laborer in the cause of his Lord and Master, believed himself called to attend the Yearly Meeting of Friends in Virginia, and some of the meetings composing it. His esteemed friend, Thomas Stewardson, kindly consented to bear him company, and they set out to perform the service in the Fifth month, 1795. From some brief memoranda which he made, the following account of the journey is taken:

"Left Philadelphia on Fifth-day morning, and rode hard in the heat to reach Elkton, forty-eight miles; arrived about eight o'clock, much fatigued.

"8th. Got off by sunrise: the day was very hot, but with diligent travelling we arrived at Baltimore, fifty-four miles. Leaving this city in the morning, we got to dear Evan Thomas's to lodge, being mutually glad to see each other. On First-day, the 10th, accompanied by several Friends, we set off for Georgetown. In our way, rode through the Federal city, then only in its incipient state, but fast advancing, both as to buildings and population. At Georgetown we put up at an inn; sent for doctor Thornton, and others, to procure a meeting at three o'clock in the afternoon. He used great exertions, and the inhabitants being generally notified, the meeting was held in a large new school-house. It was much too small to contain the people, which at first made them somewhat uneasy, but more stillness and composure taking place, the meeting was held to satisfaction. Crossing the Potomac, we rode to Alexandria, and lodged.

"Second-day, the 11th. It rained and thundered very much in the morning. I however visited several Friends, and the weather becoming more favorable, we went to Occoquan to dine, and reached Dumfries to lodge. The house being full of Virginians attending the court; they were not a little noisy.

"12th. Got to Fredericksburg to dinner, and thence to Bowling Green, and lodged, being fifty miles, and the day very hot.

"13th. Travelled very diligently, and made fifty-two miles to-day. Having imprudently drunk cold water when very warm, I became considerably unwell.

"14th. Expecting the Quarterly Meeting to be at White Oak Swamp, we rode there after breakfast, but were disappointed, as no Friends had assembled. We then went on, and soon met several Friends going to Wain Oak, the Quarterly Meeting being held there, whose company we joined. The Quarterly Meeting was a good one.

"16th. Meeting for Sufferings was held, after which we went to the meeting of ministers and elders at three o'clock in the afternoon.

"First-day, the 17th. The morning meeting very large, almost as many out of doors as within, and a favored time; that in the afternoon was also large, and a mixed congregation, as in the morning, and it was hoped was a profitable season.

"18th. Meeting for worship was large, attended by many not Friends; it proved a hard, laborious time, and a number of appearances in the ministry; after which, the business began, and was well conducted. Lodged at James Ladd's, with upwards of forty Friends.

"19th. The meeting, to-day, was a solid refreshing time: Richard Jordan's service was very acceptable, and I hope useful.

"20th. Feeling a freedom to propose that the women and men should sit together, before they proceeded to business; the shutters were opened, and there was some service to satisfaction; then went to business, in which, I thought Friends were favored. About four o'clock, the Yearly Meeting closed, and we returned to James Ladd's.

"21st. A meeting being appointed at Black-creek, a number of Friends accompanying me, with our valued Friend, Richard Jordan, of North Carolina, we reached the widow Ellison's, where we waited until meeting time. The company was large, considering the time for giving notice: many gay people attended, and it was thought to be a favored meeting. Richard Jordan was large in testimony, and in supplication.

"23d. Rode to Richmond. E. Maule and his brother have built a mill on the side of the canal, and for the privilege of the water pay four hundred dollars a year. This canal is an astonishing work, about twenty feet wide, dug through a solid rock; in many places twenty-five feet deep on the upper side of the hill. It runs about forty-five feet above the level of James river.

"First-day, 24th. Arose with much fear and concern upon my mind, lest truth should suffer by our having a meeting among a gay and libertine people, many of them much hurt by Paine's 'Age of Reason,' which has been abundantly spread in Virginia. How ever, at entering the capitol, where Friends had almost universally been exceedingly tried in their labors, I was favored with great composure. My friend Richard Jordan opened the service, which was, to all appearance, satisfactory and well received by the people. Immediately after he sat down, the way was clearly opened for me to stand up with the words, 'Verily there is a reward for the righteous; Verily He is a God that judgeth in the earth;' to illustrate and enforce which, the Lord was pleased to grant me both matter and utterance to my own astonishment and thankfulness. It proved such a time as I think I never experienced more than once or twice in all my labor in the cause of truth. A very numerous, crowded audience were exceedingly still and attentive for about one hour and a half; when, though I did believe I felt sufficient matter and concern to have supported me some hours, as well as the closest attention in the audience, yet I thought it expedient to close; with great thankfulness to our gracious Helper, who had been so marvellously with us. Friends who were present from most of the meetings within thirty miles, said, the truths of revelation rose triumphant over Deism and error, and were never more cordially received in that place. The Methodist minister having appointed to preach at Manchester at four o'clock, the time set by Friends for our meeting, we did not go to the meeting-house until five, when his meeting being over, we took possession of the house, and had a very large audience, many from Richmond. The general tenor of my labor was much the same as in the morning. This was also a solid and comfortable meeting. Returned to Richmond, and went to bed, rejoicing that truth had triumphed to-day."

The account breaks off here, and the notes of his further service in this journey, if he kept any, have been lost. From his companion we learn that on the 25th, they went to Goochland and held a meeting; thence to Cedar-creek, and taking one or two meetings in their way, reached home on the 4th of the Sixth month.

CHAPTER III.

Concern to visit Europe—Journal of the Voyage — Leave-taking — Banks of Newfoundland—Hard weather—Meetings on Shipboard — French Privateer—Arrival at Liverpool — Appointed Meetings —London — Sails for Bremen with G. Dillwyn and D. Sands, &c. — Notice of Voyage — Reach Bremen — Wine Cellar — Religious Citizens — Continues Journey—Hamburg and Altona — Religious Services — Travelling through Germany — Zell — Habits of the People—Pious Pastor—Hanover—Visits to several religious characters—Hammelin—Pyrmont—Grave of I. Pemberton—Professors with Friends — Separatists — Religious Engagements — Remarkable reuniting Meeting with both Parties—Affecting Parting — Leaves Pyrmont with D. Sands, &c. —Visits the Dutchess of Brunswick—Helmstead—Character of the Country—Magdeburg —Religious Service — Detects an Impostor — Brandenburg — Religious Meeting — Potsdam — Notice of the City — Berlin — Discouragements—Size, &c., of the City—Interviews with religious Persons—Meetings held—Visit to Freyenwalde—Return to Berlin — Disliked by the Clergy —Various Engagements— Kindness of many — Leave-taking — Start for Magdeburg.

The mind of W. Savery being expanded by Gospel love, and an ardent desire for the salvation of his fellow-creatures, he was made willing, freely, to give up his beloved home and connections, and his temporal concerns, when he believed himself called to go forth as an ambassador for Christ, to publish the glad tidings of redemption to a fallen race, through a crucified and risen Saviour. For a considerable time he had been under a concern to pay a religious visit to Friends and others, in some parts of Europe, and opening it to the respective meetings of which he was a member, his prospect of duty was united with, and the requisite certificates of the approbation of Friends were granted him.

His notes of this engagement, are introduced, as follows:

"*Journal on board the Sussex, on a voyage from New Castle to Liverpool, from the* 18*th of Fifth month,* 1796, *in company with several ministers, viz: Samuel Emlen, Deborah Darby, Rebecca Young, Sarah Talbot, and Phebe Speakman.*

"Fourth-day, 18th. All the Friends intending to embark in the Sussex, met at New Castle, a public meeting being appointed to be held in the court-house. It was large; more persons attending than could be accommodated within the walls. Our own members were desired to give place to the towns-people; they generally did so, and our dear Samuel Emlen continued at the inn with them, and was engaged in distributing spiritual bread as occasion offered. The court, then sitting at New Castle, adjourned to give us an opportunity in the house. Judge Basset, with several magistrates, lawyers, &c., were present. We believed that the great Bishop of souls granted us his presence, and directed the laborers to invite the congregation to an attentive waiting upon Him, the Leader and Teacher of his people, as the only sure means of obtaining heavenly knowledge; and they were feelingly put in remembrance, that if they died in their sins, whither Christ was gone, they could not come. A clear and decided testimony was also borne against holding our fellow-men in slavery; and the meeting closed in solemn supplication, prayer and praises to the universal Parent and gracious Preserver of men. We returned to the inn, and after dinner, the large room and balcony being furnished with seats, Friends who accompanied the voyagers hither, sat down, in number about one hundred and forty; and some of the towns-people hearing of it, also came in. The great Lord of the family was evidently with us, and favored with a precious solemnity; under which, our endeared friends, Deborah Darby and Rebecca Young, through the tendering influence of Gospel love, were again qualified to water the plants of our heavenly Father's planting, and affectionately to bid them farewell in the Lord. Two of the Friends who were going abroad in truth's service, were also exercised in the expression of heartfelt concern for the preservation of themselves in the love and life of Truth, and also of their long-endeared brethren and sisters whom they were about to leave. Holy fellowship and Gospel love being refreshingly and encouragingly felt among us, we were once more united in lifting up our hearts in prayer and praises; committing each other to the merciful and all-wise disposal of the everlasting Shepherd. This prepared the way for many near and tender friends and connections to part, in the mutual experience of that love which is without dissimulation, and in which the world's votaries are not privileged to rejoice: may it ever continue and increase throughout all the churches of Christ. About six in the evening, we went aboard the Sussex, at anchor before New Castle.

"Fifth-day, the 19th. The vessel having hoisted anchor and sailed in the night, we found ourselves this morning at Reedy island, where we waited for some addition to our poultry. The forenoon was rainy, with high wind and rough water — several of the passengers sick. The weather clearing away in the afternoon, we again set sail until about eleven o'clock at night, then dropped anchor; the pilot not being willing to go out of the capes that night.

"20th. Setting sail about day-break with a smart fair breeze, we came in sight of the light-house, and a boat coming off for our pilot sooner than we expected hurried us much with our letters. We were out of sight of land by four o'clock in the afternoon; all the passengers as well as could be expected.

"21st. A desire prevails among us to comfort and strengthen one another, and especially that the younger part of the company may manifest our duty to the elder, by every necessary attention. Our friend Phebe Speakman is weak with disease, but supported under it with instructive resignation and patience — our dear friend Samuel Emlen, better in health than when on shore, and with his usual animation, enlivens us in our watery prison with frequent recitals of interesting occurrences, and instances of Providential care and support, drawn from a long course of observation and experience. We feel as much at home on the ocean as we can possibly expect to do, in this trying separation from the tenderest ties of nature.—May the Lord increase in us and them, resignation to his holy will, until it shall be his good pleasure to restore us to each other again.

"First-day, 22nd. Fine weather, sea smooth and wind favorable. At ten o'clock Friends sat down quietly in the cabin; the promise to the two or three was comfortably fulfilled, and we hope the bond of Christian union strengthened, and something of a renewed confirmation afforded, that a wisdom superior to human, directed both us that are leaving our native country, and our beloved sisters who are returning home, in casting our lots together in this ship. Dined on deck. Retiring to the cabin at four o'clock, we informed our kind captain that his company and that of as many of the seamen as inclined to sit with us, would be agreeable; upon which he came down with the mate and six others. After a considerable time of silence, some counsel and encouragement being dropped, they received it with attention and behaved with respect. We were glad of their company, and the meeting closed to satisfaction. Our dear friends at home have laid in a great abundance of good things for us; a testimony of their care and love, though we, the objects of their benevolence, could have been contented with less, especially when we call to mind (as was the case this day at our bountiful table,) how many of our brethren by creation, and objects of the same redeeming love, are scarcely furnished with mere necessaries: the lamentable situation of the poor Africans in the slave-ships was sympathetically brought into view.

"27th. A clear morning and tolerable breeze. Retired to the cabin to hold our week-day meeting; circumstances not permitting it the two preceding days, and were favored, through much mercy, with a refreshing time, for which we all had occasion to be thankful.

"28th. Perceiving a sail making towards us, she proved to be from Liverpool, bound to New York. Both vessels backed topsails until several short letters were written and sent by our yawl, ours enclosed to E. Pryor of New York; and taking charge of theirs to their friends at Liverpool, we wished good passages on both sides. It is a pleasure to meet vessels at sea, and this opportunity of writing to our dear friends at home rejoiced us much.

"29th. Wind fair; at ten o'clock held our meeting to mutual comfort: all the Friends well but Rebecca Young, who was not out of her room to-day.

"31st. Cold and rainy: at ten o'clock perceived we were coming on the fishing banks of Newfoundland. We could not see more than two hundred yards, but heard the fishing vessels sounding their conch-shells, which we also did, agreeably to custom on these banks, where there are probably from two to four hundred English and American vessels fishing for cod. As it is generally foggy and rainy weather, they keep a frequent blowing, to apprize each other of their approach and to prevent running foul. These banks are extensive —from east to west perhaps one hundred and fifty miles, and from north to south about two hundred miles; the soundings from thirty to sixty fathoms deep. Our captain estimates that we are now about two hundred and fifty miles from the nearest land, which is the island of Newfoundland. The number of cod annually taken here is astonishing. They fish for them with lines forty or sixty fathoms long, with heavy leads and two hooks; several of these being kept out at a time. Some tend them, and others on board split and salt down the fish in bulk, until they are loaded, when they return home and dry them. We threw out a line, and soon took seven of from ten to twelve pounds weight.

"Fourth-day, 1st of Sixth month. Very wet, cold and uncomfortable, but the wind fair; we held our meeting in much quietude.

"Fifth-day, 2nd. Still wet and cold, and we were scarcely able to keep ourselves warm with our great coats on. A mountain of ice being directly ahead, we were obliged to change our course; it appeared to move southward, and was judged to be about two hundred yards in length and forty feet above water.

"Sixth-day. Little wind and a high sea; the vessel rolled much, and several of the passengers passed an uneasy night — the weather so cold and uncomfortable that we had this afternoon a fire made in the cabin.

"First-day, the 5th. Friends generally sick; we had slept little for the last twenty-four hours, which have been more trying to us than any heretofore; yet we are sensible we have much to be thankful for, especially that we are mercifully kept in near unity and sympathy with each other.

"6th. The wind and sea were boisterous and appeared awful, so that faith, hope and patience were deeply tried at such seasons. Those who venture to cross the ocean, need be well convinced that they do it upon a good foundation; such may humbly rest in confidence upon Him who gathers the winds in his fist. Our captain thinks he never before was in so hard a gale at this season of the year: the sea continually breaking over both the main and quarter deck, injuring our live stock and washing away several necessary articles. Friends almost all sick. At night the wind and sea somewhat abated, and the wind being fair, we have gained one hundred and ninety miles towards our port during the last twenty-four hours.

"7th. A rolling sea, wind ahead, and so cold that we had a fire in the cabin. Thanks be to that Power Divine that unites us in the blessed harmony of the truth. Gained little on our way, and the wind and seas being very high, occasioned an afflicting night to most of the passengers. The ship tossed very much, and we have had very little refreshing sleep for several nights; yet we are sensible that the benefits and afflictions permitted by Divine Providence, are more equally distributed than we sometimes imagine.

"8th. Wind and rain. This is the tenth day since we have had fair weather aad a comfortable sea; may we be favored to possess our souls in patience: have gained very little to-day.

"10th. Held our week-day meeting, which the wind and sickness has not permitted us to do for more than a week past: an hour and a half was spent in soul-refreshing silence, and at the close an acknowledgment was made of Divine favor. Our poultry and other live stock have been much injured during the late high seas and winds. Such is the suffering of these creatures in general on board ship, that several of us agreed in sentiment, it would be better to be deprived of the satisfaction of abounding in fresh provisions on sea voyages, than to gratify the appetite at the expense of so great oppression.

"First-day, 12th. Our meeting to-day was a favored time; hope and faith revived; thanks be to Him who is ever worthy, for this and every other mercy we enjoy.

"13th. Cool as usual; have had very little pleasant weather since a few days after leaving our capes; the main deck always wet with seas breaking over it, and frequently the quarter deck also.

"15th. Our meeting for worship was a quiet, comfortable time. The captain apprehending we were on soundings, cast the lead, but found no bottom at one hundred and twenty fathoms. At five o'clock a large ship hove in sight, which soon altered her course toward us—our captain hoisted American colors and backened sail to wait for her. Coming along under our stern, they hailed, which we returned with information that ours was an American vessel from Philadelphia. The

15

other was a French privateer of twenty guns, and appeared to have two hundred men; said they belonged to Brest, and had been cruising twelve days, was called L'Esperance. Finding who we were, they wished us a good voyage and went in pursuit of a brig we had passed, and which was still in sight. While she was bearing down upon us, the minds of Friends were unpleasantly affected, not only because it was uncertain what those sons of rapine might be permitted to do, but more so, on reflecting to what a sorrowful state of darkness men must arrive, before they can engage in the wretched business of privateering. Sounding again, found bottom at seventy fathoms.

"16th. At ten o'clock discovered the coast of Ireland, not far from Cork. Friends were mostly upon deck, and pleased with the hope of seeing Liverpool to-morrow evening.

"18th. The pilot came on board — met a number of vessels outward bound, ten of which were going to Guinea for slaves; the thoughts of which brought a gloom over all our pleasant reflections on approaching Liverpool and our kind friends there. Surely worse than midnight darkness awaits those who, with horrid presumption, dare thus trample upon the most sacred decrees of heaven. About nine in the evening a revenue boat with two custom-house officers came on board, and by them we were landed near the dwelling of our hospitable and worthy friends Robert and Sarah Benson, who received us with real cordiality.

Mercy and goodness having been abundantly evident

towards us in crossing the sea, favoring with many uniting and confirming seasons together, may we ever acknowledge it with thankfulness to the Father of mercies.

"First-day, Sixth month 19th, 1796. At two meetings in Liverpool, my American companions were all exercised in testimony acceptably, and dear Rebecca Young in prayer in the forenoon. I felt no necessity to be heard in the ministry.

"21st. Attended the Monthly Meeting at Manchester, to which Friends of Liverpool belong; the business was conducted with despatch, and in a little different manner from ours.

"23d. A number not professing with us attended the meeting on account of a marriage. I ventured, for the first time since my arrival, to say a few words in testimony; and feeling most easy to mention my prospect of having an evening meeting with the inhabitants, it was accordingly appointed. Went after dinner to Richard Routh's, and retired to my chamber. In the evening went to the meeting, which I entered in much fear, even to trembling; but came out with thankfulness of heart: a large number of the people gave us their company; and through Divine mercy, it proved a solid, comfortable meeting.

"First-day, 26th. At Liverpool, the morning meeting was large for this place; dear Samuel Emlen and our two American women Friends were engaged in Gospel labor to my satisfaction, and I hope to profit: my mind was kept still and quiet, having felt no concern since landing to appear in testimony among Friends here. Towards the close of the meeting, I mentioned my prospect of a meeting with the inhabitants of Liverpool in the evening, which was agreed to. The meeting-house was nearly filled, and the people behaved in a decent orderly manner; and it ended to our comfort; praised be the Lord.

"Having appointed a meeting to be held the 30th, for young unmarried Friends above ten years of age, it proved, through renewed condescension, a time of watering. At the close, I proposed another meeting with the people of other professions at six in the evening, which was larger than the first, and thought by Friends to be a time of favor: at the conclusion many of the people came to us, acknowledging their thankfulness for the opportunity. Samuel Emlen appointed another meeting of the like kind, to be held on First-day evening, which coincided with a prospect I previously had.

"Seventh month, 3d. The meeting in the evening was very large; it was said there were two hundred in the yard, and we had renewed occasion to say, Good is the Lord, and worthy to be served; for He crowned us with his presence, and made us joyful in the house of prayer. It was to me an affecting parting with the people for the present, my mind now feeling easy to leave them.

"7th. At Birmingham; and feeling my mind engaged to have a meeting with the people of this place, I proposed it to Friends, who readily made way for it, to be at six in the evening. Notwithstanding the notice was short, it was crowded; several ministers of different denominations were present, and there was an open door to receive what was delivered.

"First-day, the 10th. In London. Went to the meetings at Devonshire-house. They were large, both in the fore and afternoon. I was silent. A meeting being appointed by another Friend to be held in the evening at Westminster, I went to it. It was large and thought to be favored: many of the people acknowledged their thankfulness.

"11th. Attended an examination of the boys' and girls' charity school at Clerkenwell, a well-regulated school and boarding-house: the children were all dressed alike.

"14th. At Tottenham week-day meeting, and silent as usual with me. At the close, feeling my mind engaged to have a meeting with the inhabitants at large, I proposed it, and Nicholas Waln, Thomas Scattergood, and other Friends uniting with it, one was accordingly appointed, to be at six in the evening. Not many Friends came to it, being afraid of taking the room of others; it was pretty large, and through renewed mercy a solid time, my mind feeling peaceful.

"First-day, 17th. Was at Devonshire morning meeting; George Dillwyn and some others had good service. I was silent, but appointed a public meeting at six in the evening, in the house where the men's Yearly Meeting is held; which was very large, and an open

15*

satisfactory time, for which myself and friends were thankful to the Author of every good.

"19th. At Devonshire-house meeting, but could not be easy, though trying to nature, without appointing another meeting for other professors, at six o'clock this evening, which appeared to end well.

"21st. Went with David Sands and Benjamin Johnson to the American Ambassador for a passport to the continent, which he readily granted; from thence we went to the Duke of Portland's office, who is the Secretary of State, and obtained a permit from him.

"24th. At an appointed meeting in the evening at Westminster, exceedingly crowded, yet thought to be a favored season; thanks be to the God of all grace.

"25th. Went with several Friends on board a vessel intended for Bremen, and agreed to take passage in her.

"27th. Was at Greenwich Hospital, where were above two thousand pensioners, old men clothed in blue from head to foot, being ancient and disabled sailors; they looked well and were lodged comfortably, in places built like large state-rooms in a ship.

"First-day, 31st. Was at a large and good public meeting at Clerkenwell, and in the evening had a meeting at Horseley-down, over the market-house, in a room supposed to hold eighteen hundred people; all could not get in by some hundreds; and though very crowded and warm, it was a quiet good time. There being but one small stairway up to the room, sufficient only to admit one person at a time, it was more than half an hour before it was empty; and in the throng two or three women fainted.

"Fifth-day, the 4th of Eighth month. After a solid parting with my friends, Joseph Savory and family of London, George Dillwyn and myself went to Joseph Smith's, where the Friends intending for Germany were, viz: David Sands, William Farrer, and Benjamin Johnson, and a number of our kind brethren and sisters, who were desirous to take leave of us. We had a time of comfortable retirement, under a feeling of the strengthening influence of the love of Christ; after which, accompanied by Joseph Savory and wife, David Bacon, George Stacey and wife, and Joseph Smith and wife, we rode to Blackwall, and went on board the ship Victoria, Johann Borgis, master, for Bremen. Took an affectionate leave of our friends, and immediately weighed anchor.

"5th. With a fair wind we sailed by a pleasant country, interspersed with handsome villages and farms; a large number of vessels were in sight all day, and we passed by many of the large ships of war at the Nore, one of which, called the Ville de Paris, of one hundred and twenty guns, was like an enormous castle. At dusk our pilot left us.

"6th. A smart breeze and fair, with short seas; and the passengers nearly all sick: our captain and seamen behave respectfully; the accommodations are none of the best; yet we feel contented and easy, believing all is right.

"7th. The latter part of this day we were in sight

of land, being the coast of Oldenburg. At night slacked sail, and stood off until daylight, then entered the river Weser, and the tide being rapid, we lay seven hours at anchor, during which we went on shore in Oldenburg, which is governed by Prince Etienne, whose secretary was kind and courteous, inviting us to some refreshment. As he could speak French, he commenced his conversation in that language, but finding I could speak German, he seemed pleased, and was communicative. We took a friendly leave of him, and walking towards the ship, were sent for by the secretary's mother, a woman of good countenance, with whom we walked in the garden, and found her to be a pious person, towards whom we felt much love. Parting in much tenderness, we returned to the ship with her good wishes.

"9th. Sailed along between the countries of Hanover and Oldenburg to Bruck, twenty-four English miles from Bremen, and dropped anchor; here the vessels unload and send their cargoes to Bremen. Bruck is a small village, and not very pleasant: we lodged on board, and had a solid religious opportunity in the evening with the sailors.

"10th. In the morning, having hired a lighter to take us and our baggage to Fraisack, half-way to Bremen, we went on board, taking with us five poor passengers, without expense to them. The tide leaving us, we went ashore at a village, where poverty, the effect of arbitrary power, appeared in a striking point of view to Americans — the people, with their horses and cows, living under the same roof, and all very meanly; the land poor, and the people very laborious, especially the women. Arrived at Negesak in the evening, and went on shore to a large and good inn, where, after undergoing what we must expect to meet with in this journey, the gaze and observations of many, who doubtless look upon us as a strange, outlandish people, we had a good supper and retired to rest; but previously had some agreeable and religious conversation with our placid-looking landlady, and gave her some books.

"11th. After breakfast took passage in a lighter for Bremen, about twelve miles up the river, against the current, for which we paid fourteen shillings sterling. Reached Bremen in four hours, and took quarters at a public house at Walfish, outside the gates, where we were received kindly, and furnished with tolerable lodgings, &c. A man coming in, told us there were in the town some who were called Quakers, and who met at each other's houses for religious purposes.

"12th. George Dillwyn, William Farrer, and myself, visited Mooyer & Topkin, merchants in the town, to whom we were recommended. Topkin having been some time in London, spoke English, and gave us information respecting the money, mode of travelling, &c., in Germany. We then went to Cassell & Trobis, and found that Cassell had just returned from Pyrmont: he speaks some English, and lives in high style. An agreeable young man, who was employed in their counting-house, and understood the English language pretty well, walked with us round the town, showed us the public buildings and wine-cellar, which contained a vast quantity of wine, chiefly Rhenish, the trade in which is carried on for the public benefit. In this cellar there are many large tuns, containing from forty to one hundred hogsheads each, with the date of the vintage on them — some upwards of one hundred years old; this they pride themselves in, and they can only be tapped by consent of the magistrates. We returned to our lodgings with heaviness of heart, observing no openness for religious service; we however gave books to several persons. George Dillwyn, William Farrer, and myself, took a walk, and went into two houses, where we were kindly received, had some conversation and gave them a few books, for which they thanked us. In the evening, hearing of a religious woman who kept a school and was a kind of separatist, Benjamin Johnson and William Farrer went to see her. She received them gladly, and said there were about twenty or thirty of them who met together to edify each other, being all people seeking God. This revived our drooping minds, that have been much exercised, feeling something towards the people, but not knowing which way to proceed to obtain relief: hoping the Lord was working for us, we rejoiced and retired to rest.

"13th. Had an opportunity of conversation with the religious woman, who said she found by the book our friends had given her yesterday, that they were not quite the same in opinion with us, for we went beyond them. After sitting awhile with her, she sent a lad to show us the house of Albert Hoyer, one of their number, with whom we had much religious freedom, to our mutual satisfaction. We parted with him and an ancient woman, who appeared to be united with him in sentiment, and with us in the general; she making some remarks, which showed her to be one earnest for the right way. We then went to the house of an ancient man who, with his wife, a woman of a comely, meek appearance, received us pleasantly, and spent a little time, opening to each other our minds on religious subjects. He said the people called them Quakers, and sometimes pointed at them as they walked the streets, but that ought not to move them, for he knew there was nothing better to be expected from people while they continued under the dominion of the world's spirit, as they did not understand the things of God. We took leave of them in tenderness. There is no doubt these are an enlightened people, desirous of an establishment on the right foundation; but they have many outward discouragements to hinder them, as I apprehend is the case throughout Germany. They appear to have little or no dependence on outward forms or ceremonies, and confess freely, that none can be the children of God, but those who are led by his spirit; and that it is not putting away the filth of the flesh by any outward washings, but the answer of a good conscience towards God, through the regenerating power of his spirit, that is the saving baptism: but they still comply with the ceremony of water baptism with respect to their children; and they also attend the public worship. That which principally distinguishes their little company from others, is the circumspection of their lives and manners, and their frequent meetings together to strengthen and build one another up. I returned to my lodgings comforted with the interview.

"First-day, 14th. Friends sat down together in our chamber, and through Divine mercy were favored with an uniting, strengthening season, which afresh animated our spirits to pursue as ability may be given, our weighty engagements in this land. The afternoon proved distressing to us, on account of the people making it a time of merriment; drinking, singing, playing at bowls, &c., which appears to be the general practice. They attend their places of worship twice before two o'clock, that the afternoon may be devoted to lightness and foolish pastimes. I said in my heart, what will become of the careless shepherds of this people; who do not seem addicted to gross wickedness as in some other places, yet are reconciled by custom to this abuse of the First-day: and we are told the pastors do not discourage it or tell them of its impropriety. Our landlady and her children kept the house as quiet as they could, on our account.

"15th. George Dillwyn and myself visited Albert Hoyer, two others of the same religious people being present; we spent an hour or more with them to good satisfaction; they did not appear puffed up, but desirous of improvement, and were open and loving. We gave them some books, and recommended their close attention to the further manifestation of the true Light, which they had acknowledged for their guide and teacher; and to bear their testimony faithfully: thus would the Lord prosper them, and make them in his holy hand, as eyes to the blind, and as a city set upon a hill: all which they took kindly, and hoped they should treasure up our observations, and improve by them. Then embracing us tenderly, they expressed their desires that the Lord might preserve us and bless his work in our hands. We left them, comforted in a belief we had not been sent to Bremen for nought.

"After dinner, Christian Bacher came to see us, having just heard there were Friends come to Bremen. He appeared to be a man of good understanding, acquainted with the Divine Light, and separated from the public worship, with its forms and ordinances. He said there were a number in Bremen that we have not seen, who would be glad of our company, and who are seeking the truth. Being acquainted with many parts of Germany, he told us of religious people in Berlin and other places, who, though weak in many of their opinions, are honest-hearted. Some call them Mystics, and other names; and they appear to have taken many of their opinions of the inward life from Jacob Behmen, Lady Guion, and other writers of like kind. This man is acquainted with Friends at Pyrmont, and acknowledges himself to be one with us; but we thought he was too talkative, and one of those who think there is no need of uniting as a visible church, or establishing an order of discipline, which appears to be the opinion of many of the pious people in this country; and this makes them shy of Friends at first, as they know us to be a gathered people: this continually adds to the weight of exercise which Friends must experience in visiting Germany. We gave him Barclay's Apology, and several other books, to lend or give to inquiring people, which he seemed pleased with an opportunity of doing. He gave us some directions for finding a serious people in Hamburg and Altona.

"16th. Set off in an uncomfortable extra post-wagon for Hamburg, and dined at Ottenburg, eighteen English miles, travelling about three or three and a half miles an hour—and there seems no inducing a German driver to exceed that gait: the roads are very crooked, the country level and clear, so that objects are seen at a great distance. We proceeded to Tastoss, and were completely jolted and fatigued in their awkward, clumsy wagons.

"17th. Rose early: the post-horses being kept at an inn, they were in haste to have us off before it grew very warm. We were all loaded again in the same kind of wagon, which is the best that can be procured for travellers in this country, except they purchase one, and take post-horses from town to town. Indeed, the best carriages we have seen here are heavy and inconvenient. Travelled over a very poor country, as yesterday, one-third of which is a heath, where they keep boys and girls to tend cattle, and the miserable sheep we see everywhere, as we pass along. Some of the land is sown with rye, barley, oats, buckwheat, and some wheat. Hundreds of the poor peasants were employed in mowing and hauling in; the women bearing an equal share of the burden with the men. The grain was poor, compared with England or America. The villages, generally, have a miserable appearance, being composed of clay huts, without chimneys. They use turf for fuel, and the people are very laborious, living hard; coarse, black rye bread, milk, and some vegetables, being their principal diet. Their horses, cows, &c., live under the same thatched roof with the family. There are but few good houses between Bremen and Harburg, sixty-six miles, where we dined. We are still in the Hanoverian dominions: the people are shamefully fleeced, both by the government and the priests, beyond anything I have ever heard of. At our inn they were civil and cleanly; a good house, and tolerable beds.

"18th. George Dillwyn and myself went in a boat for Hamburg, about six miles across the Elbe. There were about forty passengers, several of whom were from the interior of Germany, and intending for America. After passing by many small islands, we arrived in about two hours, and landed in this great and populous city, entire strangers; but knowing the language, we soon found the London and American coffee-house; breakfasted there, and then waited on Roosen, a merchant, to whom we had letters of introduction from London. He appeared to be a high man, his countenance bespeaking little kindness to us: however, he sent his barber to conduct us in a search for lodgings, but finding none we liked, we took coach, and went to Altona, having a letter to Vandersmissen & Sons, men of extensive trade, who received us with much kindness, and appear to be religious men. In Altona we were also unsuccessful in finding suitable lodgings for our whole company. Returned to Hamburg, and took three rooms at one dollar and a half per day. Coming again into this busy city, our minds were brought under exercise, and abundant discouragement presented; seeing few or none who appeared religious.

"Having heard of a person in Altona called a Quaker, I went with two of our company, and after a great deal of walking in the heat, found him: he was an old man, named Heltman, who had separated many years past from the common forms, and met with some others at times in Altona and Hamburg of like religious opinions, and was a preacher among them. With him and his wife we had an hour's religious conversation. After I had opened our principles a little to him, and told him my motive for leaving my own country, he embraced me, acknowledging he was one with me in faith, He recommended us to two sugar-refiners in Hamburg. Having walked several miles in the dust and heat, we returned to our lodgings fatigued, yet satisfied with our visit. — 'Through many tribulations we must enter the kingdom of God.'

"20th. George Dillwyn and I went to see the two men we heard of yesterday. Upon entering into conversation, one of them showed some surprise at our coming so far from home on a religious account, and thought there was enough for every child of God to do at home, and that the Lord could make way for the instruction of the people in all places. Finding him a well-inclined man, we endeavored to convince him of the possibility of a Divine call to travel with the Gospel message now, as well as in the apostles' days, which he did not dispute; but said that some had travelled under an apprehension they were called, who had hurt themselves and did no good to others. At length he appeared satisfied with our motives, and believed we were right in making such a sacrifice. We spent two hours in conversation on religious subjects, in which he appeared to be an enlightened man, but too full of his own opinions, as having no need, or not feeling any, of anything but what he already knew. We gave them some books, and they were kind and loving at parting, and expressed a hope that we would not take it amiss that they seemed backward at first about our call.

"First-day, 21st. Four men came to see us: one of them gave me a book he had written, as an exposition of some of the predictions of the prophets and of our Saviour, &c. This man appeared too full of himself and of talk; he had suffered imprisonment at Nuremburg, on account of his not attending the public worship and conforming to the ordinances. On being brought before the magistrates and priests, he was enabled to give such reasons for his faith and practice as silenced them, and procured his discharge. The rest of these men were more solid and humble, so that we marvelled to find the clearness of sight they were favored with, and the readiness with which they brought forth Scripture to confirm their and our sentiments: on the whole, the interview was satisfactory. Stillness and more of the child's state is much wanting, but the sincerity of heart which they appear to possess will, no doubt, draw down the Divine blessing. After giving them some books, we walked to Altona, and dined with Henry and Jacob Vandersmissen. They are Menonists, but having been nine months in England, and boarded with Friends, they retain a love for the Society. They sat in silence, both before and after eating, in a reverent posture. We had some instructive religious conversation with them, and left them in much love. J. F. Reichart came to take us to his house, where we had appointed to meet some of the separatists. Twelve persons, besides ourselves, met; we advised them to get into silence, which, after some time, they did. A comfortable feeling attending, I ventured to preach Christ as the light of the world and the life of men, the bread from heaven, &c., and was more favored with expression in the German than I could have expected. David Sands then requested me to interpret for him, which I undertook in fear, but hope nothing suffered. George Dillwyn also desiring my assistance, I gave it as well as I could, though I feel myself not competent to such a work, and less qualified to interpret for others, than to speak my own feelings. Our communications were received and acknowledged as the truth, and Christ Jesus as the only foundation. If these people could see more clearly the necessity of silence, and love to abide in it, they would be made a shining light; some of them, we had no doubt, were drawing nearer and nearer to the 'quiet habitation.' They embraced and parted with us in great tenderness. The space between Hamburg and Altona having some shady walks, swarmed with people, who, according to the inconsistent custom of the country, were diverting themselves in a variety of ways, with music, singing, dancing, gaming, and drinking; we passed through them without molestation.

"Second-day, 22nd. Two of the men who were at meeting yesterday, came to see us, and in a tender frame of mind said, they felt that God was with us, and had sent us thither; were convinced of the necessity of inward silent waiting upon God, who alone can open and none can shut, and who shuts and none can open; and hoped our coming would not be in vain to them: they were very loving, and at parting expressed much desire for our preservation, and their own improvement in the true and living way. One of them, J. Abenau, appears to be the most solid and enlightened man that we have found among them; though both these men and some others, we thought were not far from the kingdom.

"The city of Hamburg is said to contain one hundred and fifty thousand inhabitants; ten thousand of these are French emigrants. Owing to its being a neutral city and free port, there is abundance of shipping in the harbor from almost all nations. It is governed by its own magistrates, but pays some tribute to the Emperor. The people enjoy the free exercise of religious opinions, yet few appear much concerned about it in any form; their places of worship, though chiefly Lutheran and Calvinist, are furnished with crucifixes, likenesses of saints, &c.; we found, however, some pious people among them, to whom we felt much love. The people in a general way, dress as their ancestors did several ages past, the Dutch not being given to change. The streets are narrow, have few foot-ways, and being every where paved with pebbles, it makes walking tiresome. Altona contains about forty thousand inhabitants, and is, of the two, the pleasanter city.

"Fourth-day, 24th. Our friends the Vandersmissens having sent their coach, some of us paid them a visit, and drank coffee, though it was but about eleven o'clock. The Germans think that coffee can never come out of season. David Sands and myself had another opportunity with our friend Heltman; he and his wife are loving, solid people, but low in the world, yet we hoped were near the kingdom; he embraced and parted with us in tears, recommending us to continue faithful unto God to the end; and said his days were drawing near to a close, but he lived in the hope, that through the Lord's mercy he should leave the world in peace. Our landlady imposed upon us by an unjust charge, which for peace sake we were obliged to pay, though it was contrary to our agreement. This is a land of impositions on strangers. We hired a boat to take us and our wagon to Harburg, six English miles, for six dollars; dined in that place, at the house where we had lodged before; the people looked pleased to see us and hoped to have our company again before we left Germany. We took four post-horses, and leaving Harburg travelled through a poor, barren country, the roads sandy and houses mean, and arrived at Walley, a village of about six houses.

"Eighth month, 26th. We were obliged to stop on the road for our postilion to take his bread, herring, and milk, which they do in the middle of every station, for which, and the feed of the horses, passengers must freely pay, or be used worse than they are. The horses eat the same bread as the drivers. We arrived at the gates of Zell about nine o'clock at night, where an officer stopped us and took our names.

"27th. Having agreed for four small rooms and beds, George Dillwyn and I went into the city, like solitary pilgrims in the midst of a strange people. It is not easy to conceive the state of mind and mortification that poor travellers have to pass through daily, but more especially on entering large cities and towns, where, at first view, all appear to be minding their own things, and where the manners, religion, and pursuits of the people are so entirely different from ours, and not a single inhabitant known to us; yet by patient waiting, the Lord hath hitherto manifested to our comfort, that five or ten upright-hearted souls are yet to be found in every place; this hope comforted our tribulated spirits in passing through the streets of Zell, as spectacles to the people. Having a letter to a merchant whose name was Helmleck, we went to his house, and were received with much civility and respect. He said, he knew a person of our religion in town, whose name was Dietrich, to whose house he took us; he proved to be a Moravian, but a kind, courteous man, and appeared to be desirous of having some books, that he might become better acquainted with our principles. On conversing with a man at our lodgings, he expressed some surprise that I, who was born in America, should be as white as a German: such is the ignorance of many. The son of a Calvinist minister, hearing our conversation, informed his father of us, who sent me an invitation to come to his house, and feeling no hesitation, I did so. I found him to be a man of about thirty-five; we conversed without restraint, on religious subjects, about an hour, he being of a candid, liberal mind, freely confessed that our simple manners, peaceable principles, and refusing to take oaths, were consistent with the Gospel and his own private sentiments, and frequently gave me his hand as a testimony of unity. He called his eldest son, a pretty lad, about twelve years old, whom I saw at our inn, and told him to take notice what I said, that I was one of the people called Quakers, from America, that I did not think it right to pull off my hat in honor to any man, but did it only in reverence to the Divine Being; that I and my brethren never went to war, nor took an oath, our yea being yea, and our nay, nay. The lad was sober and attentive, and remarked that he had read in the Scriptures a command concerning the last. We parted lovingly, both the pastor and his wife pressing me to come to-morrow.

"First-day, 28th. Several of our little band were unwell, owing, as we supposed, to the manner of living in this country. Sour wine, sour beer, bread, meat and vegetables, form the principal articles of diet; the meat cooked till it is ready to fall to pieces. Coffee, which the Germans make to perfection and drink it several times in a day, seems to be almost the only good thing at their tables. Meat is mostly poor, and the veal killed when it is about a week old. The pastor and Captain Kirchner came to see us, with whom we had some conversation, we hoped profitably. In the afternoon, William Farrer and I drank coffee with them and Professor Rock, a French Calvinist minister, who preaches in his own language to a congregation, descendants of the Huguenots, who fled here from France, in the time of the persecutions: he did not appear to be much concerned about religion. This town, unlike those we had before been in on this day of the week, was everywhere exceedingly still and orderly; few people being in the streets or on the public walks, which was very agreeable to us, and what we did not expect. Spending some time with the pastor at his house, in serious conversation, I endeavored, as well as I was qualified, to open to him the nature of our doctrines and practices; he agreed, that no man could be a Christian, but by the operation of the spirit of Christ; yet his idea appeared to be, that this spirit was so mixed and blended with the natural faculties of the soul, as not to be distinguishable from them, but that it wrought our conversion and purification in an imperceptible manner. I mentioned to him several passages of Scripture in opposition to this opinion; and at length he confessed he had never read of, or heard the subject so treated before, nor so much to his satisfaction. He said the sprinkling of infants could avail them nothing, and that what he did in that respect, was in conformity to the opinions of others, and not his own; for if he could believe any water baptism essential, he should embrace the opinions of those who administered it at mature age; and with respect to the supper, he said, he did not conceive it was intended to be of perpetual obligation in the church, for that would have been perpetuating the Passover, which our Lord was then eating, but that this and other Jewish rites he came to fulfil and put an end to. He believed no more was meant by our Lord's injunction, than that his disciples, as often as they sat down to meat, should remember him, their Lord and Master, who was now sat down to table with them for the last time before he was offered up. Clear it was, he said, that it had no effect on the souls of those who observed it, who remained from year to year in their general conduct forgetful of God. Many people, however, who took it from pious motives, he did not doubt might feel themselves refreshed. He kindly expressed the satisfaction he had felt, and near unity with me, adding with much tenderness, that it was one thing to acknowledge sound doctrines, and another to practise them. I returned to my companions peaceful, and in the hope that Truth had not suffered in the interview.

"29th. Walked through the principal streets of Zell, which is a fortified city, surrounded by mounds of earth, a wide ditch, gates,. &c., and guarded by soldiers. The promenades around it are very fine, lined with trees, and gravelled. At this time they are suspicious of strangers, and in addition to taking our names at entering the gates, every inn-keeper is obliged to return the names of his lodgers every morning to the burgomaster. The people are quiet and respectful to us; there is little appearance of trade, and the market is poor. The suburbs and city may contain twenty thousand inhabitants. As we walked along, a man looking pleasantly on us, we turned about and spoke to him, with which he seemed glad, and took us into his house. He soon opened his mind, and we found he was a great admirer of Jacob Behmen, and had a strong testimony against the priests, but very fearful of them and the people, and therefore kept himself very hidden; which is the case of hundreds in this country. He thought we were one in sentiment on religion; but on coming to see us in the evening, we presently found he was full of visions: though he confessed freely to the truth of our doctrines, and was tender and loving, yet he spoke of having found God in minerals, and that he was to be found in everything; had been made acquainted either by vision or dream with the nature of the Divine Being, of angels and of men, &c. He said he had been long separated from the common form of worship, and had but two or three acquaintances in Zell to whom he could speak his sentiments freely, and these he would bring to see us in the morning. We gave him some books, and such advice as we were favored with, which he took kindly, and left us in tears. Spent another hour with the pastor, Johann Frederick Krietsch, to much satisfaction.

"30th. Took leave of my friend Krietsch and his family, with much affection on both sides. We gave him several books. His wife said, he had never seen a stranger that he discovered so much affection for since she knew him, which he confirmed, and much desired we might return through Zell; but be that as it might, he observed, he should ever remember with thankfulness a kind Providence sending us there. He was a tender man, and I hope the Divine blessing will rest upon him. We also took leave of the family at the inn with their good wishes. An agreeable young woman, of a religious mind, who waited on us during our stay, took our attention at parting, and pressed our return if it were possible, saying she would be glad to go with us to America. The Moravian minister paid us a visit as we were about to go off; having been out of town for some days and just returned, he expressed his sorrow at the shortness of the interview. We rode through a poor country to Hanover, and put up without the city gates, where we had tolerable accommodations: the landlord was a baptized Jew.

"31st. George Dillwyn and I walked through the town and delivered our letters of recommendation. The city has the appearance of considerable trade, chiefly carried on by land, the river being only navigable for flat boats in freshes. It is fortified, has many soldiers and about thirty thousand inhabitants; the religion generally Lutheran, but there is one Calvinist meeting-house, and some Moravians who meet privately. About their places of worship and burying-grounds are many relics of popery, some monuments and imagery six hundred years old, or perhaps more. Afternoon, William Farrer and I walked about a mile and a half to see the steward to the commissary of the port-office. He and his wife received us kindly, and appeared much like Friends in principle and practice. He had been separated for some years from the common forms of religion, and was a man of solid countenance and demeanor. We spent about an hour with them to satisfaction. He gave us the names of several more separatists, persons of religious character.

"Ninth month 1st. Our friend Shaffer visited us: the cross seems much in the way of the few serious minds in Hanover, and they acknowledge they feel themselves too weak to stand forth faithfully. A person to whom we had letters came to see us, and some of us being unwell, occasioned as we thought by our manner of living, he told us that dysentery was very common here in the autumn, and many are removed suddenly, and advised some remedy to correct the acidity of the drinks and food which are commonly used in this country. He appears to be a kind man and disposed to be of use to us. The Lord makes way for us in every place. Johann Buchner visited us: he was many years a musician in the army, and had been in many battles; but growing uneasy with his profession, dropped it, and is now gardener to the king's physician. He has been in England, and there got acquainted with Friends and with the Methodists, and speaks English a little. He gave us an account of many exercises he had passed through, and of his present state and opinions, which I did not discover to be much different from ours. He is no doubt a religious man, and is separated from the outward forms used here, and more bold in maintaining his testimony than his companions.

"2nd. David Sands and George Dillwyn not being able to converse in the language, much of the labor falls upon me, and people frequently calling upon us, I am kept pretty busy; for by the time we are two or three days in a place, we begin to find out the religious characters, and they us. We went to see a shoemaker, a tender, seeking man, and his wife; both of whom were made very near to my spirit. They had left other professors and kept much retired at home. He said the people were vain, and it hurt him to mix with them, and that he was desirous of following the inward Preacher, who would not deceive, as many of the wise and learned preachers in the world did. Then we went to an old man, who was spoken of as being a Quaker; he received us kindly, but we soon found he was not got beyond the use of water baptism, and was one of the principal men of the few Moravians who meet here in a covert manner, and yet continue publicly to meet the Lutherans. By letters received from the brethren in America, he had understood that Friends had supplied the Indian brethren under the care of D. Seisberger with corn, in a time of scarcity. I told him I was one of the Friends concerned in that business, which made him more open, and he seemed pleased with our company. In the evening we had a comfortable sitting by ourselves; and have found it very strengthening frequently to retire in this manner and seek for counsel in this trying field of labor, where we feel the need of putting on the whole armor, so that nothing may suffer by or through us.

"3d. George Dillwyn, David Sands and myself, paid another visit to the aforesaid shoemaker, at his request, and he appeared glad of the visit. My companions going to our inn, I called to see Henry Wertsig, a woman's habit-maker; and after spending some time with him, he accompanied me to our lodgings. On our way we met a German nobleman, who, after passing a few steps, turned back to speak to us; and said he had been in poor health for some time, had tried physicians, the mineral waters and travelling, but all to little purpose; a dejection spread over his countenance, and he seemed in a serious frame of mind. My friend informed him I was from America, on a visit to the children of God in Germany. He expressed a wish for my preservation and success. I told him there was one Physician near at hand to whom he might yet successfully apply, who, if it were not consistent with his wisdom to restore him to health, could bless the affliction to him, and prepare him for a better inheritance; to which he assented, and parted with us in a very friendly manner. I can but admire at the clear and decisive manner in which many of these seeking people speak of their convincement of the fundamental doctrines of Friends, and the sense they have of their own weakness in not more boldly and openly maintaining them; but that time must come, I solidly believe, to many in this land.

"First-day, 4th. Though very rainy, yet eight of the friendly people, and two Moravians, came and sat down with us in silence at our inn. Some religious communication taking place, they received it in much stillness; and when it appeared about time to break up, we desired, if there had been anything said which they did not unite with or understand, they might take the freedom to mention it; to which the old man (Moravian) replied, it was entirely consistent with Scripture, and what he had found in his own mind for forty-five years. They parted with us in much tenderness and with reluctance, desiring our preservation, and hoped we would visit them again.

"A great fair of horses, cattle, hogs, merchandize, &c., is to commence after dinner; and this occasioned our getting away as soon as we could, the people beginning to collect largely about our inn. The landlord expressed his sorrow that we could not stay in his house with satisfaction, as dancing, music, and all kinds of rioting would soon begin, and continue for two days;

he also said that he thought it a blessing to have such people in his house.

"5th. Moved on to Hammeln; the country we passed through was more fertile than heretofore, the road paved, the mountains round us covered with beech and other timber, the valleys clothed with verdure, and very pleasant. Having taken some cold from riding through the rain, I was more unwell when we arrived at Hammeln, than all the journey before. This is a fortified town, and may contain about fifteen thousand inhabitants; it is now full of soldiers, and said to be the strong hold of the Hanoverian dominions; its handsome gardens and valleys of grass land, with a water course through it, give it a pretty appearance.

"6th. Feeling poorly, and but little prospect of religious service in Hammeln, we set out for Pyrmont, travelling through a handsome, hilly, and well cultivated country, thickly settled with villages—the people were gathering in their harvest. Arrived at Pyrmont, and alighted at our friend Frederick Seebohm's, and were provided with accommodations. Lewis Seebohm, and several of the friendly people, coming to see us, we had a comfortable religious opportunity with them, in which Lewis interpreted.

"7th. This being their week-day meeting, about twenty men and women attended, and it was a solid baptizing time. The people stayed with us some time after the meeting was over, and seemed much pleased to see us. We concluded to have our dinner ready cooked from an inn, and a young woman, named Lena

Spannagle, who had been with George Dillwyn and Sarah Grubb, and also with John Pemberton, until he died, having heard of our coming, walked twelve miles to offer us her services, which we freely accepted.

"8th. Walked out to Lewis Seebohm's, about one and a half miles. The valley which he occupies, was given him, about four years past, by the prince of Waldeck, to erect a manufactory of edge tools, which he has accomplished, and improved the place very much, for the time. He has a pretty good library, and is a man of good talents, acquainted with the English and French languages.

"10th. Visited the family of Lewis Heydorn, consisting of his wife and six children. Being obliged to act as interpreter, I did it in much fear, lest I should make some mistake; sensible that we have daily need of Divine help, that we may keep a conscience void of offence: we hoped the opportunity was profitable.

"Went to see a person, named Galla, whose family consists of himself, wife, and two journeymen. The language of 'peace be to this house,' went forth freely; the spring of everlasting love and life being mercifully opened, we rejoiced together in the feeling of near unity and affection for each other. One of the young men was especially made near to us, as one who, if he kept faithful, would be made an instrument of good to others. At the burying ground we saw the grave of dear John Pemberton. When I think of this brother being brought, in so singular a manner, to lay down his life among this handful of professors, who are like the first fruits in Germany, that saying mostly occurs, 'the blood of the martyrs is the seed of the church.' He is remembered here with much sweetness.

"First-day morning, 11th. About forty* Friends attended the meeting, which was a solid, profitable season. A woman who happened to be at the meeting at Hanover, last First-day, walked with her brother-in-law six miles to the meeting, over a high mountain. She is the wife of Huber, at Hanover, dined with us, was very tender, and said the Friends at Hanover sent their love to us, and hoped we would visit them again —she thought the Lord had brought us there for their sakes. Afternoon — some notice being given of the meeting, about sixty attended, some of whom were of those who had separated from the little society here; the Lord was pleased to be with us in a remarkable manner, and most present were broken into tears. It held three hours, and ended in solemn prayer and praises to God; several persons continued with us, until nearly ten o'clock, conversing on religious affairs.

"12th. In the afternoon, visited the family of Herman Shutamire, who had separated. We asked him some questions concerning his separation, which he answered in a good frame of mind; and after recommending him to dwell near the Fountain of love, that would reconcile and unite all the children of our heavenly Father together, we parted in much tenderness.

* These people, though professing our principles, are not accounted strictly in membership with our religious Society.

"13th. Visited several families, which service was attended with much openness and satisfaction. The valley where the Factory is, they call Friedenstall or Peace-dale; it is a quiet, sequestered fertile spot, and I believe that great harmony prevails among the inhabitants, who are four families, chiefly connected with Friends.

"16th. Herman Shutamire visited us, and brought three papers, one from himself, one from Henry Munthang, and one from Anthony Shonning; being a vindication of their conduct in separating from Friends. On reading and considering the contents, we agreed to request the principal Friends who remained united as a body, to meet us to-morrow.

"17th. The Friends having drawn up the causes of their disunity with those who had separated, we found it was likely to prove a very exercising affair to us, and were much discouraged, feeling but little hope of a reunion.

"18th. First-day: held a meeting at nine o'clock, which ended solidly. In the afternoon meeting about fifty were present, two of whom were Jews, and it was thought to be a favored time. The young women who are in families, and work either in or out doors, as occasion requires, and very hard at times, are paid about seven dollars a year: and a young man, a Friend of good capacity, says, if he makes his pair of shoes per day, he earns about two shillings and sixpence our money, a week, and is found board and washing; yet he keeps himself decent, and is dressed like a Friend of our country. Provisions and clothing are about two-thirds of the price in America; but they make but little clothing and mean diet do. Several of them express their desire to go to America, but we dare not encourage or unsettle them. Our concern for the right ordering of things among this little society, keeps our minds closely exercised, as well as for the restoration of those who are scattered—the eyes of the people are much upon them and us, some for evil, and some for good. Having had my mind especially turned to this place, I feel at home for the present, and desirous of bearing my part of the burden while we stay.

"19th. Anthony Shonning, a sensible old man, who was separated, brought a paper he had drawn up, containing a large sheet closely written, which he said he could not be easy to omit. We made such remarks as occurred to us, and afterwards David Sands and myself visited him and Henry Munthang at their home; they were loving, and evidenced a strong desire to be reconciled upon a right ground. We proposed a meeting at six o'clock, with all that had gone off, and Friends together, and desired them to seek for a preparation of love and charity, that they might meet each other in a state that the Lord would condescend to bless. Most of the men Friends, and three women, met in the meeting-room. Henry Munthang, Herman Shutamire, Henry Land, his son, and Margaret Wint, being the heads of the families of those who had gone out from Friends, came also. After a season of silence, David Sands was drawn to prayer; then we, the visitants, expressed our minds to them fully; setting forth the opportunity it gave the enemies of Truth to triumph, seeing them at variance, and the importance of their mutually laying down their prejudices against each other, and seeking after a spirit that would bring about a reconciliation without many words. The three principal separatists then expressed themselves in great brokenness and humility, and in a spirit of forgiveness of those who they thought had dealt hardly with them, and caused the separation. I marvelled at the clearness with which they expressed themselves. The Lord graciously condescending to favor, in a remarkable manner, with his blessed presence — all hearts were humbled, the high untoward will of man was brought down, and the spirit that loves contention, and delights to have the superiority, was cast out, and through mercy, the meek, teachable state of little children appeared to predominate in most present. Our minds being deeply baptized with an undoubted feeling of the Lord's goodness, we were opened with clearness to set before them the nature of our holy profession, the love of Christ, the good Shepherd to us all, and the necessity of dwelling in that charity, which, instead of magnifying each other's weakness, and entertaining groundless jealousies and surmises of each other, would cast a mantle of love over them, remembering that we also were weak, and liable to be tempted. A truly contriting and heart-tendering time it was, and most of the company were melted into tears, under an extraordinary sense of the Lord's compassion to us.

"It was then proposed, as it appeared that in a time of weakness many things had been said and done on both sides, that did not savor of that Divine love and charity in which all the children of our heavenly Father ought to dwell, that all present should now, under the humbling visitation of God's power, without bringing up the occasion of offence, or going into many words, forgive one another, and cast all that they had counted offences, as into the depths of the sea, never more to be brought up again. Both sides freely, and in great tenderness, confessing their readiness so to do, and to begin again under the direction of the heavenly Master-builder, in an united labor for the edification and building one another up in the most holy faith. They rose, embraced and saluted each other with manifest tokens of unfeigned love and thankfulness to the great Searcher and softener of hearts, who, in an unexpected time and manner had revealed his power to the uniting of brethren who had been seven months in a state of separation, after having for some years walked in harmony and suffered together for his name's sake.— The meeting then concluded in heart-felt praise and supplications to the Fountain of love and mercy, who had in so remarkable a manner blessed the labor and exercise of the evening, and crowned us with gladness, when we parted at almost eleven o'clock. For my own part, I thought myself amply paid for all my exercise, the long journey and voyage, and the trying separation from my dearest natural ties, by being made a witness to the love of God poured forth, I thought, as in the beginning among

18

Friends. We went to rest, sweetly refreshed in spirit, and I did not marvel that my mind had been so remarkably turned to this place before I left home.

"20th. Made several visits to the different classes; many told us in brokenness of spirit, that they had never before witnessed so much of the love of God shed abroad, as was manifested last evening. It appears that these people, in a time of weakness, had been scattered through the influence of one Brown, with whom John Pemberton had labored because of his erroneous opinions.

"21st. A large meeting, most of the Friends and professors, with the families of those who had not been at meeting for more than six months, attended; it was a solemn tendering time, and we were favored to relieve our minds in loving counsel, caution and encouragement, to hold fast the profession of their faith in a good conscience and love unfeigned. It was like completing the bonds of union; we rejoiced together and gave thanks to the Author of every mercy. In a conference with all those who were accounted members, we were made acquainted with the business of their Monthly Meeting, in which they had hitherto kept no minutes, but had visited and received some as members, and in a book for the purpose, had recorded their births and burials, and raised a small stock for the uses of society. We recommended several matters to their attention and care, and the necessity of promoting the school education of their children, for which purpose our dear friend John Pemberton had left them thirty pounds sterling, and another Friend had given them five pounds. Our advice was received kindly, as they had long felt the necessity of a regular established discipline. The meeting concluded in much harmony. Thus we are favored, through Divine help, to get along step by step to our comfort.

"Fifth-day, 22d. Visited a family consisting of a man, his wife and four children; they appeared to be the lowest in the world of any we have visited. A number of persons who were near the house at their work, both men and women, hearing our voices, drew near, and it proved a time of distinguished mercy and encouragement, both to the family and those that came in, who were not Friends. The man is a day-laborer, about the Factory, and has to maintain his family with about one shilling a day, Pennsylvania currency.

"23d. Visited Henry Munthang and family; consisting of his wife, Anthony Shonning, an old Friend removed from Rinteln, and six children; we hoped it was a uniting time, both to visitors and visited. In the afternoon called upon Klapp, the governor of the town, who received us kindly.

"24th. Friends sat down quietly together, and apprehending we were nearly clear of Pyrmont, I expressed my prospect of going to Berlin.

"25th. The morning meeting was the largest we have had, though there were but three or four who did not profess with us; yet, with the addition of the families lately re-united, they made a respectable appearance: three Friends from near Minden, and two from Boetter were present. It proved, through mercy, a solid favored meeting. Afternoon had a meeting at Leibsen, a village one mile and a quarter from Pyrmont, in the same valley as the Factory; most of the Friends and a pretty large company of others attended; we were considerably exercised, and it was thought to be a season of profit.

"26th. Sat down together to seek for best counsel. I mentioned my prospect of Berlin, which still continued with me. David Sands expressed his unity with it, and thought we should go together. George Dillwyn thought he was not yet clear of Pyrmont. The governor having sent an invitation, I went with some of our company, and had much conversation with him; he spoke well of Friends, and I hope he is a friend to them. The people who saw us with him with our hats on, appeared astonished, for the great men in Germany are approached with much servility. In the evening being quietly together, Lewis Seebohm thought it his duty to offer himself as a companion to David Sands and myself to Berlin, which was a trial to George Dillwyn. Christopher Reckefus, and the Friends who had been here some days from Minden, came to see us, as we expected soon to leave. He has passed through many trials for his testimony, and lately had a child taken up out of its grave, in his garden, by the priest, after it had been buried nearly six months. The priest had it interred in their burying-ground, and then seized upon Christopher's property for his dues.

"A number of our friends having come to see us, the house was so full that all could not sit down; a solemn covering prevailing, Friends were made near to each other in the love of Christ. It is a special day of renewed visitation to many, both youth and others: indeed we are bound to them and kept here in a singular manner. After the opportunity, some young women had a conference with a few of us, as to the means of giving them employment in spinning, weaving, &c., that would afford them a more decent living and less exposure in the fields. Women in this country are obliged to labor very hard, both in and out of doors, for about one shilling a day, Pennsylvania currency, and about three shillings if they find themselves. The men get about two shillings and six-pence per week, and their diet and lodging, both which in a general way are very poor, and do not probably cost more than half a dollar.

"27th. Sat with the company of Friends in the capacity of a Monthly Meeting, which held four hours, was a solid time, and I hope our being with them was of some use.

"28th. Attended their week-day meeting, which was large, and through renewed mercy a tendering parting season.

"29th. Almost all the Friends came to take leave of us. We sat down with them about an hour, and it proved a favored contriting season; having been nearly united to them, it was one of the most affectionate partings I ever experienced; many of the dear young people held us by the hand, and would scarcely let us go, and testified their affection by many tears. We reached Mela about dusk and had entertainment at a good inn; this is the territory of the bishop of Hildesheim, mostly Roman Catholics.

"30th. Got to Hildesheim to breakfast; gave to the landlady and her son (Protestants) some books. Hildesheim is a considerable city, surrounded by ramparts, is the residence and capital of the bishop's dominions, in which the Lutherans are tolerated and have one place of worship: the city may contain fifteen thousand inhabitants. Rode to Brunswick, forty-two miles, and lodged at an inn where we had good accommodations. The country we passed through is thickly set with villages, the land excellent and the roads good, with many crosses and crucifixes on the sides of them.

"Tenth month 1st. The Duke has built a noble orphan-house here; the city may contain thirty thousand inhabitants, and abundance of trade is carried on during the fairs. The Duke not being at home, we had a desire to see the Duchess. The palace is large, in the form of a square, with one side open. After waiting some time, we were ushered into a large room; — she seemed pleased to see us, conversed freely on various subjects, told us our people were as much attached to her brother, the king of England, as any of his subjects; and if all were like us, there would be no troubles or wars in the world. We told her our business in Germany, and she asked if we found people of our profession there? We mentioned our friends at Pyrmont, and that we found religious and awakened people in almost every place. As we were going to Berlin, we asked if it were probable we could have an interview with the king (of Prussia,) whether he was a man easy of access? She said yes; but he was opposed to them on political principles. We told her our religious concern for the people was, that they might come unto Christ, and find rest in him. Presented her with Penn's No Cross, No Crown, in French, which she received kindly, and wanted to know the meaning of the title, as she supposed no person could pass through life without their crosses. We told her the saying of Christ, 'If any man will be my disciple,' &c., and that the cross here spoken of was not anything outward, or the common disappointments of life, neither such as were made of wood, stone or costly metals, but an inward and daily cross to our corrupt inclinations; a being crucified to sin and worldly vanities. She said she now understood the title of the book, and would read it with pleasure. Before we parted, I mentioned the words of our Saviour to a beloved female. 'Mary hath chosen the good part,' &c., that crowns and dignities were perishing and transitory things; but if those who wore them were concerned to rule well and fill up their duty as good stewards, they would receive a crown of unfading glory in the world to come. She thanked me, wished us a good journey, and we parted with satisfaction of mind. Afterwards we visited some religious people, and gave them some books: they appeared to be measurably enlightened men. Passing through a fine country, a city called Kings-Lutter, several villages, &c. we arrived at Helmstead.

"First-day, Tenth month 2d. Walked round the

town,—the people gazed much at us; and when we asked what place of worship they were flocking to in such numbers, they told us the Lutheran; but supposing us to be Catholics, said our Church was outside the gates. Some asked if we were Brabanters: when we told them we were not, nor Frenchmen, nor Catholics, nor Lutherans, but of a different religion, and came from America, they looked surprised, and said it was very far off. Waited on professor Beireis, who is esteemed a very learned man. We gave him Barclay's Apology in Latin, which he received respectfully, said he read every thing, and was visited by kings and princes, whom he should now have an opportunity of informing of our principles. He remarked, that he was glad to have the company of religious people, and willing to do us any service in his power; but said there were no separatists in Helmstead. Finding this to be the case, we took an early dinner, left some books at the inn, and went off for Magdeburg, thirty-six miles, Passed through a very fine country and many villages: three-fourths of the ground was covered with wheat and rye stubble, the roads good, and horses excellent. It is the greatest grain country which any of us have ever seen, and the people raise great numbers of sheep and geese. Arrived after dark at the gates of Magdeburg, where we were examined, and all our trunks and packages searched. A little further on, an officer stopped us, took our names and places of residence, and sent a soldier to conduct us to the inn; here again the landlord took our names and places of abode, in a book kept for the purpose, where the names of all strangers that have lodged here for several years are to be seen. The landlord and waiters were obliging, and the accommodations good.

"Tenth month, 3d. Walked round the town, which is handsome, cleaner, and better built than most we have passed through in Germany, and is well lighted with lamps. We excited the curiosity of the people, who looked at us as far as they could see us, yet there was nothing like scoffing or ridicule. We were informed of a number of religious people, who met in companies once a week, in different parts of the city, to sing, tell their religious experiences, &c.; and one of the companies being to meet this evening, we inquired whether we could be admitted to sit with them, which they agreed to, and appointed to meet at six o'clock. We found about twenty-five men, but no women. We kept our hats on, giving them our reasons, with which they appeared satisfied — they had a short hymn at this time on account of our being present, after which the tutor made a prayer. David Sands then spoke, and was enlarged on many subjects; during which, many coming in, the room was crowded, and in the entry there were many women; in the whole there were about sixty or seventy persons. My mind being drawn to prayer, they all kneeled, and it appeared to be a solemn time; they seemed to be filled with love toward us, and expressed their thankfulness. We mentioned our desire to have a more general collection of the seeking people in Madgeburg, both men and women, as we felt much love in our hearts to them. They said their situation required such a matter to be well considered, and to be moved in with much caution and wisdom, on account of the jealousy of the priests and government. Poor creatures, they are like so many Nicodemuses, and therefore much sympathy is due to them, when all things are considered. On parting with them, they embraced us with many prayers for our preservation, and thanks to the Author of all good, who had sent us among them. They do not appear to have any idea of our Society, and perhaps have never heard of the name of Quaker; indeed, we seem now to be beyond where our religious Society is known, and on this account I feel some hesitation in handing them books which hold up a name given us only in derision by our enemies, and not our acknowledged title. The river Elbe affords a communication between this city and Hamburg by flat-bottom boats: in the river are a number of curious grist-mills, that float upon large boats, and are worked by the stream.

"An honest hearted simple friend, who was with us yesterday, and who had a very high conceit of a man that had made these people believe he possessed extraordinary powers, came to see us, reflected on what we said in the meeting, and appears now to be much changed. Some of us accompanied him home, where this wonderful man was, and also another person who had visited us yesterday. The magician put on an air of consequence, and with great rapidity went over a number of incoherent expressions, without any sense, which his two disciples seemed to catch with great eagerness, and thought he was very deep, because they could not understand him. After slipping in a few expressions, which was hard to do, Lewis Seebohm told him we were in much doubt about his schemes, and that if he was possessed of the power he pretended to, he would not have occasion to live at the expense of other people, for several months, as he had done. Finally, we told the people that the things he had promised them, would never be brought to pass, they were only deceiving themselves with a golden dream. This touched him to the quick, and he flew out of the door of the room instantly. Lewis called to him, but he did not return; so the false prophet was manifested before several witnesses, and they convinced of the delusion; their hopes of receiving a quantity of gold, which he had said the angels were to bring him, and in which they were to be sharers, were at an end. They thought it was worth while for us to come to Magdeburg, if it were only to break up this delusion, for he had many disciples upon whom he lived, and had so done for a long time. I notice the occurrence, as an instance how far the credulity of people is carried, especially in Germany. Those two persons were simple, well-meaning, religious men, and one of them had separated from all outward forms of worship, for several years.

"We visited a few families to satisfaction; the people look upon us with very friendly countenances in this city, and speak kindly; and there is something more courteous and engaging in their manners, than any other town we have been in. Our two friendly visitors were with us this evening, and gave us a full opportunity of explaining our principles and doctrines; they heard us with great attention, and appeared to be sensible men, saying that the longer they were with us, the more they loved us: we gave them some books, and parted in much affection.

"5th. At the best inns in Germany, the charges are very high, but they are remarkably decent and quiet. We rode through a beautiful country, about three miles, when it became more sandy and barren; and arrived at Brandenburg about nine o'clock at night. The king of Prussia suffers no smoking in the streets of the cities or villages, under a penalty of fifty dollars, or being sent for some months to work at the fortifications; this is trying to the Germans. Here is a fine river, about one hundred yards wide, which runs into the Elbe, and goes up to Berlin, with a number of good mills upon it. There are many people in this place, who, though not in strict communion with the Moravians, seem much inclined to them. That society have a town and large congregation in Saxony, perhaps fifteen miles off.

"6th. Lewis Seebohm found a man of a religious character, who said there were upwards of forty men and women, who met at times in his house to edify one another. Lewis asked if we could have an opportunity with them before we left Brandenburg; he thought it would be acceptable, but would let us know soon. A pious young man came to our inn, and invited us to the house where they met at four o'clock, which, though some of our company had gone out, I consented to. At four o'clock we all went, and found several religious people, who received us in a very loving manner, said they were a people seeking God, and were very willing to collect at six o'clock in the evening, to give us an opportunity of opening our minds to them. They were rejoiced to find that we were come to Germany on so important an occasion; said the love of God was great and unsearchable, that He should thus send us among them at the risk of our lives, and enable us to leave all for his sake; and they shed tears of gladness. At six we went, and found forty or more gathered in an upper chamber—the man of the house gave out a short hymn, which they sung; he then told them where we came from, and our concern to visit this land, and desired they might all retire in their minds, and be attentive to what the Lord might give us to say among them. After a time of solemn silence, David Sands and myself were severally opened in testimony, and the meeting ended in prayer. They were very solid, and most of them much tendered, seemed scarcely able to part with us, and expressed with many tears, their thankfulness to the Father of mercies for sending us; we all thought it a favored, contriting season. Surely the Lord is preparing a people in this land, who shall not be afraid to own him and his testimonies, in his own time. We left them a number of books.

"7th. Just as we were setting off for Potsdam, a

good-looking woman came up, and said in an affectionate manner, we must not go until we had seen her father, who, being out of town last evening, had not seen us, but was not easy to let us go without requesting our company. We went to see the old man, who is about seventy years of age: he had been the first promoter of the meetings of these pious people, and appeared like an Israelite indeed. Some religious communication being offered to him and the family, they were much broken, and were made near to us in the covenant of love and life. O! the simplicity of these dear people! they parted from us with regret, and said those who were with us last evening at meeting would not forget us as long as they lived. The people every where in Prussia are astonished when we tell them we are from America, and entertain us with the strange ideas they have formed respecting the country. They suppose our homes are quite on the other side of the world—that when in our own country our feet were toward theirs, and asked if the sun rose and set as it does here: they lift up their hands and are astonished that we should come so far from home, and we can scarcely convince them that we have no lucrative motives.

"On arriving at Potsdam, we underwent a strict scrutiny, had our names taken, and a soldier sent to see us to the inn, where another officer took our names and examined all our trunks. They not only take our names as we pass through every town, but also the place we last came from, our several places of residence, our business in this country and the character we travel in, whether officers, merchants, &c., to all which we have learned to answer generally, that we are on a visit and travel as '*particulars*,' a word they have taught us, which mostly satisfies them. This town is pretty large: the river Havel, which leads into the Elbe, affords them a water communication with Hamburg, two hundred and thirty miles. The streets are wide, the houses large, the palace and many other buildings being very spacious, have an appearance of much grandeur, and it is by far the most magnificent city we have seen.

"8th. The new palace and the buildings attached to it, far exceed anything to be seen in England, as well as the ideas I had formed by reading of human pomp and grandeur. As a description would be foreign to our principal concern, it will be wisdom in us to turn our minds from such things, and stay them upon God, who alone can strengthen us to finish the important work He has required us to be engaged in, to his own praise and the peace of our minds. The more those who love the humble path of Jesus, see of the greatness and glory of this world, and how empty and vain it is, the more they will be constrained to draw nigh unto him, who is their dignity and their riches, and will finally be their everlasting glory. Thus I hope it was with us, in turning away from these sumptuous palaces. The road to Berlin is through a poor sandy soil, much of which is covered with scrubby pines. It is paved all the way, and lined on each side with Lombardy poplars; we passed through two or three villages, and entered Berlin at the Brandenburg gate, which is lately built, and must strike every stranger with its magnificence: there we were again examined by a polite young officer, who sent a soldier with us to the Inspector's office, where, after a good deal of persuasion, they consented to examine our trunks and bags this evening, which at first they did not seem disposed to, intending to lock them up until to-morrow. This took up so much time, that we did not get to the inn until it was quite dark.

"First-day morning, 9th. Lewis Seebohm went out to seek for some religious characters, and while absent, two Jews came into our rooms, one after the other, wanting to trade with us, either to buy, sell, or exchange money. I mention this, because in all the large towns, strangers will find such people exceedingly troublesome, for custom seems to have given them, and also women with fruit and trinkets, and other persons of that class, liberty to come into the inns, open your room doors, &c., and impose themselves upon you when they please; and so importunate are they, that it is difficult to get rid of them. Generally, the people are respectful and complaisant, especially those who have had a tolerable education. In our retirement, our minds having been much exercised during the morning with a feeling of discouragement, the spirit of prayer was granted, and through renewed mercy we were strengthened to put our confidence in that gracious Arm that had hitherto preserved us in this trying field of labor, and enabled us to discharge our duty, so as to leave every place so far peacefully. Two of our company going out to seek for religious persons, brought back some of the books we had left at Magdeburg, in the hands of . . . ., the tutor in the college there, who appeared very kind when we parted, and gave us a letter, speaking favorably of us to a person here, named Herman. But it appeared by a counter letter, which was read to Lewis Seebohm, that though he acknowledged we were religious men, and had preached the Gospel to them to their comfort and satisfaction, yet upon reading our books, he says he finds we hold erroneous opinions, reject baptism and the supper, and do not hold the Scriptures to be the Word of God; so that he could not unite with us, and had therefore sent the books with this information to Herman, requesting him to return them to us. This brought us under additional exercise and suffering from an unexpected quarter. Herman being a leading man among those who meet for the edification of each other in this place, who are pretty numerous, we did not doubt but he would spread sentiments among them to our prejudice, and we feared our way would be quite shut up in Berlin; for the subjects of the letter had taken a deep hold on his mind. Lewis had much conversation with him, which appeared to soften him in some degree; but not to convince him.

"The tutor at Magdeburg was a man of learning and of some influence, but evidently puffed up with his own importance, and could not submit to be deprived of it by adopting the simplicity of the doctrines of Truth; but if he had been a man of candor, he would have replied to us when we were present, as we had much conversation, particularly on the points he lays most stress upon in his second letter to Herman, viz. the Holy Scriptures, our views of which we fully explained to him at that time, apparently to his satisfaction; so that after it he wrote of his own accord our letter of recommendation, embraced us and parted from us with every token of brotherly love. We left at Magdeburg a number of books besides those sent back, which we hope will still be of use to a number of valuable seeking persons there, who were made near to us. Our present situation at Berlin is as trying as any I was ever in. In addition to the exercise we are under, in feeling the darkness and gross depravity of many of the inhabitants, it appears as though we should obtain but little intercourse with those who are religiously inclined. We sat together in a low, discouraged state, almost ready to wish ourselves away, but concluded that here we must stay, endeavor to clear ourselves, and contend for the faith as ability might be given, through suffering. While thus engaged, a religious man whom Lewis had seen in the morning, came to invite us to their meeting at seven o'clock. He said he had acquainted several, and he believed we should be kindly received; but we felt most easy to decline it at present. We continued thoughtful where it would end, as we were among strangers with whose laws we were unacquainted, and things might spread among them to our disadvantage; yet a secret confidence was afforded, that we were under the protection and care of Him, whose cause we were drawn here to espouse; and that if we abode in patience, He would make way for us; yet it was a deeply trying, and almost a sleepless night.

"10th. Conversed with several religious characters, who promised us a visit in the evening. Berlin is a very large and populous city, said to contain one hundred and fifty thousand inhabitants, including the soldiery. There are between three and four thousand Jews; thirty-three places of worship, of which the greater part are Lutherans; but the Calvinists, Moravians, Roman Catholics, and Jews, have also their houses for public worship. There are several large palaces for the king, queen, and royal family, which, as well as the public buildings, and many private houses, bridges, &c., are crowded with statuary. The streets are wide, and the houses generally the largest of any place we have been in; and taking it altogether, the city is superior in grandeur, perhaps, to most places in Europe. Many of the inhabitants are rich, and a considerable number of coaches are kept.

"11th. In the evening six religious men visited us, one of whom was a man of rank; they appeared glad to see us, and asked us many questions concerning our faith and religious opinions, which we answered to their satisfaction, and we hoped the three hours we were together were profitably spent. Near the close of the interview, quietness prevailing, some religious service ensued; and after prayer, during which they all kneeled, we parted. This gave us encouragement, and a hope that it would be introductory to further service; they said the letter from the tutor at Magdeburg had not prejudiced them—they owned us as brothers in Christ, and thought he did not do right. In the evening two religious young men came to see us, who appeared very loving and tender. They were rejoiced to see brethren who had taken so long a journey for the Gospel sake, and said there were great numbers of awakened minds in Berlin; but they were scattered over the town, and met in separate companies; that a man named Drewits held meetings at his house, to which many, especially young people, resorted; and that they were now going thither, and would conduct us if we thought proper. Apprehending some persons might call to see us, it was concluded that Lewis Seebohm and David Sands should go, and the rest of us continue in our chambers. About nine o'clock they returned, having attended the meeting; the man preached and prayed, which was the common practice, but there was no singing. David Sands had an opportunity of speaking before they broke up, to his satisfaction, though they were shy of them at first entering the room, seeing them keep their hats on; yet they parted lovingly: there were about thirty men and women. We make our way by inches in this place, the people being very wary, afraid of being interrupted by the authorities, and meeting with suffering, as some have heretofore; so that our trials are great; yet we do not doubt that our being here is in our heavenly Master's appointment, and desire to abide in patience all his appointed time.

"Fourth-day, 12th. Several of the friendly people visited us; and we proposed a meeting in the evening, which was agreeable to them. We took a walk round the city, the magnificence of which is surprising; many of the houses are from one hundred to one hundred and fifty feet front, and ornamented in a beautiful manner; it being the residence of many of the great officers of the kingdom, both civil and military; and one thing is remarkable, we have not seen a beggar, and but few miserable looking people in the streets, though many are low in the world; but the employment they receive from the army and grandees of the court, with the many charitable institutions, supply all their real wants. In the evening at six, between thirty and forty persons collected in our rooms, which are convenient and retired; among them were two parsons, one a Lutheran, the other a Calvinist. I had conversation with one before the people were all gathered, and found him possessed of some lovely and valuable traits. The company being gathered into silence, a solemnity covered us which was precious, and we were favored with the spirit of prayer; after which David Sands and myself were engaged in testimony: the people were solid, and through Divine mercy it proved a satisfactory season to us and them, as far as appeared. They all took leave of us in a very affectionate manner, and some stayed late in religious conversation. A pious young woman, in particular, took our attention, who continued for some time after the meeting was over, lifting up her eyes and pouring forth pious ejaculations and praises to the Father of mercies, who had thus favored us together. Here we had fresh occasion to acknowledge the continued goodness of God, who thus unexpectedly made way for us: 'Surely there is no rock like unto God.'

"13th. We felt our minds drawn to visit Freyenwalde, a town about thirty-five miles north-east of Berlin, where the Koenig's Rath Albinus had retired, after laying down his lucrative office for conscience sake. We arrived there in the evening, and finding a number of awakened people lived in the place, our friend Albinus proposed to collect as many as he could in about an hour, in the house where he boarded. We went there at the time appointed, and about twelve persons came in, with whom we had a solid meeting, in which the Lord favored with matter and utterance, we believed suited to the states of this tender people, and we parted in much love and brokenness of spirit. Albinus accompanied us to the inn, after ten o'clock, where he stayed and supped; his countenance and spirit bespoke him to be a brother beloved in Christ. He is a single man, about forty years of age, of good education and polished manners. He proposed taking a seat in our wagon to accompany us to Berlin, which was very agreeable to us.

"14th. The woman of the house where the meeting was held last night, having requested us to visit her husband, who was sick in his chamber, and could not have the benefit of the meeting, we breakfasted early, and had a precious opportunity with him, his amiable tender spirited wife and our friend Albinus in the chamber, and parted from them and divers others who were at meeting last evening, in near affection and with their prayers. On the way to Berlin, at the place where we dined and changed horses, I accidentally fell in with the president of the Chamber of Justice at Berlin, who conversed with much freedom respecting America, and was particularly desirous of information on the subject of our abolishing corporal punishments, with which he seemed pleased; but had doubts whether it would answer the desirable end in view. Travelling in a convenient wagon with our friend Albinus, gave an opportunity of much free religious conversation, for which his mind was prepared, and he made several very pertinent remarks and inquiries; he is, by the teaching of Divine Grace on his own mind, nearly united with us in principle, and earnestly endeavoring to conform in practice; though he sees plainly, as we do also, that the cross will be great if he is altogether faithful to the light he has received. If he is favored to stand fast on the foundation, of which we do not at present see any room to doubt, he may be made an instrument of much good in this country; though it undoubtedly will be through suffering.

"We arrived at Berlin about seven o'clock, where we were subjected to an examination of our trunks; this is a trying circumstance, and occasions great detention to weary travellers, but must be submitted to at every fortified town, though it may be twice in a day. Albinus took up his lodgings with us at the inn where we staid before — the landlord and servants received us gladly. Some conversation taking place respecting the mode of cutting the hair and powdering it, common here even among the religious people, it appeared that he had felt himself restrained from the general custom; we sympathize with him, and have strong desires he may be favored to go forward, step by step.

"15th. Lewis Seebohm and Albinus visited several religious people, and a minister named Jenike, who was at our meeting on the twelfth. He holds an assembly every seventh-day evening in a large room at his house, to which many young people come. Lewis queried, whether we could not attend and hold the meeting in our way. He behaved kindly, but informed our friend, that he found by the letter Herman had received from Magdeburg, that we did not own water baptism nor the supper; and that our preaching tended to draw the people from a dependence on their teachers; that it had already been under consideration among the ruling clergy, to apply to the magistrates to send us out of the city; though for his own part he should have nothing against our coming to the meeting, but it would give great offence to his superiors; said he had been well satisfied and edified the evening he was at our meeting, and wished us well.

"Concluding to hold a meeting in our chambers tomorrow evening, we wrote a note to Jenike, requesting he would give the people notice who assembled at his house this evening; which he did according to his promise; but told them at the same time, that we were no doubt good men in our way; yet we held some doctrines tending to lay waste their ordinances, and to draw people from their pastors, and that the superior clergy had already taken into consideration to apply to the magistrates to send us out of the city. Our friend . . . . . ., being present, vindicated us, and came from thence with the information. At the request of some, we met them at six this evening, and had some discourse respecting baptism and the supper. They were men of talents, and furnished with arguments in support of their opinions, equal to most who attempt it; — a small degree of warmth appeared at one time in the course of disputation, for they were very zealous, religious men, and were very loath to give up their strong holds; but that soon subsided, and much brotherly love prevailed; and though they did not acknowledge themselves fully convinced of our doctrines, we had reason to believe the opportunity had been blessed to them; several others coming in, the evening was closed in prayer, and we parted in a friendly manner, having fresh occasion to say the Lord hath not forsaken us.

"First-day, 16th. Held a meeting in our chamber, with a few of the most serious of our friends here, among whom was secretary Hoyer, one of those who were with us last night; it proved, through the renewing of our heavenly Father's love, a time of refreshment and comfort. Dined by invitation with Johann Christopher Henefusz; and several other religious people being present, there was some service in the ministry. The family were made very near to us in the love of Christ. A young woman of good countenance and innocent manners, daughter of one who dined with us, came in; she had not seen us before, but on hearing her father speak of us, she sent a book with a collection of religious scraps in it, to our lodgings, requesting us to put our names in it, and each to add a text of Scripture, such as might occur to us for her instruction; which we did; this appears to be a practice among the religious people here. In the evening, the people began to gather an hour before the appointed time, many crowded into the meeting whom we had never seen before, so that our four rooms, which communicated with each other, were soon filled; some who took an account of the number, thought there was not much short of two hundred, divers of whom were people of rank in the world. Our minds were much humbled in the prospect of the necessity of Holy direction, that Truth might not suffer among this discerning people. Our heavenly Father, who is graciously pleased to be with those who trust in him, was in a very remarkable manner, mouth and wisdom, tongue and utterance to us; an uncommon solemnity prevailed over the assembly, such as I have seldom seen in my own country amongst a mixed multitude of strangers, and great brokenness was among them. Although the meeting continued three hours, and many had to stand in a crowded situation the whole time, yet nothing like restlessness appeared; we rejoiced in the hope, that Truth was in dominion over all; for which favor, the glory and the praise was rendered unto God, to whom only it is due. The Lord causes all things to work together for good to them that fear him. We had reason to believe that this meeting was increased even by the opposition we had met with from Herman and others.

"17th. Many of the tender people who were at meeting yesterday, visited us, and acknowledged their unity and satisfaction. A young man also came with some money, which his mother desired we would accept, towards bearing our expenses: we thanked them for their kind intention, but could not receive it, and it gave us an opportunity of explaining ourselves to the satisfaction of several respecting the free gift of Gospel ministry. Another poor woman sent us a pot of honey and some cakes, and many appeared ready to do us any service in their power, which manifestations of their love for us, were grateful and encouraging. A Roman Catholic hearing there were some priests arrived from a foreign country, came to see us, and inquired if we received the confessions of the people: we told him it was best to confess his sins to God, who would forgive him upon repentance; and he went away satisfied. At the request of the people, we gave away almost all the books in our possession, and those sent back from Magdeburg answered a good purpose. Several parents brought their children, desiring we would give them some counsel; and in many ways they expressed their attachment to us. Truly the Lord has a tender-hearted people in this place, whom he is gathering to the spirituality of his kingdom. We visited an ancient woman who had been many years helpless from palsy; the people of the house had been at our meeting, and several neighbors coming in, we had a truly refreshing, tendering opportunity, which we trust will not soon be forgotten by some of them. At our return found several visitors had taken possession of our room, to whom we had some religious communication. In the evening there were several with us, some of them men of considerable rank in the world, of enlarged understanding, and measurably enlightened to see the spirituality of Christ's day; they rejoiced to see us on our present errand, and say the Lord's hand is in it.

"18th. We are here kept day after day, through the Grace that is mercifully granted us, without murmuring. The Lord has many sheep, whom in his own time he will gather, and establish upon that foundation, which the fear of man will not be able to overthrow. We were united in appointing another meeting at six in the evening; and though the time was short, and the seeking people much scattered, yet upwards of one hundred attended with great readiness, many of whom we had not seen before: and what is remarkable and different from any other places is, that the zeal of these people occasions them to be mostly collected before the hour appointed. The time of silence was solemn, and David Sands appeared largely in the ministry, being much favored; after which, having travelled with him in near unity, I felt excused from any addition, and the meeting ended in prayer and praises to our heavenly Helper. The people took leave of us in great brokenness of spirit, with many tears and prayers for our preservation; so that we are made thankful that Truth is making its way in many minds, although there are not a few adversaries, who, we fear, are watching over us for evil. Experience teaches that where Truth is gaining in the hearts of people, Satan raises up enemies to it.

"19th. In the morning we had some hopes we might have left Berlin in the afternoon; but many of the people coming in, we were engaged with them until dinner-time in religious conversation. A Major Marconnay, who had been a man of note, and held an office under the king, had been several times to visit us, and attended the meeting last night; and now came with a desire to open to us the religious exercises of his mind. He related how he had sought the Truth among a variety of professors, and had not been satisfied, though divers of them had held up high pretensions; at length he had left all, laid down his office and lived a retired life; but he had found *that* among us, which he never was acquainted with before; saying, he believed we were sent there in the will of God, for his and others' help. He had a few questions to ask us, which he did in a very tender frame, and was much broken with the answers that were given him; and after some religious communication and prayer, we parted; his mind being relieved, and we hope convinced of the way of Truth as professed by us, and with desires to walk in it.

"Time will not admit of particularizing our almost continual engagements in this great city, where we find a large number of seeking souls, and every day brings new ones to see us; who, while they are honestly striving to find the new and living way, are very various in their opinions, but all appear glad of an interview with us, and open their minds with great freedom. Some have separated themselves from all outward ceremonies and modes of worship, and walk alone. Our being with them brings them into acquaintance with each other, and we do not yet find ourselves easy to go away. Towards evening we proposed another meeting to be at six o'clock; the notice was short, but about one hundred and twenty came. Our minds were engaged to enlarge upon most of our fundamental doctrines, which they received with great stillness and attention; some staying a little after the meeting, professed their full unity with the doctrines, and I believe received the word with gladness, as it corresponded with what they had secretly felt for years. They took a solemn leave of us in tears, recommending us to the heavenly Shepherd, and requested our prayers when we were separated from each other. One young woman of noble countenance was much broken, and seemed to part with great reluctance. Dear David Sands and myself, on comparing our sense and feelings at different times, were united in belief, that we never were among people to whom the love of God more richly flowed, than to many in this place, nor any that were made more near to us in the love and life of Christ. Our whole company (the travellers) were frequently much broken among them, and led to marvel at the goodness of our heavenly Father, who had thus unexpectedly been with us in this distant and strange place; and more especially so, as we were sensible that the priests and worldly-wise professors were much alarmed, and there was every reason to suppose they would interrupt and probably persecute us. Yet we were strengthened to hold our meetings and distribute our books openly; and though clouds seemed to gather about us at times, the Lord was graciously pleased to dispel them all, and great freedom we had in our labors among them, to our encouragement and holy confidence in Him that puts forth and goes before. Though many in this great city are very dissolute, and have proceeded to great lengths in pride and vanity, the Lord hath many sheep and lambs, whom if they keep steadfast, he will doubtless bring home to his fold of rest in his own way and time, and to him we commend them at present. Our friend Lewis Seebohm being so devoted to the cause we are engaged in, and clear in our testimonies, is able to unite with us in our services, and to deliver what we offer to the people, with so much energy and quickness, that nothing seems to be lost by his interpretation; and though we cannot but feel for him in long meetings, his frame not being strong, yet it is cause of thankfulness that he is enabled to go through it with great cheerfulness.

"20th. Several came to take leave of us, and a tender parting it was. Our kind landlord and all his family, children, servants, &c., embraced us, and with many tears manifested the place we had in their minds: they have been very kind and attentive to us all the time of our stay, have forwarded our meetings with cheerfulness, preparing seats, showing up the people, &c., so that we believe there was a Divine hand in sending us to this house.

"Left Berlin at ten o'clock, after visiting the mayor, and leaving with him a note and a copy of Barclay's Apology for the king, whom we had a desire to visit; but he being only a short time in the city, we could not obtain an interview, and were easy to go on for Brandenburg. We were obliged, in consequence of the road being very sandy, to put up nine miles short of this place, at a poor inn, where we found several Jews, who looked like pitiable objects, dressed little better than the American Indians, and little, if any, more polished in their manners. We were informed that great numbers of the poor Polanders were driven through this place like cattle, having very little clothing, and some clad with skins of beasts; their living only the coarsest rye bread and water; and in this condition they were taking them to the army. O the miseries of war!

CHAPTER IV.

Magdeburg — Halberstadt — Journey continued — Reach Pyrmont — Religious Meetings — Again leave Pyrmont — Rinteln — Reconciliation between separated Friends—Minden—Uncourteous treatment at Ufeln—Trials at Bilefield—Lemgo—Bad roads—Return to Hanover—Various religious services—Leave for Amsterdam—Disasters on the road — Revisit Minden — Religious Meetings — Counsellor Borges and Consistorial Rath—Osnaburg—Impositions upon travellers — Bentheim — Deventer — Amsterdam — Friends in Amsterdam — Hague — Rotterdam — Religious reflections — Meetings with the inhabitants — Voyage to Sluys — Proceed to Dunkirk — Markets, &c. — Journey to Paris — Thomas Paine — Irreligion in the city—Journey to Congenies—Origin and character of Friends at Congenies — Religious services — Minutes made in former years — Affecting parting — Journey renewed — Gilles — Character of the people and country — Professors with Friends — Leaves Congenies.

"Seventh-day, 22d. Reached Magdeburg before night; the inn-keeper and servants received us again with gladness. The reason of our return to this city was to show ourselves to the school-master, who had endeavored to do us much harm in Berlin, by his letter to Herman; and generally to defend our principles, if he had spread anything to our prejudice. We therefore desired he might be informed that we were returned, and ready to answer for ourselves to him or any who were willing to meet us with the Bible in their hands; we also desired our being here again might be spread among our religious brethren. Two religious men came to see us, whom we had not seen when here before; one of them was full of the necessity of the supper, but yet in a loving frame of mind; and though he endeavored to defend his doctrine, he found himself more deficient than he had contemplated; — the other appeared to be a solid man and in good measure united with Friends in principle.

"First-day, 23d. One of the men who was with us yesterday, came with one of his friends, and attended our little meeting; and something being said to them by way of ministry, they received it kindly. In the afternoon, one of those men who had been deceived by the magician, came to see us, and was glad in being released from the impositions of that person. It appears that the poor Magdeburgers have often been deceived by persons professing to have the philosopher's stone. A meeting of a company of serious persons, different from those we had been with when here before, was to be at four o'clock this afternoon; and though they invited us, we felt some objection to going among them in the time of their singing; they therefore concluded that we should come near five, when their service might be over. We accordingly went, and found about fifty men and women; one of them asked if we would be easy until he read two letters from some religious people who lived near the Rhine, at the seat of war; they were very affecting accounts of the sufferings of the people by the French, particularly at their taking possession of a city where one of the persons lived. Being gathered into silence, the meeting opened by prayer; after which considerable was said in the ministry. The people were generally quiet, and several much tendered, though it was evident, by the conduct of some of their principal men when we went in, that their minds had been somewhat prejudiced, and that they were not pleased with our keeping on our hats; yet through renewed mercy Truth prevailed, and we parted in a tender affectionate manner, with their prayers and good wishes for us.

"24th. Left Magdeburg, and not finding a convenient house for our accomodation in the town where we stopped, were compelled to proceed to Halberstadt, where we put up at a poor inn. Our landlord's son, a sensible agreeable young man, soon became acquainted with us, being bred up for a minister. He said he was sorry that he was destined for that station, and would rather do anything for a living than to take orders, because he did not think he was called to it.

"25th. Two religious men came to see us, who belonged to a little company that held conferences on religious subjects with a view to each other's edification. We proposed seeing them together this evening, which they gladly assented to; one of them, whose name was Kein, took me to his house and was very kind.

"Halberstadt is a very ancient town, and the houses are built in a singular manner. It appears to have but little trade, and few of the inhabitants are rich; it contains about two thousand houses, has seven Roman

Catholic cloisters for nuns and friars, and the places of worship are very ancient; one is said to be eight hundred years old. We went to Kein's house, and found but about ten persons gathered; the service in general was close and searching, and not so much openness felt as at some other places; yet some were tender; on the whole we were relieved by the opportunity, and believe it will be blessed to some of them. We afterwards heard there was a deist present, who appeared touched with the doctrines, said he had never heard such before, and hoped he should improve by them. Kein, and the young man educated for a priest, coming to our inn, some suitable remarks were made to them, to which they assented. The young man thought it an unhappiness that he had not been brought up to some other means of getting a living; said there was a great falling away from the primitive church; that the priests were very mercenary, and that he could not bear the thought of their exacting money from the poorest class of the people, when they took the sacrament, so called, which was the practice of most of them. We gave him Barclay's Apology in Latin, and are in hopes that our observations will not be lost upon him.

"26th. The young priest and a lad came to take leave of us, and at parting embraced us affectionately; the family also all manifested their love for us on parting. We passed through a fine country, thickly set with villages and large towns, among which was Wolfenbuttle. The people tell some extraordinary stories respecting what occurred to Luther, while he was writing some of his works there. We arrived before dark at Brunswick, being forty miles. Doctor Neimire and Simon Lobenstine came and spent an hour with us, and mentioning to them our thought of having a meeting before we left the town, they cheerfully undertook to open the way for it.

"27th. Finding that although the doctor had offered his house for the meeting, yet from some cause had again declined it; but another person, a serious man, opening his house cheerfully, we went there and found a small room full of men and women, being such as met at times privately for the improvement of each other. Our gracious Helper being near, it was an open satisfactory meeting; they did not seem restless in the time of silence, but were solid and attentive to what was offered. Several were very tender, and after being with them nearly three hours, they seemed loath to part, and embraced us affectionately.

"28th. Our kind friend who had given up his house for our meeting, came by sunrise with his wife to bid us farewell, remarking they had wept together last night after we left them, in considering how we had left all for Christ's sake, and were travelling at our own expense, and they knew not how to administer to us, though they felt willing according to their little ability. This morning, however, they thought they could not be easy without bringing us some sausage of the woman's own making, to the value of about half a dollar, as a token of their good-will; it was made in such manner as to be eaten without warming, and was very agreeable to take in our wagon. There was something so simple-hearted and full of love in these dear people, that their little present was enhanced to us an hundred fold, and we parted with them in near unity, and in the love of Christ, wishing one another's welfare here and for ever. The family at the inn parted with us again in much affection, and passing through many villages and a fine country, we dined at Hildesheim; then through a rich country with many crosses on the road-side, arrived at Oelsen, a considerable town, but dirty and irregular. Here we were taken to a large inn, where there were nearly thirty guests before us, mostly of a low class of people, who had their music, card-playing, &c., the landlord an unpolished man, and the fare very mean. David Sands being very poorly, we procured a pretty good bed for him; the rest of us were but meanly accommodated.

"29th. Got off early, and rode to Mila, where, as there was a good inn, and David being unwell, we breakfasted. Finding we were not likely to get to Pyrmont to-night, if we kept the common post-road, and our postilion not being allowed to go out of it, we were so anxious to be with our friends, that we discharged him, though we had paid the whole sum for the station he was to take us to. We then agreed with our landlord for a certain sum to take us over the mountains before night to Pyrmont. Passed on a rough road, over very high mountains; the atmosphere being perfectly serene, and descending from them we crossed the Weser in sight of Hameln in a boat, a beautiful stream about one hundred yards wide. Here we found a mean-looking town, and poor, dirty people—got very coarse fare, and hastened on and arrived at Pyrmont, to the joy of ourselves and our friends, before dark. Here we found George Dillwyn, who had continued all the time of our absence, having met with divers matters among the little flock which engaged his care and labor.

"First-day, 30th. At two meetings, which were satisfactory. Before we arrived here, a letter had been brought from Major Marconnay of Berlin, expressing in a grateful and thankful manner, the goodness of the great Shepherd in sending us to Berlin; that he hoped he should never forsake the Truth as it had now been discovered to him. He had undertaken to open our way for an interview with the king several days before we left Berlin, being acquainted with the Prime Minister. We waited as long as we thought necessary, and then left the city, he having received no answer from the Minister. The next day after, he was informed by him that the way was open, and the king ready to see us. Finding we were gone, the great men expressed regret, and despatched a courier after us to Potsdam; but we had left that city also. Thus by their needless delay, their curiosity and our concern for an audience with the king, had been frustrated. On the way back, we frequently looked at it as the only thing we had left which caused us regret; however, as there are many serious people in many places in Prussia, we cannot doubt but other instruments will, in the Lord's time, be sent among them, who may have the same concern laid upon them, and which he may open a more effectual door to discharge. We cannot charge ourselves with wilful omission, and therefore hope it will not be laid as matter of accusation against us. The journey into that country, and the Divine mercy so evidently extended to them and us, must remain as cause of reverent admiration and thankfulness as long as we live. In the tour to and from Berlin, we travelled about six hundred miles, and were out thirty-one days.

"31st. We have received several letters from Philadelphia, which were very acceptable, though there was also some cause for exercise; yet I must endeavor after resignation in all things, which has been my prayer this day. This world and the fashion of it passeth away. O may we secure an inheritance through our Lord Jesus Christ in an ever-abiding mansion in the world to come. David Sands and I walked to Conrad Galla's, spent some time with the kind family, and Charlotte Laaer, who had come to this place, and was glad to see us. She was in a loving frame of mind, and we hope the breach between her and her friends will be healed; she appears to be an innocent, sincere young woman, but through the influence of Brown has imbibed some opinions not congenial with the harmony and unity of this little body of professors.

"Eleventh month, 1st. Spent much of the day alone, my mind discouraged and much exercised from a fear lest we had hastened from Prussia too soon. In the evening my friends perceiving my depression, endeavored to cheer me up, but I retired to my chamber and obtained but little relief for body or mind.

"Fourth-day, 2d. The meeting was large, nearly all the Friends residing here were present, and some from Hanover, two of whom were a father and son, who had a strong desire to spend some time with us, and came forty miles on foot: the son is a youth of a sweet innocent countenance, and was much broken in the meeting on First-day and to-day; thus the Lord is at work to bring sons from far, and daughters from the ends of the earth. The meeting was a solid good season; both my beloved brethren were engaged therein, but my mind was not in a state to enjoy it as at other times. I took an opportunity when my dear friends George Dillwyn and David Sands were alone with me, to mention what I thought was the principal cause of my depression; not waiting at Berlin for an opportunity with the king lay heavy upon my mind, and I thought I could do no less than stand resigned to go back again, if it was the Lord's requiring. They were led into sympathy with me, and in a little time George Dillwyn said, what I had mentioned had taken so much hold upon his mind, that he apprehended it was his duty to stand resigned to the further openings of Truth with respect to going to Berlin, if it should be called for at our hands—and the concern now resting on the minds of my friends, I felt more at liberty.

"First-day, 6th. The meetings in the fore and afternoon were thought to be seasons of profit.

"7th. The Monthly Meeting held near six hours: we were all engaged in labor for the preservation of this little flock in love and unity, and leading them into such order and discipline as was suited to their circumstances. Several new members who had made application, were received into membership; and on the whole, it was thought to be a solid, well-conducted meeting.

"Fourth-day, 9th. We had a tender instructive parting from this dear little flock, who are made very near to us.

"Fifth-day we rose early, a number of the Friends coming to see us; after a season of contrition we again took leave of them in many tears, leaving George Dillwyn still at Pyrmont, with a hope to meet at Hanover, if the Lord will. Christopher Reckefus waiting upon us with his four horses to take us for a few days, we put on and arrived at Rinteln; the roads being very rough, our wagon was almost broken down, and we had but poor accommodation at the inn. Rinteln is in the Landgrave of Hesse's dominions, where several have been imprisoned for their religious principles, and others banished. There appears much of the spirit of intolerance and great darkness among them; yet there are a few awakened people, for whom we feel sympathy. It contains, perhaps, five thousand inhabitants; is a poor dirty place, and garrisoned by many soldiers. Had a small meeting at a house, the owner of which, when near his end, directed it should always be kept open for religious meetings — there were but about eight people met, yet through mercy it was made a time of refreshment and comfort; most of them were acquainted with our principles, but being afraid of the priests, had declined meeting together since the decease of the former owner of the house. We encouraged them to a revival, and left them in much sweetness.

"General Worms hearing we were from America, offered us a visit; he spoke some English, and said he had seen David Sands when on Long Island—inquired affectionately after several Friends there — appeared glad to see us, and wished us a safe return to our families. All the officers and soldiers who have been in America treat us with respect.

"12th. After paying an exorbitant bill for very poor accommodations, we passed through a fine country to Minden, where the inns being much crowded on account of fair time, it was difficult to get lodging; however, we at length met with a tolerable inn, but were obliged to eat at the Table d'Hote, which is not pleasant, though the people behaved respectfully.

"First-day, 13th. Had a meeting this afternoon about a mile out of town, where about sixteen beside ourselves attended; it was rather a laborious time, but ended well. Some years past, there were upwards of sixty who used to meet on First-day, being mostly separated from the public forms; but Emanuel Brown and others have been the means of scattering them, so that at present there appears to be but five or six families, who meet once a week at this house, and hold their meetings mostly in silence, acknowledge all our doctrines, and we hope are honestly seeking a right foundation.

"14th. Yesterday we thought of leaving this place; but feeling a stop in our minds, we now became more acquainted with the state of the little company professing with us, and were enabled to account for the feelings we had in the meeting. Three of the principal members being at variance among themselves, we requested to see them all in our room, when with tenderness and caution we labored with them to search out the cause; and they being brought into a tender frame of mind, opened things to us and to each other with great freedom; the humbling power of Divine Grace attending, they freely forgave each other, and desired that every thing which had caused uneasiness might now be buried; and we had the satisfaction of seeing them embrace one another with much cordiality and brotherly affection. After their reconciliation, we had a comfortable religious opportunity with them.

"15th. We went to Frederick Smith's; breakfasted, and took leave of the family and others who had come in, with much brotherly love. Our dear Albinus was much broken at parting, having travelled about four weeks, and upwards of three hundred miles with us, was very near to us in the love of Truth, and it was a trial on both sides; he said he hoped he was now, through mercy, favored to know the Truth, and had faith to believe it would set him free. We proceeded on to Henford, and in our way stopped to feed our horses at an inn, where a number of the family were sitting down to a meal of potatoes, some salt, and rye bread, which looked as coarse as if it had been made of bran; yet they all had the appearance of health. Thus vast numbers of the people of this country live; their houses are very dirty, and pigs, goats, cows, geese, &c., mingle together with the family. A young lad being ill with the cholera morbus, David Sands administered to him, and the family appearing very thankful, would have made him some pecuniary compensation. Our friend Christopher Reckefus still continued with us as our postilion; and the country being every where crowded with Prussian soldiers, feed for horses was very dear, so that we paid a Spanish dollar for a bushel of oats.

"Fourth-day, 16th. We were much discouraged, and doubted the propriety of staying to appoint a meeting; but as we waited in patience, it appeared best that some inquiry should be made after religious people; and meeting with some encouragement, we agreed to stay, and appoint a meeting for this evening, at the house of . . . . . . Bude, a town officer, where our dear friend John Pemberton had had a meeting; a few religious seeking people came to see us. This town, like many others in this country, is dirty, the streets narrow, and paved with pebble stones; the houses with the gable-ends towards the street, have generally a mean appearance, the people poor, and few of respectable mien, except the officers of the army. It was crowded with soldiers, billeted on the inhabitants, which is the case with all the adjacent towns and villages, there being thirty thousand soldiers quartered in the neighborhood. This place seems to be in a dead state as to religion. The meeting was small; ability was given us to hold up our principles, and the spirituality of true religion, and it ended to satisfaction.

"17th. We set off for Kiepshagen, the place of abode of our friend Christopher Reckefus; the roads so bad that we travelled only four and a half miles in two hours. A meeting being appointed to be held at his house this afternoon, about fifteen persons met us. Christopher and his brother have thirty acres of land, for which they pay about forty dollars a year to a nobleman; they value their property in the whole at six hundred dollars; but the various demands upon them of a public nature, for some of which they suffer distraint, keeps them poor and bare; yet they appear contented.

"18th. After a religious opportunity with these families, we parted in much sympathy, the two brothers accompanying us to Ufeln: we passed through the finest piece of woodland we have seen in Germany, the timber almost as tall as in America, which it is not common to see here. Christopher took us to the house of a person whom John Pemberton mentions in his Journal. This man's wife being a religious woman, and inclined to Friends, had provided a dinner for us;

but her husband not being united with her in religious concern, and having always treated Friends with indifference, and there being eight of us, we thought it best not to stay, though the woman pressed us very kindly. With considerable exertion we found a poor inn, the people of the house not well disposed to receive us, and there was no retirement or satisfaction to be obtained. Officers and other light persons were crowding into the room, and the residents of the inn cross and disobliging, evidencing clearly that we were not welcome guests, which we endeavored to bear with patience; but at length they told us what was to pay, that we must discharge it and leave them. This excited in us some admiration and disgust. We went and dined at the house of the person before mentioned, who treated us with kindness. A young officer in the army offering his room for a meeting, we sat down together; he, the woman of the house, and about five others, with eight of our company, made up the number. Upon the whole, it appeared to be a satisfactory season, and we hope will have a tendency of uniting the man of the house more fully to his tender, religious wife, and opening the way for Friends to be more kindly received in this town than they have hitherto been; the minds of both priests and people being very dark and prejudiced. We were nowhere so much stared at, so ill-treated, nor so depressed in our minds. After meeting, the affectionate woman got us a dish of coffee, we took a kind leave of the family, and through Divine favor left them rejoicing. Arrived at Hereford, and on the 19th got to Bilefield. Though the appearance of the inn bespoke but poor accommodations, yet the widow and her children who kept it, seemed disposed to do as well as they knew how. This town contains about eight thousand inhabitants, who are chiefly employed in the linen manufacture; and it is filled with soldiers.

"First-day, 20th. Several religious people stepped in to see us, with whom we had a satisfactory time; one of them was a soldier, had been with the King of Prussia against the French, and was in several battles, but had never fired his gun. One was a general engagement of the two armies; the night before it took place, he being upon guard on the out-pickets, and perceiving a general attack likely to come on in the morning, felt great repugnance to shedding the blood of his fellow-creatures, and kneeled down and besought the Lord to preserve him through the coming day, which was mercifully granted: his company were divided into five parts, which were to follow each other as they were called out, and those who remained alive after expending their ammunition, to return and be succeeded by another. He was first placed in the second division, but afterward was providentially transferred to the last; many of his comrades were killed, and the last division being called, was prevented from getting into action by night coming on; thus his prayers were answered. There being several religious men in the regiment he belonged to, and others in the same brigade, during the campaign they frequently met together to edify one another in the spiritual life: so it appears that the Most High may be sought even in the midst of wars and armies. He was a tender-spirited man, and desirous of finding the right way, though under many discouragements and burdens, in consequence of his employment as a soldier: we advised him to patience, and encouraged him to look to the Lord for help. In the evening we were invited to a meeting outside of the walls, where Sarah Grubb and a company had had one to their satisfaction: about thirty serious people attended; the Lord favored us together, and Truth rose higher than I remember it to have done since we left Berlin; so we parted and returned to our inn refreshed.

"21st. Things appeared rather discouraging — no way opening for a meeting in the town. David Sands, Lewis Seebohm and myself dined with C. Wellman, who, with his wife and children, used us very kindly, were very free in conversation, deeply acquainted with the mystic authors, high in reasoning, and seemed much fixed in their strong-holds. There are several families among those that are called rich, much in the same circumstance; they do not attend at any public worship, and plead that there is no necessity for meeting together, but that each one may seek the Lord in private; yet they would fain attend a meeting if it was in a private way, being afraid of the cross. Some opportunities and close labor being had with them, we hope the observations made may hereafter be blessed.

"22nd. William Farrer and myself visited Charlotte

Laaer at her father's house, she having come here from Pyrmont; her mother appeared very friendly and pleased to see us, but her father was not so kind, though he used us more respectfully than we expected. This poor young woman has much to try her faith and patience; we felt great sympathy with her; she is of a loving, tender disposition, and honestly laboring to be what she ought to be in the sight of her heavenly Father; this leads her in a tribulated path—her family being people of distinction in the world. Lewis Seebohm and myself took coffee with a merchant who had married Charlotte's sister; she met us there; they were kind and appeared to be religious people. In the evening had a meeting in our inn, where about thirty or forty people came, many of them of the first rank; it held about three hours. David Sands and myself were led to preach the Gospel, during which much solemnity prevailed; it proved refreshing to us, and we believe to several of them.

"Fourth-day, 23d. Had much conversation with C. Wellman and his family, who appear to be drawing nearer to the spirit of Truth in themselves. In the afternoon had an opportunity of more free conversation with Charlotte Laaer's father and mother, in which he seemed tender; and we parted friendly. It has been a day of much exercise, in which my mind has been more tried about the way of moving from hence, than I have ever experienced before; and the same also with my companions: indeed this has been a very trying place to us during the whole time of our being here.

The state of things among those called Separatists, who are ashamed of the cross, has exercised us much; yet there is a little remnant who are desirous of standing faithful, whom we hope we have been made a means of strengthening. To the flesh it looks pleasant to turn towards Amsterdam, the days being very short and the roads exceedingly bad; but our minds are not fully settled to proceed that way.

"24th. After a time of waiting on the Lord under much concern to be rightly directed, it appeared most safe to proceed to Lemgo. We parted with several of our acquaintances and with the people of the inn, in an affectionate manner; our landlady and all her household have been very attentive and obliging, which has been a relief to us during our stay in this exercising place. Dear Charlotte Laaer, who has had our sympathy in her trials, was much affected at parting. The roads were bad, and we did not arrive at Lemgo until afternoon; the landlady received us kindly, but the house was crowded with Prussian officers. Lewis and myself visited an ancient man named Buckholz, who passes here for a Quaker, has been brought under suffering several times for his testimony, and is very near to us in principle; with him and a few others, we had some religious service tending to their encouragement. I was glad of the visit. There are many precious souls scattered up and down in this country, struggling with discouragements. Lemgo is the Prince la Leppes' dominions, believed to contain five thousand inhabitants.

"25th. Undetermined which way to turn; these two

weeks past have been very trying, hardly able to see a day before us; thus there is need to pray for patience. Being nearer to Amsterdam now than we have been before, it seemed as though we might be permitted to turn that way, but after solid consideration, all seemed closed for the present with respect to Holland, and our minds were most easy to proceed in faith towards Hanover, directly back. It was a trial to be thus kept in Germany. Passed through several villages, and the roads so bad that our wagon stuck fast, though all our company were out of it, and the horses were not able to move it; our good driver, Christopher Reckefus, was obliged to go back about three quarters of a mile to get a chain to draw it out, which detained us an hour and a half in the cold.

"26th. The roads continuing very bad, I hired a horse and a man to bring him back from Hameln: here we found three of the young Friends from Pyrmont, who had come on foot twelve miles to meet with us; showing the love these tender young people have for the company of Friends. We took an affectionate leave of them and our attentive friend Christopher Reckefus, who had continued with us eighteen days, and endeared himself to us. We took post-horses and went on to Spring, the road being a turnpike, it was a great relief to us, but there are few such in Germany, as the princes are not willing to spend their money on roads, and the people are too poor to improve them.

"27th. Arriving at Hanover, we found our dear friend George Dillwyn with his interpreter; they had held a meeting in the morning and appointed another in the afternoon, which we all attended, and it appeared a satisfactory time; several of the religious people having evidently gained ground and come nearer to Friends. There are several here who have scruples respecting some parts of the business on which they are dependent for a livelihood, similar to that which was among Friends in the beginning, and from which testimony many under our name are now departed: and when we think of the occupations of many who have had an education among us, and some who are in high stations in the church, it has a painful influence upon our minds, while we are endeavoring to cherish that which is of the right birth in those who have not had the same advantages; but Truth is the same in all places, and Wisdom is everywhere justified of her children. David Sands and myself have had our minds turned to think of a meeting in a more general way than has yet been in this place, but no opening has hitherto presented; — there wants more firmness and boldness for the Truth among those who appear to have a love for it and its friends.

"30th. Had a meeting at George Dillwyn's lodgings: about thirty attended, among whom were two candidates for the priest's office; it was a humbling time, and one of these young men was much broken, and all his former fabric destroyed; he seemed like a man in amazement, that he should have found the truth in so simple a way and so unlooked for, and we endeavored to strengthen his exercised mind.

"Twelfth month, 1st. A number of people coming in, we had another meeting in the evening.

"First-day, 4th. A meeting being proposed at the house where George Dillwyn lodges, outside of the gates, a number of people collected; the landlord, who had heretofore cheerfully given us his commodious room, now refused, being afraid of the magistrates, and he turned away many of the people who were collecting; some of the most zealous, however, persevered, and about thirty being assembled, the Lord favored us with his presence and it proved a solid, contriting season. The magistrate sent a civil officer to tell the landlord he would be fined twenty dollars; and his wife being in great passion at this, I endeavored to pacify her by offering to go with the officer to the magistrate, and to take all the consequences upon ourselves; but after some conversation with him, I found he had no orders to take us there; and showing him the tenor of our passes, he went away, and afterwards came back to the inn and said he had informed the magistrate what sort of people we were, upon which he did not incline to send for us. In the afternoon we held a meeting at the house of J. Buchner, who had freely offered it; about sixty were collected, and many went away for want of room; two civil officers came in while we were speaking, but offered no interruption. It was thought to be a meeting of the most information to them of any that had been held; they expressed their thankfulness, and we parted with tenderness.

"5th. The knowledge of our being in town being

much spread, many of various characters and ranks came to our lodgings throughout the day, and a number sent their children for books, so that all we had were presently disposed of, and if we had had a large number more, they would not have been sufficient for the applications. The school-masters in this place make it a practice to tell their scholars any interesting matter that occurs, and as several of them had been to see us, the children got information that we were from America, a great way off, and come to preach the true religion to the people of Germany, without taking any pay for it. This news the children communicated to their parents, and it thus spread fast, and accounted for the city being so generally acquainted with it. In a conference with some of the principal men who make profession with us, we found a necessity to guard them against appearances by way of ministry that were not duly authorized, some instances without proper weight having been manifested among them. Several said, they desired rather to continue always in silent waiting than to admit any ministry not from the right fountain, as it would only scatter. In half an hour after we returned to our inn, we found ourselves surrounded by one hundred people, with whom we sat down in silence. Emmanuel Brown being come to Hanover was also present; David and myself were engaged in religious communication, and the people were very quiet and serious, and the meeting appeared to be owned to our humbling admiration; hence we have cause to say continually, Good is the Lord, and worthy to be served in all things. Frederick Seebohm and two other Friends from Pyrmont being present, we had a short opportunity with Emmanuel Brown, who appears like a Friend. After a day of much labor, we retired to rest in the enjoyment of sweet peace. The Lord has not raised such a remarkable inquiry in this place, but with gracious design to bless it, if those who have now been called remain faithful to him.

"6th. Had another full opportunity with Emmanuel Brown, George Dillwyn being present; he freely acknowledged the doctrines of Friends, with respect to Christ's baptism being spiritual, the non-necessity for those who had come fully to enjoy the spiritual communion with Christ, to partake of the ceremony of bread and wine; and also the benefit and duty of meeting together for Divine worship. He favored the doctrine of celibacy, believing it right for him to continue single, but did not think it was obligatory upon all. This man had been the means of sowing discord and leading off many innocent persons in this land with his vain imaginations, and his professions of love and attachment are not to be relied upon. Many came and took an affectionate leave of us, and we were renewedly convinced that the Lord has a precious seed in Hanover; to him we must leave them at present, feeling now clear in our minds, and humbly thankful to our great and gracious Lord, who has been with us and granted strength to go through the various and almost continual labors and exercises in this place to our own comfort, the encouragement of the little honest-hearted flock, and we hope not to the dishonor of the blessed cause we are engaged to promote. Here we parted with dear George Dillwyn and his wife in near unity, he proposing to stay a few days longer, and then to proceed towards Berlin: as we now are likely to travel in contrary directions, there is little prospect of meeting again on the continent, Berlin and Amsterdam being near five hundred miles apart. Our landlord and servants were very respectful and affected at parting; a number of gay women having come to get a sight of us, they waved their hands and wished us a happy journey, as did also the people in the streets. There appears great encouragement for Friends to visit this place who may be rightly called to such a service. We rode on about ten miles, and our postilion having taken up a man and woman without our consent, when we came to the house where the horses were to stop, they called for drink and victuals which the landlord charged to us. As it was an imposition we were not disposed to submit to, being of violent passions, he stormed and swore we should pay it, that it was the practice to charge all to the herrschaft and let the poor go free; so for peace-sake we were obliged to submit; he was in such a rage, I heard him tell the postilion he would do right to overset us on the road, which he fully executed about one and a half miles from the stopping-place. It was extremely cold, windy and snowing, and near night, when we were overset; my companions were bruised and much injured, I escaped with little damage, but it was with great difficulty we could get the wagon up, and were kept in the snow and wet a considerable time. It being now dark, William Farrer and myself walked to the village, not being easy to trust ourselves to this bad man again, who we believe was in league with the inn-keeper; the conduct and appearance of whom, and of the people in his house and other circumstances, convinced us that Satan reigned there. The inn where we now arrived was a decent house: the wounds of my friends were dressed as well as we could, and the people being of more kind and accommodating manners than is common in the villages in Germany, we felt tolerably comfortable, and retired to bed in thankfulness to a gracious and ever-watchful Providence, who so preserved us that no limbs were broken nor lasting damage sustained; thus we have daily fresh occasion to sing of his mercies.

"7th. Our wagon being much damaged, it was near mid-day before we could get it repaired so as to be fit to proceed: rode on to a village eighteen miles, when it was near dark. The place was very dirty, and the houses crowded with soldiers; and though we offered high pay, yet no beds could be obtained fit to lie on, and the rooms were so filthy as to be quite unsuitable to spread straw upon; we were therefore obliged to go on to Minden, twelve miles in the night, and where we were in great danger of being overset again. We however got to our former quarters, and were received by the landlord and family gladly.

"9th. Had a meeting in the evening, which proved

to be a tendering season: several returned with us to our lodgings, and appeared comforted.

"First-day, 11th. Attended the meeting of those professing with us, held at Frederick Smith's; about fifteen persons were present, and though it was mostly silent, yet it ended to our satisfaction. In the evening we had a meeting in a chamber at the orphan-house, where two hundred at least attended, and behaved well. Among them were people of note, and officers of the army; it was a solemn season, and we parted in much tenderness, returning thanks to our gracious heavenly Helper, who thus in an unlooked for manner made way for us. It is not likely that such meetings were ever before held in Germany, and we humbly hope that the cause of Truth has been promoted by them. There was much expression of unity with us, and thankfulness for the opportunity. O! what occasion we have to say, 'Good is the Lord, and worthy to be served.'

"12th. Not feeling ourselves at liberty to go forward, we were visited by several who were at meeting last evening, and informed us that many who had not been there expressed a desire they might have such an opportunity; after weighing it, we concluded to put off the appointment of another meeting until to-morrow. The little company of Friends in this place seemed much relieved by the public meeting, and said they felt as though a great burden was taken off their shoulders. We dined at counsellor Borges's; his house and heart seemed to be opened in an unexpected manner, and we had much religious conversation with him and his two daughters, we hope to profit. This is the same man whom Sarah Grubb mentions, and who being involved in a multitude of business pertaining to his office, and much looked up to by the people, had not ventured to avow openly, what no doubt he had been convinced of, and so appeared to have fallen back, and not inclined to see us at our first visit to Minden. He attended the meeting at the orphan-house, but stood in the entry. It was said by his son-in-law, Lewis Seebohm, that he never received Friends with so much openness before, and manifested great attachment to us.

"13th. We were informed that the Consistorial Rath, who is a director of things relating to the church within his precincts, as well as a priest of the first dignity, had forbid any more meetings being held in the orphan-house, and had said things which reflected upon us and our Society. We felt most easy to appoint another meeting for this evening, at such place as our Friends thought best; and with respect to the priest's reflections, we thought we should not be clear in leaving Minden without paying him a visit, lest it might tend to the discouragement of the little flock here. David Sands and myself went and found him at home; and on inquiring the cause of our being forbid the orphan-house, he affected to be friendly, and said we might freely have held meetings there as to his own particular sentiment, but that the edict of the king of Prussia admitted of no public religious assemblies in his Westphalian dominions, but Lutherans,

Calvinists, Roman Catholics, Moravians, Jews, and Menonists; and therefore as the king's servant, he was obliged to forbid our public meeting; but that we might meet more privately at our inn or any private house, without interruption, for the edification of the people; to which he was not at all opposed, but said we might do so in the Lord's name. We told him we could not resort to secret places as some did, to hide their testimony, or for fear of suffering; and that we held our meetings open for all in the city of Berlin. We also asked him, if he did not believe liberty of conscience was the common right of all men? To which he answered in the affirmative; but thought it was not abridged in this place. We conceived it was; but not finding it necessary to go into much controversy with him, turned to the other subject. This confirms me in the expediency of encouraging those upon whom it may be laid, to visit the king of Prussia; perhaps it may fall upon dear George Dillwyn. For my own part, I feel my mind relieved from it at present. With respect to the other subject (reflections upon the Society), he appeared startled that it had come to our knowledge; but was not able to tell his author, and said it was a matter of little consequence, that we ought rather to rejoice when evil was falsely spoken against us — it was what every true Christian might expect; but for his own part, he did not believe there was the least foundation for it. We replied, that the character of ourselves and the Society was dearer to us than our lives, and that we were bound to defend it; which he acknowledged was right, and that if it was possible to find his author, he would inform us before we left the city. After making some general observations, and placing the reflections cast upon us to the account of the old root of bitterness in the priests, we parted in a friendly manner, himself, his wife and daughters shaking hands with us, and wishing us a good journey. One of our Friends here not being free to bury his wife in the manner of any of the religious societies, buried her in his garden, for which the priests took from him six dollars as their fee. Thus these poor people are under suffering many ways for the testimony of a good conscience.

"Made another visit to counsellor Borges and had some religious service, which was an humbling time. The old man embraced us affectionately, and said he had not words to express the thankfulness he felt for our visits—followed us to the gate and took a final farewell, recommending us to Divine protection and care, with the tears flowing down his cheeks. We hope our intercourse will remain with sweetness, and be beneficial to our few sincere-hearted brethren who hold a meeting in this place; this counsellor being a man of extensive influence. Had a meeting this evening consisting of about sixty persons, besides a number in the entry. A man of genteel appearance came in, who was a Calvinist minister, stayed the meeting through, although our principles respecting true Gospel ministry and the freedom of it, were largely treated upon. It was a confirming time to most present, and a solemn parting with our dear Friends, who came one after another in the most affectionate manner to take leave of us. Some of these partings in Germany must remain with me as long as my memory.

"14th. A cold damp day; the ground covered with snow and the roads deep and dangerous; our wagon being too high and top-heavy, we rode in fear; but arrived in safety at a town where we stopped a short time and proceeded to Bomte, having travelled six Dutch, or thirty-six English miles.

"15th. Got to Osnaburg and dined at the Table d'Hote with about twenty persons, who treated us respectfully; one of them expressed his surprise that we adopted in our writings, and otherwise, a name that was given us in derision; there being something inviting and consistent with the character of our Society, in the appellation of Friends; but foreigners must be at a loss for a reason why we continue the name of Quakers. Such remarks have been frequently made in our travels; and if the Society had not continued it, it is very probable the name of Quaker would scarcely have been known at this day.

"16th. Osnaburg is subject to the king of England, and contains about ten thousand inhabitants. There is a convent in this town, composed of young women of noble families. It appears that the German nobility who have many daughters, persuade some of them to go into nunneries, to save the portions that are expected at the time of marriage. At the Table d'Hote, it is very unpleasant to be obliged to hear the music which is almost continually playing, so that we can scarcely hear one another in conversation. We expressed to the priests and the landlord our objections to it; and some of the company finding us uneasy, took up the subject, and an elderly man told the landlord, he thought it a great imposition upon many to please a very few; and although he had lodged there for some months, if it was continued he should be under the necessity of shifting his quarters. In the evening we had a meeting at a private house, where about ten sober people convened, who behaved in a becoming manner, and we hope the service will prove profitable. Although they are separated from the public worship, they are more like Moravians than Friends — they remember Sarah Grubb with respect.

"17th. Proceeded to Rheine: the roads being very difficult and filled with snow and ice, we thought it a mercy that we got on without being overset, as our wagon is so top-heavy. Rheine is a small Roman Catholic town subject to the bishop of Munster; the people in these parts appear to be very poor, and the whole seems to be a country of darkness.

"First-day, 18th. The people were crowding by day-light to matins, with their beads and crosses: my feelings are heavy and unpleasant. O! sweet liberty of conscience, thou restorest men to their proper dignity, if thy blessings be used to the glory of God. Passing on, we halted at a village, where the language, manners and cleanliness, evidently indicated we were drawing near the borders of Holland. Got to Bentheim, a considerable town on a rocky hill, with a strong castle. This town being Protestant, and we finding a decent, clean house kept by the post-master, took up our abode for the remainder of the day. The rooms, beds, furniture and people, are much more cleanly than we have met with for some time. Had a satisfactory opportunity with the people of the house and some others, in the evening, which left my mind easy and pleasant. The Lord is good; and though trials inwardly and outwardly attend us, yet he favors with times of refreshing from his presence, which is an ample reward for all our toil and suffering.

"19th. Left Bentheim, and the roads being difficult, did not arrive at Delden till two hours after dark. Our expenses at inns are extravagant; and all over this country, travellers are fleeced in almost every way, especially foreigners; and without submitting to multiplied impositions, there is no getting along with any degree of comfort. It is far more expensive travelling than in England; their movements are slow and tedious, generally about three miles an hour, and make great demands upon our patience. The country is in general handsome and fertile; many houses in the villages are of good brick and look well, though but one story high. Their fires are made in grates, fixed in the chimneys, the fuel being turf and some wood, which might do very well if there was enough of it. With considerable danger we arrived at Deventer, a pretty large town; with clean streets, many elegant houses and open squares. A very spacious and ancient piece of architecture claimed our notice; it had been used as a worship-house for the Reformed, for centuries past, but is now totally in ruins inside, the French army having made a stable of it; such are the effects of war!

"Fourth-day, 21st. We travelled through a highly cultivated country, extensive meadows, fine planted woods, houses, gardens, and all around conveying an idea of great regularity and order. The city of Deventer and its environs, the river Yssel, with a handsome bridge upon boats, and the cleanliness of the people, formed as agreeable a prospect as any we have seen on the continent—the city may contain ten thousand people. Travellers become more numerous as we approach Amsterdam: we were taken for Hanoverians, could understand but little they say, though they can readily comprehend us in German. The Holland language appears to be a mixture of bad German, French, and English. The roads being good, we made thirty miles to-day, travelling, for the first time since we have been on the continent, at about six miles an hour.

"Sixth-day, 23d. Passing through a fine country, we arrived at Amsterdam; the houses in the main streets of this great commercial city are generally large; and although they are built with the gable-ends to the street, and from three to five stories high, yet they have an appearance of grandeur. The river Rhine empties into the Zuyder sea, which a few centuries past was a valley filled with towns and villages; but the ocean breaking the banks, overflowed the country and drowned most of the inhabitants. The public buildings are magnificent, and the whole city crowded with shops. This is indeed a beautiful and populous city; neatness is conspicuous through its borders, but the number of beggars is considerable.

"First-day, 25th. We were at meeting in a room of J. Vanderwarf's house; a number of strangers came in, and through Divine favor it proved a good meeting.

"26th. Held another meeting, and though the people, as is their practice, were restless in time of silence, yet it was thought to be a serious opportunity. The weather was very cold, and no fire in the meeting-room, except in foot-stoves for the women. In Holland, it is not customary for women to draw near or sit by a fire, that being a privilege for men only; hence the women are furnished with wooden boxes, with a bason of coals or turf in them to put under their feet. It is so cold here that the hair of the men is frozen with their breath, as they pass along the streets; and fuel being dear, chiefly turf, with a few coals from Germany and England, or a little fine wood to kindle it, they keep very small fires, and having few stoves, the rooms are so cold that we had to keep on our thick overcoats most of the day. Meat costs from about nine to twelve cents per pound, which is for the best kinds. In almost every thing they are the reverse of Germany; the furniture, &c., being kept very clean and nice; they drink a great deal of tea and coffee, but do not use much sugar.

"27th. We were examined by the Committee de Surveillance, who treated us with much civility, and recommended us to the French consul for a pass to go towards France. The Stadt-house where they sit is a very large and noble building, highly ornamented with marble sculpture. All religious professors now have liberty of conscience, and to meet openly for worship; but private meetings are forbidden. Their funerals are attended by men only; no bell rings, nor do they wear mourning after the interment. Our passes being certified by the American consul, he advised us to go by the Hague to see the American and French ambassadors there.

"First-day, 1st of First month, 1797. Had two meetings; about fifty persons attended each, and we hope they were to some profit.

"2d. Our passes being endorsed by the French consul, we exchanged our old wagon for a coach, which will be safer and warmer, and we hope to travel with two, instead of four, horses. Notwithstanding the beauty and opulence of Amsterdam in general, travellers are beset every few paces with beggars. In the Jews' quarter especially, the misery, nakedness, and dirtiness, exceed anything of the kind I have ever seen before. In Berlin I was never asked for charity. The neatness of everything in Amsterdam, its shops, streets, canals, bridges, &c., is very pleasing to strangers; yet the Jews' quarter is an exception. The vessels that trade up the Rhine are drawn by horses; are very capacious, being about one hundred feet long, and have several handsome rooms upon deck, where the families of the captains reside.

"First-day, 8th. Were at two meetings, the largest we have had; there were six American captains present, and these meetings were thought to be the most solid and satisfactory of any since we came to this place: many of the people were affected and parted with us affectionately; thanks to our great and gracious Helper, who hath not forsaken us in any place. If any good remains on the minds of the people in any of the cities and towns we have visited, let the name of the Lord be magnified, and we humbled in the dust.

"9th. Sat with the few Friends in what they call their Monthly Meeting. Their principal business for several years, appears to have been only to meet and make a minute that they did so; and once a year, to transmit an account to Friends in London, of the condition of the estate of Friends here; as the house where John Vanderwarf lives, and in which the meeting is held, belongs in part to Friends of England and part to Friends of Holland; there is also some other estate under their care. The books for one hundred and thirty years back, the minutes of the Monthly Meeting, records of births, burials and marriages, &c., are still preserved in very neat order. By these it appears, that from about 1676 to 1720, there was a considerable number of Friends here, sixty or seventy signing their marriage certificates. Since the last date, there appears to have been a gradual decline, until it has come to what it now is; two ancient Friends being all that keep up the Monthly Meeting, who appeared concerned what might become of the property when they should be taken away. After reading and minuting our certificates, the meeting concluded. In the evening we had a religious opportunity with young J. Vanderwarf and his wife, which we believe was right, and hope it may have its use.

"10th. Set out for the Hague; passed through Haarlaem, a large town, and over a fine country, many beautiful villages, elegant country-seats, &c., to Leyden, a large city, containing about sixty thousand inhabitants; the neatness, decency, and size of the houses, makes it rank among the first cities of this rich and populous country: thence travelling through a country very pleasant and highly cultivated, we arrived at the gates of the Hague, and took lodgings at a good inn.

"11th. Visited the American ambassador, who received us very courteously, endorsed our passes, and gave us such intelligence respecting our journey to France, as was in his power. We went also to the French ambassador, who treated us respectfully, but said he had no authority to give a pass to an Englishman; but thought William Farrer would meet with no interruption while he remained in our company, engaged in the good work of promoting religion among the people; and remarked, that he was satisfied we were what we appeared to be, without deception. This beautiful city may contain forty thousand inhabitants, and is said to be the handsomest town in Europe: the principal street, which is magnificently built, and about three hundred feet wide, has a promenade in the centre, of about one hundred feet wide, shaded and ornamented by five rows of stately and beautiful trees; the woods round the town, are also laid out in fine walks with seats at proper distances. All the principal streets have trees on each side, and canals in the middle; the trimming of those trees in the winter, serves for fuel for the poor. The inhabitants appear civil, very neat in their houses and decent in their persons.

"12th. Got to Rotterdam, and met with several Englishmen and some Americans: we were received by those to whom we had letters, with great openness and friendship.

"Sixth-day, 13th. Found an open reception at Cornelius Lloyd's, who is of English descent, and was the last person who contributed to support a Friend's meeting at this place. Although there is something pleasant in meeting with so many who can converse in our own language, yet the general state of my mind for some days past has been far from joyous; having travelled under daily exercise, though concealed by a cheerful countenance, partaking in secret of copious draughts of the bitter waters of Marah, from a consciousness of my natural disqualification for the work of Gospel ministry. Travelling so far, through many outward difficulties, for the promotion of the Redeemer's kingdom, brings me into deep reflection on the degree of redemption which I myself have experienced; which alas! I often have cause to acknowledge before the Searcher of hearts, is far short of what I am persuaded the power of redeeming love is able to effect; yet some consolation is afforded by the conviction, that I most sincerely desire a higher degree of attainment, even the state of a perfect man in Christ Jesus — that I may be thoroughly washed in the laver of regeneration, until I am prepared, through adorable mercy, to be presented faultless before the throne of his glory with exceeding joy. In passing through these European countries, a secret sadness has frequently covered my soul, on viewing the pompous palaces, the crowded cities, the vanity of the great, the avidity of the merchants, the oppression and wretchedness of the poor, and the depravity of many in all the different classes; that I am ready to cry out, O! when shall the Son of righteousness arise with healing in his wings, to recover mankind from the many maladies which encompass them! A few there are, scattered over this continent, whom he hath gathered, and is gathering under the shadow of his wing; who have appeared to me, though many of them are hidden in solitary places, to be like the salt of the earth, which prevents the whole mass from sinking under its corruption. With these my soul has rejoiced, and will rejoice; they have been like stakes of confirmation to me, and with all the infirmities I feel, I am satisfied that my lot has been cast here for their sakes. On taking a retrospect this morning of the five preceding months of wearisome travel, labor and exercise, I feel the reward of sweet peace; and the tribute of thanksgiving to the Beloved of my soul, who hath not forsaken me in the hour of trial, but mercifully preserved me, though faint, yet pursuing the mark, for the prize of the glory of God in Christ Jesus, my Saviour, whose service is perfect freedom.

"14th. Visited the ancient place of meeting for Friends, and it being now used as a carpenter's-shop, we requested it might be cleared out and made ready for meeting to-morrow. Rotterdam is about one-third the size and population of Amsterdam, lies nearer the sea, and has fine canals running through it in different directions, in which the largest merchant-ships may lie conveniently. The number of English and Scotch people, the appearance of sociability among the inhabitants, and other advantages which it possesses, would make it a more desirable place of residence than Amsterdam; though it does not equal it in grandeur. Many of the houses here, as well as all over Holland, are built with the front from one to three feet from a perpendicular line, the upper part of the walls having the gable-ends to the streets, project over the footways, which they say, is to prevent the water that falls, from running down the walls and windows. The new houses project very little, and some not at all. When a fire happens, as the streets are narrow, these projections occasion a communication of the flame to those opposite. There are people paid to put out fires, and the citizens trouble themselves but little about it. Pumps are fixed in the canals, and by means of leather pipes, convey the water to the engines, so that they use but few buckets. In the principal towns, the houses are almost universally occupied by shops below, and the family sit up stairs.

"First-day, 15th. About sixty persons attended the meeting, mostly respectable people, and it was a solid good time. Dined with Cornelius Lloyd, a merchant of considerable wealth: his wife was so terrified at the noise of the cannon, and the fear of the French army entering the city, when Dumourier was on the opposite side of the Maase, that it deprived her of memory, so that she cannot retain anything a minute at a time. His mother, an ancient woman, was educated a Friend: on visiting her, she appeared glad to see us; her faculties are good, and she remembered William Brown being here on a religious visit; her son has now the care of the meeting-house, which he rents out, and has some stock in his hands to pay for cleaning it, finding candles, &c., when wanted; but the funds of Friends here, have sunk by the failure of one of the descendants, who held them to a large amount. In the afternoon, about one hundred and fifty attended the meeting, which, through renewed mercy, proved a satisfactory season; many were tendered, and it was a time of refreshment to ourselves. Thanks be to the Author of every blessing.

"16th. At the meeting in the evening, it was thought that half the people who desired to be present, could not get in, and the place being so crowded and warm, they were, for a time, rather restless; however, through Divine mercy, Truth rose into dominion; they became solid, and parted in tenderness.

"17th. In the evening had a meeting at the Episcopal worship-house, built by Queen Anne, for the benefit of the English residing here; it is not large, but a decent, plain building. Many of the English and Scotch people having gone away from Rotterdam in the heat of the war, among whom was the priest, it has been shut up for some time; the remaining part of the congregation, seeing that Friends' house was too small, offered it freely, but the construction of the room is such, as to produce a great echo, so that we are informed many who sat in the centre, heard but partially; however, they behaved remarkably well, and on the whole it was thought a profitable meeting; the Lord is good to us poor unworthy creatures, from day to day.

"18th. The inhabitants are civil and respectful; the water here is better than in Amsterdam, where they drink little but rain-water, here the canals ebb and flow with fresh water, which, at this season, is pretty good. The canals render it dangerous walking in the evening, when the weather is foggy. A few years since, in very thick weather, there were said to be three hundred people drowned by falling into them; since which, they have increased the number of lamps, and ropes are extended from tree to tree, when there is danger of the like disaster.

"First-day, 22d. The meetings both in the fore and afternoon, were, through the mercy of our heavenly Father, solemn seasons; there are doubtless a number of seriously visited souls in Rotterdam, and the prospect of Friends visiting this city on a religious account is much more promising than in Amsterdam. Though

Friends are almost extinct as to supporting meetings, yet I cannot but feel a prayer in my heart, that the Lord might be pleased to send his servants into this part of the vineyard.

"23d. Expected to move towards France, but our minds not being clear of the people in this place, we concluded to tarry some time longer.

"First-day, 29th. Have been unwell for several days. A pass was procured for our going into France, except for William Farrer, who could not obtain one on account of his being a British subject. We had three meetings to-day, and through the renewing of Divine favor, they were satisfactory; we took leave of the people in much tenderness and affection, believing we might soon be at liberty to go.

"30th. We hear many discouraging reports of the difficulty of travelling in France, and are much exercised about the right way to proceed; believing our religious concern in this place is now fulfilled. We have none to lean upon but the Lord alone, who, blessed be his name, has been hitherto excellent in counsel and wonderful in working for us, more so than I feel myself worthy of. We visited several of our friends here, who advised us to go to Sluys in Flanders, by water, and our minds settled to turn that way.

31st. Went on board the packet: the commander was an honest-looking man, and I made out to understand his half Low Dutch and half French.

"1st of Second month. Wind ahead, stormy and some rain; sailed about twenty miles, our cabin having no fire, and the weather being very damp and cold and the beds small, we did not feel very comfortable.

"Fifth-day, 2nd. The wind was very high; lay to all day; very cold and no prospect of getting on, added to which, we understood we should be arrested on our landing if we did not wear the national cockade, which we could not comply with; everything looked more gloomy than at any time since leaving my native shore; a little hope and some confidence however remained, and an humble trust in the Almighty Arm that hath hitherto preserved, which settled us in calmness.

"4th. Got on pretty well, though the wind continued nearly ahead. Passed by several handsome villages on the islands, which are in the province of Zealand. The wind being very small and a thick fog, the anchor was dropped.

"5th. Much detention on account of the fog, but it breaking away, we sailed by the beautiful island on which are the cities of Middleburg and Flushing; reached Sluys in Flanders, about dusk; here we underwent an examination by the officers and also a search, but all ended without long interruption. The dampness of the vessel, and scarcely anything comfortable, kept David Sands unwell most of the voyage, which was about one hundred miles; I was also taken poorly, having got a heavy cold. The merchants to whom we were recommended visited us. Many exercises crowded in, so that it was a trying time.

"6th. David Sands and myself both very unwell; the prospect of proceeding to Dunkirk is, from a variety of circumstances, very discouraging; it was indeed a gloomy day, faith and hope very low. The two merchants to whom we had letters coming to see us, did not encourage us to proceed to France, supposing it to be impracticable without a national cockade, which was also the sentiment of others.

"7th. Weighing seriously what was best to be done in our trying situation, and the various reports of difficulties that would interrupt our journey, our minds being calm and composed, we concluded to pursue our journey to Dunkirk, in humble confidence on the Divine Arm, that is alone the defence and preservation of them that love the Lord in sincerity. We left Sluys in the afternoon, and arrived at Bruges before dark, having passed through a poor country. This city is thought to contain sixty thousand people, but has a dark uncomfortable appearance, the houses like prisons with iron bars across the windows.

"8th. Hired a post-chaise to take us to Dunkirk, thirty-seven miles, and passed through a flat fertile country; met with the American consul on this station, an agreeable young man, who told us that with our passes we might go over all France; this relieved us much from the anxiety we felt, both for our testimony and our safety, and our hearts were lifted up with praises to our heavenly Benefactor, who can at his pleasure dispel the clouds and darkness that at times surround. Riding on the side of the sea, we arrived at Dunkirk in the afternoon. I put up at Judith Gardiner's, a Friend from Nantucket, whose husband died at sea since their settling here, and she keeps a boarding-house.

"9th. Unwell, the consequence of travelling so long in this damp foggy climate, where we have not seen the sun for fourteen days, and but very little for six weeks. Our landlady, who is a motherly woman, attended me kindly.

"10th. This town is supposed to contain forty thousand inhabitants, has a gloomy appearance, the houses being closely stowed; the people here, as well as in Flanders, are mostly Roman Catholics. The harbor, which is about a mile from the sea, is narrow, walled at the sides, and almost bare at low water — two men who supped at the house being Deists, I had to contend against them till near eleven o'clock, yet we parted friendly.

"11th. The poultry market is pretty good, and fifty per cent. cheaper than in Philadelphia. Though this place is in France, the people speak Flemish and French alternately; their markets, as well as at almost every place where we have been in Europe, are in the open air, without any shelter; the buyers and sellers are for the most part women; the articles are brought to market on the smallest species of asses that I have seen; their loads being so very large that the poor animal is scarcely seen.

"First-day, 12th. Had a good meeting at B. Hussey's, where about thirty attended, among whom were some American captains, and several citizens of Dunkirk. In the evening attended a large meeting, consisting of Americans, French, and a number of Scotch and English. The company were remarkably quiet, the doctrine delivered was much opposed to Deism, with which it was believed some present were tinctured; the labor was with tenderness in Christian love, and we hoped it had an effect on some. Prayer and thanksgiving were offered to the Author of all our mercies; the people parted in much kindness, and we felt an evidence that we are in our places, though it was through many exercises we got here.

"13th. The few Friends who remain here are respected by the inhabitants, the magistrates, &c., through whose kindness they have been exempted from bearing arms, and at the times of general illuminations they have been signally protected, which must be esteemed a favor from Him who rules and disposes the hearts of men to be kind to such as keep his testimonies.

"14th. Owing to great industry and exertion in cultivating the land, which is naturally poor and sandy, vegetables are abundant and very cheap; potatoes and turnips may be bought for about twenty cents a bushel; apples are good, and in greater plenty than in America at this season of the year. The people are civil and respectful, especially to Americans. In the evening the meeting was as large as the room could hold, and the people very orderly, none appeared restless or went out until it concluded. It was a favored time, much tenderness being evident in those assembled. It is indeed cause of admiration to me, that in passing from one nation to another, we find a tender-hearted people everywhere: the Lord has a precious people in this city.

"15th. It appears as though we might soon be at liberty to leave Dunkirk for the present. The people go to their chapels at any time of the day and perform their devotions, thus at all hours they are going in and coming out; I could not help feeling a love for them, though I cannot own their superstition, believing they will be accepted according to the sincerity of their hearts, when many who think themselves wise philosophers, will have nothing to yield them consolation. Got our passes endorsed by the American consul, who went with us to the municipality, and at his request they gave us new passes, inserting in them that we were Friends, called Quakers.

"17th. Leaving Dunkirk, we passed through the city of Burgh, and before dark arrived at Lille, where, with difficulty we procured a passage for Paris, one hundred and fifty miles distant. Lille is a large city, and may contain seventy thousand inhabitants.

"18th. Proceeded in a cabriolet,* which is a very heavy carriage, takes a great deal of goods, and has eight horses, two postilions, and a director; we had four passengers besides ourselves.

"19th. Passed through a number of towns and villages, and saw many of the people going to their mass-houses, over the doors of which is painted, 'The French nation acknowledge the Supreme Being and the immortality of the soul.' Arrived at Paris.

"20th. The country is populous, but we see much

less travelling than about London. The city of Paris is crowded with inhabitants, the houses are of white stone like the plaster of paris; the streets are not kept clean, and have no paved side-walks for foot-passengers.

"22d. We rode to the municipality, where they endorsed our passes; and going into another apartment to have them sealed, one of the principal men ordered us to take off our hats. We told him we were of the people called Quakers, who did not use that compliment to any; he appeared warm, and said it was no matter what we were, no person could be admitted before them with their hats on, and came towards us, as we supposed, to take them off, but one of his companions in office, observing to him, that we made a religious scruple of it, he withdrew, and growing more mild, said he always paid respect to religion, and had no more to say if that was the case. He sealed and signed our passes, and we parted friendly. A law of France, which obliges all others to appear uncovered before the National Convention, exempts Friends by a special clause — there were a number of persons present waiting to do business with the municipality, who appeared surprised at our thus bearing our testimony; perhaps some may reflect on it to profit.

"23d. There seems no probability of much religious service in Paris, except in conversation and distributing books; and our minds have been much exercised both before and since arriving here, under a sense of the difficulty of passing through this country at this time; and laboring to keep to our righteous testimony among a gay and dissipated people, many of whom make light of all religion. Over their chapel-doors is placed the inscription before mentioned. These places are frequented by many pious people, and mass is performed by a priest who has taken an oath to the nation, none else being allowed. I do not doubt that with all the vices and infidelity which reigns in Paris, there are many of Sion's true mourners there; with such I was favored frequently to feel a secret sympathy. May the great and universal Shepherd of the heavenly fold, stretch forth his arm to this nation, and gather many thousands to the standard of truth and righteousness, where their tossed souls may lie down in safety and none be able to make them afraid. In the evening, David Sands and myself fell in with Thomas Paine, and spent about an hour and a half in conversation about his opinions and writings. He made many assertions against Moses, the prophets, Jesus Christ, &c., which had much more the appearance of passionate railing than argument; to all which we replied. I felt zealously opposed to him, and believe that nothing was said by my companion or myself that gave him the least occasion to exult: we bore our testimony against him firmly.

"Our path on this continent has been through many trials of faith, and contentions for the faith; may they all end to the glory of the great Head of the church, whom I honestly desire above all other things to serve, with my time, talents, and substance. This city contains almost everything to gratify the eyes of the curious, the desires of the voluptuous, the talents of the learned, and the dissipation of the gay and fashionable world; but has little to satisfy the soul longing after celestial riches, and but few in appearance are seeking after it. . The street called the Boulevards, is about two hundred feet wide, encircles the whole of the city, and is, perhaps, the most extraordinary street in Europe. It contains a great number of shops and stalls for the sale of every species of goods, many places of vain amusement, and handsome walks with seats, and is almost constantly crowded with passengers. It is a great inconvenience to persons walking that there are no foot-ways, or very few in any part of the city, so that at the approach of carriages they run in crowds into the houses, shops, &c., adjacent. There are many objects in this great city which excite astonishment, but the mind grows weary with the iniquity which abounds, and desires rather some quiet retreat even in the interior of America than to dwell in such a city; it made me feel sad and disgusted at the ever-lying vanities of a delusive, uncertain world. A passage offering to proceed towards the south, we concluded to embrace it and leave Paris in the morning.

"25th. Arrived at Fontainbleau, which has but few manufactures and little trade, and may contain ten thousand inhabitants. This morning for two leagues before we got here, there were neither houses nor farms, but the road bordered by uncultivable mountains, consisting almost entirely of rocks, or else by wood-land, the towns and villages on the road, looked as poor as the country around them.

"First-day, 26th. The weather has been very fine and serene, the country though not rich was beautiful; the villagers dressed in their best clothes appeared lively, walking about in their wooden shoes, which they almost universally wear. Some were attending their places of worship, but more diverting themselves in the fields, and appear not to be deeply impressed with trouble for the miseries of war. The people have many conjectures about us, sometimes supposing we are Spaniards, Hollanders, Swiss, British or Germans, sometimes Italians, &c.; we generally inform them soon after our arrival to quiet their minds, that we are not in any of the characters they suppose us to be, but Americans and of the people called Quakers, travelling to see our brethren in the south of France; this with a present of a few books sets them right, and they use us respectfully. We endeavor to maintain a conduct void of offence; but are often much tried, and it frequently appears to me as though I was travelling in the midst of darkness and could see no light; yet I greatly desire to be preserved from murmuring, having had hitherto to acknowledge the mercy and goodness of God, who has extended his care and protection in the course of the present arduous journey, in many a trying hour.

"27th. At Nogent. It is the time of the carnival, an occasion of feasting and rejoicing all over France, but the Catholic religion being at present at a low ebb, this festival is not celebrated with as much pomp as it used to be.

"28th. Passed through a handsome country, but many of the people live very hard. The weather being raw and cold to-day, I pitied the poor shepherdesses, who sit on the sides of the rocks and mountains, tending, perhaps, a few sheep, hogs, asses, and goats, on very barren pasture. They spin all day long, and follow their flocks; and sometimes ride about the country on very small asses, two women on one, one of the women looking one way, and the other another way; but the habits and manners of this people baffle my powers of description. The country appears to abound in wine, and little else is drunk, it being generally a very light claret.

"1st of Third month. Being a remarkably fine morning, I set off alone before the carriage, and after walking six miles along the side of the Loire, and passing two villages, stopped for the voiture; the country was pleasant and hilly. Passing on, we met about two hundred German prisoners, who had been taken at Mantua, and were in a most deplorable situation, almost exhausted in every respect, many of them having neither shoes, stockings, hats, nor shirts; the miseries of war were very affectingly painted in this spectacle of wretchedness.

"2d. Arrived at Moulin in the afternoon; a considerable, but not a handsome city, principally occupied in making muslins, which the women spin, while walking in the streets. Our cabriolet leaving us, we were obliged to take what they call a chariot de post, which is nothing more than a small cart without sides, at each end a basket, and in the middle a straw bed for the passengers to sit on, back to back, with their legs in the basket; they carry four persons, have a little horse or mule, and a postilion, and these appear to be the only carriages that travellers can obtain in France, except they travel in the national cabriolets with eight horses; or have their own carriages, when they may obtain post-horses. This was a very trying day to my mind; darkness seemed to cover my spirit.

"3d. Left Moulin in the disagreeable chariot de post or potache; passed through a mountainous country, mostly covered with vines, and got to Pallisee in the evening. There are but two inns in this place, kept by father and son, who were the only persons from whom we could obtain a convenience for travelling, and they did not fail to take advantage of us, charging at least fifty per cent. higher than the best inns and carriages in America.

"4th. Finding no other way of travelling, we resumed our potache, passed over a country more mountainous than any heretofore, until we arrived at ~~Rouen~~, situate on the side of the Loire, a city that may contain twenty thousand inhabitants. At the Table d'Hote, were a number of Frenchmen, who treated us politely, and finding they had a desire for religious information, we gave them some books.

"5th. The country, as yesterday, is covered with vines and mulberry trees; arrived about dusk at a large town closely environed by mountains, the inhabitants employed in manufactories of muslin and silk. They were differently dressed from any we had yet seen, and remarkably friendly; indeed the frankness of this nation does not suffer us to remain strangers more than an hour; seeing but few strangers, especially from other nations, they are curious in their inquiries. We passed a very disagreeable night, and as soon as it was light, were glad to rise and proceed on our journey.

"6th. Arrived at Lyons in the afternoon, and put up at an auberge, perhaps the largest we have seen in Europe, forming a hollow square about two hundred feet on each side: this city contains about one hundred and forty thousand inhabitants; one-third is built on a very steep mountain, on the side of the Rhone; many parts, however, now lay in ruins, being battered during a long siege. We are a spectacle to many; my mind is heavy and disconsolate: the ways of the Lord are a great deep, but I dare not murmur, he is good and worthy to be adored, both in suffering and reigning.

"7th. Finding a boat that was to go off at eleven o'clock for Avignon, one hundred and thirty miles, we took our passage, there being about twenty of us in all, and sailed down the stream eight leagues. The country, on each side, is very beautiful; arrived at a village in the evening, where the keepers of the inns rushed down to the shore, and almost compelled us to enter their houses, and perhaps twenty girls and boys were waiting to take our baggage, and earn a few sous.

A genteel man, a merchant, who had a coach on board, took us under his protection, and we got to tolerable lodgings.

"8th. Proceeded early down the river and met a number of boats going up to Lyons, loaded with wine, &c. Three or four of these being fastened together, are drawn by horses, as many as twenty being necessary to draw them up against the stream, which, in some places, is rapid—the mountains are planted with vines to the tops, but in some places interspersed with olive, almond, and mulberry trees. The Alps, about eight miles distant, are covered with snow. It being uncommonly low water in the Rhone, our boat got aground twice, but having four stout horses in a smaller boat which they tow after them, for the purpose of relieving them when aground, after an hour's labor we got afloat again, and arrived at Valence in the evening, which, like most of the cities in the south of France, is very ancient, and may contain eighteen thousand inhabitants.

"9th. Embarked early, but having a strong head wind could not proceed far. We went on shore and walked to a city about a mile distant, said to be built and fortified by Julius Cæsar, and called Montlemar; it has high strong walls, and bears all the marks of great antiquity, has little riches or trade. No auberges or taverns, within the walls, being permitted to lodge travellers, we went to several outside, but could find no lodgings; it being on the main road from the south to Lyons, they were filled with guests; at last we got to a poor inn where they took five of us: my state of body and mind rendered me more unfit to endure hardships than at other times. Most of these ancient cities have more or less of Roman monuments yet remaining.

"10th. The wind continuing very high and right ahead, and the waters so low that our captain thought with such a wind it would be impossible to proceed; we accepted the kind invitation of our friend, the merchant of Circasson, who had a coach that would take four and offered us places in it as far as Nismes; so taking post-horses at Montlemar, we arrived at Point Esprit before dark. This city is a very ancient, dark-looking place, may contain eight thousand inhabitants, and was built by the Romans; the streets are so narrow generally, that no wheel-carriages can pass; their fagots and other things are carried upon asses. These ancient cities generally have a melancholy appearance, so as to damp the spirits of the most animated stranger; the bridge at St. Esprit, which crosses the Rhone, is a very ancient and handsome structure, more than a mile long.

"11th. Went on about seven miles: there is great danger in travelling on account of robbers and assassins who infest the roads, so that none care to travel after night. The mail was robbed on a mountain which we crossed to-day, and some travellers have been robbed and murdered lately in this vicinity, which makes it a very trying time to travel in France. We went to the municipality, who endorsed our passes and behaved friendly; and some persons being desirous of information, we gave them several books. Our kind friend, the merchant, inclining to stay here a few days, we were obliged to take a potache for Nismes; the people of the auberge taking us for priests, behaved respectfully.

"First-day, 12th. I was very unwell, and the weather being misty and cold, and the chariot de post open, with only a little straw to sit on, and there being two women passengers besides us three, we were uncomfortably situated, and travelled very slowly, having only a little horse and a mule to carry us and our baggage. The country is highly cultivated, covered with vines, almond, olive and mulberry trees. We passed several crucifixes and images on the road, but most of all within six miles of Nismes. As we travelled only about three miles an hour, we did not get to Nismes until candle-light, not quite thirty miles.

"13th. Nismes contains about forty thousand inhabitants, chiefly employed in silk manufacture; it was the first place in France where we were questioned about the national cockade, but our reasons satisfied them. We hired a voiture to take us to Congenies, about three and a half leagues. The country between Nismes and Congenies, though somewhat mountainous, is fine; the people seemed pleased at seeing us, and immediately judged we were Friends, having seen those who were here eight or nine years ago. We went to Louis Majolier's to lodge, and several of the Friends being there, they received us with strong marks of affection and joy.

"14th. Our friends flocked to see us, and saluted us with tears of joy; much mutual consolation was felt, and they furnished us with the best provisions the village afforded. In the evening about thirty-five of them being with us, we desired them to retire into silence, for which they appeared prepared: mercy and goodness were evident in covering us with a precious solemnity, a few sentences being offered in much brokenness, they received it like the thirsty ground; after which, our friends Pierre Robinel and Magdalene Benezet, both bore testimony to the continued goodness of the great Shepherd, towards the few scattered sheep in this remote corner of France. Our valued friend, Louis Majolier, also added his grateful acknowledgments and confession of unworthiness of Divine mercy, in much tenderness and with many tears.

"15th. The weather is very fine, the almond and peach trees are in blossom, and the olive, figs, &c., out in leaf. I never was in a country where there was more unaffected simplicity than here. Shepherds and shepherdesses, are scattered about tending their flocks, and knitting or spinning at the same time; having very few cows or goats, they milk the ewes, which affords them a sufficiency, and they think the milk richer than cow's milk. In the evening we had some conversation with them on their present state as to religion, and from the information of . . . . . . Robinel, an ancient man, it appears that for sixty years at least, there has been a number of religious people in this neighborhood, who had separated from the common ways of worship, and were by some called Inspirants. Their attention was first turned to Friends by information in the public papers, of a young man who came to Paris and advertised that the owners of a vessel and cargo, which was taken by the British in the war with America and France, were requested to come forward and claim their several proportions of the said vessel and cargo; and that his father, who was part owner of the ship which took the French vessel, was a Quaker, and did not desire to hold their property, as it was inconsistent with his conscientious scruples. They then made inquiry respecting the principles of Friends, and found them much the same as their own. After this, being visited by Sarah Grubb and company, and confirmed in their sentiments, they continued to profess the principles of our religious Society, and have passed through many trials lately, some having been imprisoned; they were truly glad to see us, believing we had come in an acceptable time.

"16th. We visited twelve of their families. When speaking to Louis Majolier in imperfect French, he repeated it in better, or rather in what they call the Padua language, which is bad French and Italian mixed, and hard to be understood. Dined with Jean Benezet, the husband of Magdalene; being affectionately desirous to serve us, they provided a great variety of food: the wine is of their own manufacture, such as is commonly drunk here, being similar to the American cider, and not stronger. In the evening we had the company of many of these Friends, and hope it was a time of encouragement to them. I could not but repeatedly contrast the circumstances of these persons, with that of my dear friends at home and in England. O! the sweet simplicity and innocence of this poor, industrious, but apparently happy people.

"17th. Taking a walk, on our return we were met by a number of our friends, who took us into a house where they had spread a table with bread, butter, and a variety of fruits, showing their assiduity to make us comfortable; the innocence of their manners and their desire of improvement by our visit among them, was so forcibly impressed upon me, that I was constrained to turn aside and pour forth tears of gratitude and joy.

"18th. Visited the remaining families, and find there are seventeen in all; the men, women and children, are mostly employed in vineyards, or cultivating olives and making oil of them, or raising silk-worms; though there are some weavers of silk, and some of wool and linen for the use of the villagers. They appear to have but little in the world, and yet are contented, as much so as any people I have seen on the continent; their dispositions and manners evidently different from the other nations we have visited. The village contains about one hundred and fifty houses and six hundred and fifty inhabitants, all of whom have been civil and respectful to us. There does not appear to be any person of high character or riches among them, but a remarkable equality reigns throughout the whole.

"19th. Attended meeting in the usual place, where several not Friends were present; the whole number supposed to be about eighty, and it proved to be a solid good time. Having yesterday felt our minds turned to write our views and feelings respecting the state of the Friends here, and to add some admonition, encouragement, &c., Louis translated it and read it at the close of the meeting, during which most of the assembly were much contrited. We then separated under a thankful sense of the goodness and mercy of the gracious Shepherd of the sheep. Their usual practice being to hold but one meeting on First-day, we appointed another to be at three o'clock in the afternoon: before the time, the room was filled, many coming from Fontanes and other villages not far off; the opportunity was satisfactory, and ended in prayer and thanks to Him whose is the power and the glory. In the evening, about eight or ten men and five women, the most noted among them, came to have a free conference with us respecting establishing some order and discipline, and a Monthly Meeting, which has been dropped several years, though there had been some little care of the poor, and also over the moral conduct of the members; but as the time was short, we separated without attempting anything.

"20th. Walked to Calvisson, a village three miles distant, containing three times the number of inhabitants of Congenies. None appear to profess with Friends, except the father of Louis Majolier and his sister-in-law, who do not attend the meetings at present. In this part of France, villagers and peasants seem to be the only inhabitants, few or none of rank or wealth.

On a mountain by the way, we saw the Mediterranean sea, and had a most extensive prospect of vineyards and olive-yards: the air as fine and pure as France affords, or perhaps any other country.

"21st. In the evening, about forty men and women Friends assembled to revive their Monthly Meeting; many of them lament the want of proper discipline, and are very desirous of adopting as much of our order as may be suited to their circumstances. Louis Majolier being chosen clerk, it was agreed to procure books for entering fair minutes and for recording births, marriages and burials: they then nominated two men and two women overseers; some remarks were made and we gave them such information as appeared proper; they then recorded our visit on their minutes, and agreed to hold their Monthly Meeting at a stated time in future.

"22d. I looked over the old minutes of the Monthly Meeting, where they had recorded some certificates and letters, &c. It appeared that two men and two women had laid a concern before them to visit the families of Friends at Gilles's, which they performed; that there were several marriages solemnized nearly in the same order as Friends; that they had issued advice to be honest and punctual in their dealings, and to walk in all respects consistent with their profession; that they had dealt tenderly with some who walked disorderly, and at length disowned one who would not be reclaimed; they also took care of the poor, and recorded the certificates of our friends, George and Sarah Dillwyn, Robert and Sarah Grubb, Mary Dudley, A. Bellamy and John Elliott, who visited them in the year 1788. Upon the whole, there was more consistency than I expected to find — and as they now appear reanimated to commence again, I feel a hope they will be supported; many of them are in a state of weakness, and they know it, and are willing to receive counsel. On inquiry, I find there are a number of families scattered in different villages, who hold the same religious opinions, and at times attend their meetings.

"23d. Benjamin Johnson was very poorly, and but little medical aid could be obtained. We deferred going to Gilles's, and our minds are closely exercised, yet thanks be unto Him who in mercy has hitherto carried us through all; I endeavor to cast my care upon Him in this sequestered corner of the world. In all the village of Congenies I believe there is not one shop for the vending any kind of goods, yet the simple wants of the inhabitants seem to be supplied, and they are continually bringing us various kinds of fruits, preserves, nuts, &c.; no people need be more kind or sympathetic than they appear to be. Their fuel is principally the trimmings of the grape-vines, olive, mulberry, fig and almond trees, and at times the wood of such trees as die or are blown up by the roots; it is sold by weight. I have not seen a forest of timber-trees, for two hundred miles. The olive-yards endure a long time, and do not arrive at their most fruitful state in less than fifteen years; I have seen several from one hundred to one hundred and fifty years old, which are highly esteemed — they trim them almost to the stump every year.

"24th. Walked with Louis to a part of his ground where we planted some potatoes, which are not much known or used here; observed many men and women pruning their trees and vines; they work diligently among their olives, almonds, mulberries, vines, &c., but do not appear to be as laborious people as the Germans, yet they generally live better.

"25th. Our friends Louis Majolier and Pierre Robinel accompanying us, we rode out to a village about one and a half leagues from Congenies, and were met in the road by an ancient woman who goes under the name of a Friend; much pleasure was pictured in her countenance, and she conducted us to the house of one also professing as Friends; they set before us some bread, honey, and wine, with a little cheese, made that morning of ewes' milk. After waiting about one hour, eight of those called Friends came; others being gone into the fields, we did not see them. We sat down in religious retirement with this little company, who appeared to be less conformed to our practice than those at Congenies, yet were serious. Something was given to express for their encouragement in pursuing the way of Truth as it opened on their understandings, and to meet together to wait upon God on First-days, and to visit, as frequently as convenient, the meetings of Friends at Congenies; after which we returned. Though the roads in France are generally pretty good, there is scarcely any such thing as travelling fast, their poor little horses, mules, and asses, seldom going more than three miles an hour.

"First-day, 26th. The meeting in the school-room, which is at present their only meeting-place, collected about ten o'clock; the fore-part was somewhat interrupted by a number coming late, and the room was crowded, but being at length gathered into stillness, the great Master of assemblies favored with his presence: a remarkable solemnity continued for near an hour, very refreshing to our spirits, and we were persuaded to many of theirs also. Feeling my mind at liberty, I expressed a number of Scripture passages among them with some addition, and thought I had never been so favored to express myself in French before; great tenderness prevailed among both old and young: Louis made a very suitable addition, and the people parted, we believe, through infinite condescension, comforted — there were upwards of eighty present; several professors came from the adjacent villages, and shed tears of joy at meeting with us: there were also some who had never been at a meeting of the kind before.—Louis's religious father and mother-in-law from Fontanes dined with us. In the afternoon, about the same number attended the meeting, and the people who came from other villages parted with us and their friends here in tears. In the evening, had a conference with the overseers, with those who speak in their meetings, and with some other leading members; on their own motion it was agreed to hold henceforward two meetings on First-days, and one in the middle of the week, if the next Monthly Meeting united with it; this opportunity afforded us a free expression of sentiment on subjects relating to their welfare.

"27th. Louis, his wife, and myself, went to visit her parents and family at Fontanes; the country is hilly, yet covered with vines, the soil very poor, though there are delightful valleys among the mountains; but I have seen neither cows nor oxen since leaving Nismes; but sheep and goats for milk. Passed through a village where were several large and once elegant buildings, gardens, &c., belonging to a cidevant nobleman, now totally ruined; a cross and a crucifix of enormous size, lay in scattered fragments on the ground. As we advanced towards Montpelier, I felt desirous of visiting it, but it was not practicable. Arrived at Fontanes, where the good old people and family of Samuel Brunn were much pleased to see us; the kindness, simplicity, and genuine hospitality of this house, was truly grateful; after spending about three and a half hours with them, we took a most affectionate leave, not expecting to see them again: most of the family walked half a mile on the road with us, loading me with fruits, nuts, &c., accompanied with their blessing and desire for my safe return home. We got back to Congenies about dusk, and found Benjamin still very unwell.

"28th. In the evening, accompanied by Louis, I visited seven families, which appeared to be agreeable and reviving: having found my mind concerned to leave with them in writing, some further counsel respecting holding their meetings for worship and discipline, with that solemnity becoming the occasion, I got it translated, and concluded to have it read at their Monthly Meeting. I believe these tender, good people, would find their meetings more useful, if they were kept more in silence; they have four persons who appear by way of ministry in their meetings, three of them we cannot doubt have received gifts; yet one or more of these, we hope may improve in weight and usefulness, by an increasing disposition to wait all the Lord's appointed time, to qualify them to administer to the greater edification of the church. Our friends here have not yet banished that lively activity of spirit and quickness of imagination, so characteristic of their nation, and may be in danger of carrying it into their most serious concerns; they do not appear to have that visionary disposition and desire of penetrating hidden mysteries, so observable in the Germans; and indeed the two nations differ in almost everything.

"30th. Our friends collecting at ten o'clock, we sat down with them. The silence was truly solemn and affecting, and the thought of parting was deeply felt on both sides. I took leave of them in the best French I could, Louis mending it in some places; after which, David Sands concluded in prayer: we embraced them all with tenderness, and parted in heart-felt sympathy and affection, with many tears and pious wishes. We mounted, David on a bidet, I on a very poor little mule: Louis Majolier, Pierre Robinel, Pierre Marignol, and Pierre Benezet, having two asses between them, accompanied us. I rode about a league, when my mule kicked and flounced about, and showed so many obstinate airs, that I was willing to exchange it for an ass, but had not rode two leagues more, before the little animal stumbled on his knees, and slipped me over his head, without damage, however. I then remounted my mule, but soon after arriving at a village where it had an inclination to stop, he kicked, and refused very obstinately to go on; however, at length, with the assistance of the spectators, I got through the village, and he afterwards behaved with more decorum during the journey, travelling at the rate of two and a half miles an hour. Our whole business on this continent has one tendency, viz., to learn us patience; and we shall be poor scholars, indeed, if we return with as low a stock as when we came from home. My mind feeling sweetly relieved, at parting with my dear friends at Congenies, I passed along without complaining, the weather being fine, and the country covered with blossoms and verdure. I did not wish myself at any other place, nor in any other company, for the present, believing we were moving in the way of our duty. The country, in the vicinity of Gilles's, was more hilly, and the whole, with a very few trees interspersed, was covered with vineyards, the cultivation of grapes being almost the sole occupation of the people; yet in the valleys they raise some wheat and rye. There are very few cattle in this part of the country, though as a rarity we saw two young oxen; horses are very scarce, but they have excellent mules for their wagons. We arrived safe at Gilles's in the evening, the road being the nearest way from Congenies, was in many places not practicable for carriages; the distance, said to be five leagues, occupied six hours, without halting. Our guides took us to the house of one professing with us, where we were received kindly, and several of those, called Friends, came to see us, and supped with us. Our landlord is an old man, and perhaps the richest of those, called Quakers, in France; we were well accommodated, both as to provisions and lodging.

"31st. Several of those called Friends came to see us, and with some of them we walked about three quarters of a mile to the Rhone: the land between the town and the river, was mostly sown with wheat and rye, which looked well. After we returned, there being several present and a good deal of conversation, David, Louis, and myself, retired to our chamber. It is not beneficial to enter too freely into conversation about things which have little or no connection with our main business among this people, and therefore we find it best sometimes to withdraw, for they are a people very fond of talking. In the evening, about forty attended our meeting and behaved orderly, though we sat in silence about an hour, when I thought it right to deliver a few expressions, to which they paid attention; yet, except in a few instances, there did not appear to be that preparation to receive the word which was so evident in our friends at Congenies. Louis afterwards urged the necessity of their adding more of the works and fruits of the Spirit to their faith, without which the good profession they had made to the world would neither yield them peace nor be a light sufficient to guide others into the Truth. There appeared some tenderness, all were quiet and seemed retired in their minds, yet I thought it altogether a time of suffering, and there was less of the cementing power and love of Christ to be felt than in the meetings at Congenies.

"Fourth month, 1st. From the top of the hill above the town, there is a prospect of a fine extensive valley with a canal in the middle. On the side next to the Rhone, it appeared to be as handsome and rich a spot as I had seen in France; but one of the Friends in company said it was not of more than half the value, nor did it yield half the profit of the hills of gravel that surrounded all the other side of the town, extending several miles, and covered with vines, but so poor that it appeared as though it would yield little or no grain or grass, yet produced the finest wine in all Languedoc: the valley was too rich and damp for wine, and two acres of it would be given for one of vineyard, and the vineyard cost as little labor per acre as the grass or grain. The grapes raised on rich land make the poorest and thinnest wine; but the more dry and poor the land, if the vines will grow at all, the stronger and more excellent the liquor; this is a fact established by experience.

"This city contains six thousand inhabitants, a few of whom are Protestants. Before the revolution, they had twenty-nine Catholic priests to support, at present they have but one large and very ancient chapel remaining, and but two priests; the women appear to be going in and out of their chapel all day and seem devout, but very few men pay any attention to religion. It is a lively industrious place, and has a considerable trade in wine and brandy up and down the Rhone — they sell almost everything by weight, as apples, nuts, oranges, &c.; in the market they were weighing live eels, and had much difficulty to keep them in the scales. The Friend at whose house we are, has a large family of children, and is a great cultivator of the vine, &c.; having about five hundred acres of land on rent, at from two to three guineas per acre; another of the Friends has also about the same quantity, and they appear to be men of the first rank in this place. Those professing with us, appear generally to be in more easy circumstances than at Congenies. Dined at one of those Friend's who had a plentiful table and the finest fruits, raisins, figs and grapes, almost as fresh as on the vines. After dinner, sitting down with the family, a solemnity covered us, in which David Sands and myself had something to offer. Mary, the daughter of David Ventigole, also bore a lively and tendering testimony in much humility. I thought I had not heard the Gospel preached more in the demonstration of the Spirit in France; she has appeared a few times in their public meetings. Going out to take a little walk alone before dark, one of the Friends came to me, and I went back to his house and spent a few minutes with him and his wife to much satisfaction, they being a valuable couple who love the Truth. The more we know the people here, the more our love increases toward them. I was at the house of a lame man, a tailor, who appears to be a steady, religious person, and says he never asks one price for his goods and takes another.

"First-day, 2d of fourth month. At the meeting this morning in the house where we lodge, about sixty or more attended, who behaved with remarkable decency and solidity. About an hour passed in silence, then Pierre Robinel, Pierre Marignon, Louis Majolier and myself had each a few words to offer; after which, Mary, daughter of David Ventigole, bore her testimony, which was edifying and sound, delivered in much humility, and had considerable effect on the audience. After the meeting closed, Louis read the same writing that was read at Congenies; the truths contained in it touched divers of them sensibly: we were satisfied with the meeting, believing the great Master of assemblies favored with his presence. In the afternoon, the meeting was attended by some Catholics and some Protestants, and concluded in much brokenness, and an humbling sense of the renewed love and mercy of our heavenly Father. At seven o'clock in the evening, we had about ten men and four women of the principal persons in our room, to propose for their consideration the propriety of establishing an order and discipline; some of them expressed their opinion of its fitness, and we then left it under their consideration.

"3d. Dined at David Ventigole's; he told us he owned about eighteen hundred sheep, seven hundred and fifty of which were milked by the shepherds and shepherdesses twice, at noon and midnight, and do not afford quite a pint per day each; he has also fifty-six oxen, fifty horses, seventeen mules, and ten asses, and employs from one to two hundred persons, according to the season, but seldom has much less than one hundred. Our landlord has about the same amount of stock, and employs as many people, but he has twenty-seven hundred sheep; the reason we have seen no oxen is, that they keep them on the mountains. Those professing with us here, who employ so many people, have no small influence in the town and neighborhood: they are very generous and hospitable, but in general not quite so susceptible and tender as our Friends at Congenies. Some of the young women wear crosses of gold; one of them said that hers cost more than a louisdor, but she and some others had taken them from their necks. We had a free conference with those under our name about some matters in their dress, &c., which they received in love, acknowledging their weakness. The Society here, as well as at Congenies, has been subsisting for sixty or more years under the name of Inspirants, until they became acquainted with the principles of Friends. I believe if the Lord should put it into the hearts of other more qualified brethren or sisters to visit them, it would have both its use and reward, especially if they understood the language well. In the evening, the meeting was attended by about forty, and I thought it the most solid of any we had with them. I believed it best to speak without the assistance of an interpreter, and by attending to my concern and proceeding deliberately, I found myself more relieved and satisfied than since I came into the south; the meeting for worship concluded in prayer by David Sands. Louis then read some of the thoughts I had written respecting worship, and the solemnity in which all our meetings ought to be held; then we had a free conference respecting the nature and necessity of church discipline, and parted with serious impressions.

"5th. This forenoon, after a short time of retirement with the family where we lodged, and some others who came in, we parted in much love; many were waiting without to take leave of us, which they did affectionately, but many more not being present, I felt tried at leaving them. We went on, however, accompanied by several of our friends, some of whom went a mile or two on foot, and appeared affected at parting. Proceeded to Nismes three leagues: several persons came to offer us a conveyance to Paris, but we thought we had better buy a carriage and take post-horses. In Nismes, there are many curious Roman remains of great antiquity—an amphitheatre, said to have been built before the birth of our Saviour, capable of containing seventeen thousand persons; a temple of Diana, and an extraordinary fountain and castle of the same age. Having procured a carriage, after dinner all our dear friends from Congenies and Gilles's, except three, took a most affectionate leave of us, such as I trust will not soon be forgotten by any of us.

CHAPTER V.

Leaves Congenies — Impositions — Vienne — Lyons — Incidents of travel — Poor quarters — Robbery and its event — Accident on the road — Difficulty of religious labor — Renewed imposition — Mean fare—Catholic chapel and ceremonies—Arrival in Paris—American consul — Renewed difficulties — Notice of Paris — Ruins of Prince Condé estate — Dunkirk — Character of the French — Rejoicing at the prospect of peace — Difficulty of procuring passports — Arrival in England — Renewed religious engagements — Printed sermons — Isle of Wight — Island of Jersey — Descendants of M. Dyer — Guernsey — Prisoners at York — Liverpool — Isle of Man —Interesting interviews and meetings — Swarthmore — Services in the north of England — Scotland — Edinburgh — Dundee — Urie and R. Barclay — Aberdeen — Penitent hearers — Return to Edinburgh — Glasgow — Ireland — Belfast—Boarding-school—Poverty of the people—Romish funeral—Dublin—Distribution of alms.

"6th. Parting affectionately with our three friends from Congenies, we passed through a number of villages, and arrived at Bagniol, took some refreshment, and proceeded to Pierrelatte, having travelled nineteen leagues to-day.

"7th. Leaving Pierrelatte we got to Montelemar, and while we were in the auberge, a smith, without our order, put a piece of iron round one of the wheels of our carriage under a pretence of mending it, and demanded three shillings sterling for his labor; but as we had not employed him, we endeavored to show him the unreasonableness of meddling with our carriage without consulting us; and not without a great many words we obliged him to take it off, as we saw it would rather injure than help the wheel. The postilion also demanding an unconscionable fee, we were obliged to dispute it; but many people gathering round, we felt unpleasant, and to rid ourselves as well as we could, paid our money for the sake of peace. It is not uncommon to have a host of importunate people to contend with in France and other places where we have travelled on the continent, which with other things, makes it very exercising for Friends to travel; that we have need of a double supply of meekness and wisdom to pass along and keep a conscience void of offence. We got to Tain and lodged, being twenty-three leagues.

"8th. Passed over a mountainous country. I alighted from the carriage and walked through the city of Vienne, on the side of the Rhone, with the Alps to the east. It is very ancient, and has some remarkable places of worship, much defaced at present; it is about a mile long, and crowded with inhabitants; after crossing a high mountain, we arrived at St. Symphorien and put up at a poor inn. The postilion seemed desirous of taking advantage of us as we were strangers, and with some pecuniary sacrifice, I got him quieted.

"Fourth month, 9th. Arrived at Lyons about twelve o'clock. Benjamin Johnson being much weakened with his late sickness, had now another attack, and having a long journey before us, it was a time of discouragement and trial to us all, yet not without a ray of faith and hope in that mercy and goodness, which has been our support and preservation through the course of our journeying both by sea and land. His company has been useful, and the giving up his time and substance to accompany one so unworthy as I often feel myself, will I trust be recompensed to him by the gracious Dispenser of every blessing. We travelled but four leagues to-day, and had to pay double the usual rates for the last two, it being established by law that the last post entering in, and the first going out of Lyons, Paris, and other great cities, travellers shall be subject to that additional price; the fixed rate in common, being thirty sous for each horse for two leagues. In our circumstance the law requires us to be furnished with three horses and to pay for four, but they generally incline to go with two and take pay for three and a half. Having arrived at Lyons without deciding what auberge to put up at, our postilion took us to a good one opposite the grand promenade. The Rhone and the Seine pass by this city on opposite sides, and meet a few miles below it. Many of the shops were open, although it was First-day, and many booths of goods were exhibited for sale. It is very thickly inhabited, perhaps no city that we have seen, more so, except London and Paris. We were informed there was some worship to-day, both Protestant and Catholic, but that the priests who had not taken the oath, performed their devotions privately in chambers, &c. The people are in an unsettled state respecting religion, yet doubtless there are many pious souls all over France, who lament the decay of religion among the people. It appears to me that the all-wise Ruler of the universe, is preparing a way for the Truth to be preached in this country. We distributed some books and left Lyons about twelve o'clock, though my mind and also David's were not a little turned towards Geneva, but on account of several circumstances, we were upon the whole induced to move towards Paris. At the end of the first stage, we were again brought to some hesitation about going to Geneva, yet concluded to proceed as far as Macon; our way is strewed with circumstances unusual to Friends.

"11th. Passed through fine roads, and a delightful country, nine leagues to Macon, lodged at one of those immensely extensive inns which are found in many places on this continent, exceeding in size any I have seen in England or America. The kitchen and other offices are so far off, that it was with difficulty we could get what we had need of, though the waiters seemed active and ready to oblige us when they knew our wants. Here we were told there were thirty priests who would not take the oath, and remained in confinement, assisted by the charity of the people; there were also both Protestants and Roman Catholics who held open worship. The people had their different opinions about us as heretofore, not a few pleased themselves with the thoughts of our being priests in disguise. Seeing the castle where the thirty priests were confined, about a mile distant, I took a walk in company with a young man that way, but not being permitted an entrance, and it being warm, stopped at a little cottage, where was only one person, a woman; we asked for some water, which she got, and said she had something better for travellers, and brought a fine bunch of half-dried grapes; said she had lost a son in the war, and whether her husband was living, she did not know. We observed to her that her's was a solitary life in a place so hidden; she replied that she had some neighbors who wanted her to live with them, but she had the company of the good God, who was better than ten husbands, and all her children. Macon is a considerable city: the Saone passes through it.

"Fourth month, 12th. Left Macon, and proceeded through a delightful country, which I thought might be called the garden of France; got to Sennez, about nine and a half leagues; the women here work in the fields, and appear to be a hardy race of people.

"13th. Benjamin Johnson continuing very poorly, and the people of the auberge being agreeable, we concluded to stay here all day.

"14th. Passed on through Chalons; the stable for the post-horses and carriages, a large building, was formerly a magnificent chapel, some part of its ancient grandeur still remaining. In the evening got to St. Emilian, a poor village, and as it was raining hard, and near night, we were obliged to stop and take up our quarters at a very sorry inn. After a poor supper, having occasion for something in our saddle-bags, they were not to be found. A number of people, apparently of bad character, being at the inn, we made our loss known, searched in all the places we thought it probable they were, but in vain, and we went to bed. The rain came down on us through the thatched roof, and the people were coming in and going out of our room frequently, which, with the idea I had of their ill-character, and the probable loss of our bags, kept me in such a situation as to allow of but little sleep.

"15th. Rose early, went into several houses and informed of our loss; I also inquired the character of our landlord, and found they had little to say in his favor. I then thought of going back to a town, about two leagues off, in order to obtain advice and assistance, and had procured a horse for the purpose, but a person sitting in the house, told me my going back would be quite useless, that I might rest assured the valise was in the village. I inquired for a magistrate, and the people of the inn denied any being there, but a man somewhat more respectable than the rest, took me aside, assured me there was one, and he would conduct me to him. The magistrate appeared to be a man of integrity, and offered to assist us: I gave him a description of our property, and promised a reward to the person who should produce the valise; he had a drum beat round the village to alarm the people, which succeeding, a man in half an hour came to the auberge with the valise, said he had found it in a stable, at some distance, covered with hay, but his countenance was evidently marked with guilt and confusion. We gave a reward of a louis, and prepared to leave a place we were heartily tired of. The bag, besides clothing, contained a number of letters, papers, &c., and we did not perceive that anything was missing. Passing along a fine country, and through Autun, a handsome and beautifully situated city, we got to Chissey, a small village, where we had some repairs done to our carriage, but had proceeded only about a mile, when one of our springs breaking, we had to return. The innkeeper had taken possession of an ancient castle of some cidevant nobleman, which he converted into an auberge.

"First-day, Fourth month, 16th. Passed through Salies, a considerable city, and it being, what is called, easter, the people were dressed in their best clothes, and collected in large companies, amusing themselves agreeably to the customs of France, and appeared all activity and vivacity. Arrived at a small city called Avalon: great numbers of people, of both sexes, were on the promenade, which all the large towns have. David and I walked through the place among them; they behaved respectfully, but gazed much at us: there can scarcely be a more exercising service than we are engaged in, to minds like mine. We frequently feel as though there were some religious people in the places we pass through, but are at a loss how to select them, or be of much use to them, as none of us know the language sufficiently; we, however, at times converse freely, and sometimes spread books. I doubt not but the day draws nigh, when the word of the Lord will be sounded under his own authority to many who have hitherto sat in darkness. At present we feel rather a spirit of heaviness and mourning than any pointings of Truth to gather the people to the true standard; probably the time is not now, and may we possess our souls in patience.

"17th. Passed through Auxerre, Bassou, &c.; this seemed to be a high day with the inhabitants: all the country was full of mirth, and shall I say wantonness? Arrived at Joigny, a large town, where also the people were scattered like flocks all over this beautiful country, round the city as well as in it, dancing, &c. O! France, how dissolute and thoughtless are many of thy inhabitants, who have certainly not learned the things which belong to their peace, though their chastisement has been heavy.

"18th. This is a fine country of wheat, but few people at labor, mostly engaged in diversions and sports: at Sens, a considerable city, we had to stop to have our carriage mended, the rough pavements of France being very destructive to carriages. The people in this country seem to think it is not improper to get all they can from travellers, and therefore charge for their work, about three times as much as would be a just compensation for their trouble. The blacksmith charged us twelve shillings and six-pence sterling, for two hours' work; these continual impositions make our travelling amount to three and a half guineas a day, though we have often no full meal but supper. The charges for post-horses are high, and we content ourselves almost all day with bread and cheese, some smoked herring, apples, nuts, and some poor wine. The chapel of the former bishop, in which a priest was officiating to several hundreds of the people, mostly women, was the largest and most magnificent I have seen in France; the paintings, the multiplicity of ornaments outside, &c., bespoke it to be very ancient, and were also a testimony to the unnecessary and inconsistent manner in which these buildings were erected, six or nine centuries past. The people go in procession, near kindred and acquaintance, two and two, to the chapel, with an infant to be baptized, and return with a drum and music before them, and sit down to a feast. In this chapel an invitation to all good Catholics was pasted on the pillars to bring in their gifts liberally, for the support of the priests and the altar, that their holy religion might not fall to the ground.

"19th. The country is thickly set with towns and villages as we draw nearer to Paris; we passed through Chatelet, Melun, Charenton and many other towns, and got to our former lodgings in Paris, and were received with pleasant countenances. In the afternoon, went in search of the American consul, Skipwith, but the office was shut. A number of Americans have been in this city nearly a year, seeking some indemnification for their property taken by the nation, and have no prospect when they shall be at liberty to return.

"20th Went again to the consul's office, but were told to come again or wait an hour; we returned and after some time went back. It is exceedingly trying to wait from time to time on men in public stations before any business can be accomplished; they only think fit to attend from about eleven o'clock to three each day. He used us courteously and appeared willing to oblige us, but has little in his power at present, as there is some disagreement between the French government and ours. He told us that for about two months past, all communication between England and France had been prohibited, so that no passes could be obtained but for Hamburg or some other neutral port. This was an additional affliction to us, to think of travelling six or seven hundred miles from hence in our wearied state; apprehending it was more than we could accomplish in time for the Yearly Meeting in London. Being much cast down, I quietly reflected on the mercy and goodness of our heavenly Shepherd, who has condescended from time to time, to 'make darkness light before us, and crooked things straight;' and then felt easy to leave the business of procuring passes and forwarding them to us, to the consul, and proceed to Dunkirk. We then took post-horses for St. Dennis, to go on a different road from that we came here upon. Paris, for the licentious and men of pleasure, is perhaps more fully calculated than any city in Europe; there may be found everything to gratify their desire, to feast their eyes and delight their imagination; but for persons of our character, and engaged in the weighty business we are, it is altogether undesirable. France is a country in which my mind has been much exercised and sunk, and I think every hour long till we get out of it. Our cabriolet needing some repair, while it was doing at the second stage, a man arrived in his own cabriolet from Paris, and being an Englishman, spoke to us in that language. He was of genteel appearance; had been in France about ten years; told us he lived at Chantilly, and would be glad to have us at his house to-night, which we agreed to. When we got to Chantilly, our carriage being badly broken, we had to get it repaired again. Our friend, the Englishman, whose name is Christopher Potter, sent a young man for us, and received us with great frankness; he is a man of ability, and having a genius for manufactures, has succeeded admirably; says he gives bread to about six hundred people in his different establishments; lives on part of the estate once belonging to the prince of Condé; his wife and children continuing in England.

"21st. Having breakfasted at Potter's, he took us to view the former seat of the prince, which for magnificence and extent, exceeds anything we have seen in Europe, belonging to a subject, though at present its grandeur is defaced: the mansion-house, stables, green-houses and other buildings, are in their extent and style, such as I have no talent for describing; the gardens, fish-ponds, canals, cascades and fountains, are said to have been, when in their best condition, preferable to anything in Europe. These ruined palaces, once replete and surrounded with all that could please and gratify the voluptuous inclinations of their inhabitants, are some of the most striking monuments the world can exhibit, of the instability and vanity of all earthly enjoyments, and bring with them, to a wise, reflecting mind, an antidote against setting our hearts on any terrestrial thing; and cast a melancholy shade over all human glory.—Lord, teach us to aspire with increasing ardor, after that glory which is celestial and eternal, and those mansions of immutable felicity, which thou hast prepared in the riches of thy mercy, for all those who love thee and keep thy commandments. The prince and his family, who, it is said, had above one thousand people who wore their livery, are now wandering emigrants in foreign parts. Potter is a very extraordinary person, as a man of this world, and no doubt of great use in employing the poor in his neighborhood; yet one thing is lacking, worth a thousand times more than all he can otherwise acquire; a desire more ardent after the peace of God, which passeth all understanding, and those riches which will never perish. We felt a desire to have a meeting among his people; he said, he hoped the time might come, when he should forward such a proposal with pleasure, but as they were a body of English people, and were watched over with rather a jealous eye, the object of the meeting might be misconstrued by evil-minded persons, and bring them into suffering. He returned with us to our inn, and we distributed nearly all our books among his people. We parted from them in kindness, and he pressed us to direct any of our friends who came that way, to call on him, and he should always be glad to see them.

"22d. Passed on to Doulen. The sheep here are kept pretty much under care of the shepherds' dogs, whose sagacity and attention is admirable. There are very few hedges in France, and no fences except a few of stone, where there are intervals of pasture on the sides of the road; the dogs let the sheep feed along the borders of the grain, continually watching them at all quarters; and if one or more transgress the bounds, they immediately bring them to order. The shepherds have so much confidence in them, that they sit down on the side of a bank and work at making baskets, or some other employment, leaving the management of the flock very much to their faithful subordinate keepers.

"24th. Having passed through several towns and some fine country, we arrived at Dunkirk in the afternoon.

"25th. Felt refreshed after a laborious journey. We find, by computation, that we have rode fourteen hundred miles in France; about fifty of which was over the same road twice, so that we have had an opportunity of seeing and feeling the state of the people in a religious sense and otherwise, and my judgment is, that the French are an open-hearted, unsuspicious people; we passed through them without any material interruption, such as we frequently met with in Germany, as searching our baggage, inquiring our names, characters, and business, &c. They are generally civil and polite; the country pleasant, and in many places fertile, abounding in corn, wine, and oil. Though not remarkable for pasturage and cattle, yet the air is pure and serene, the waters good, the necessaries and even luxuries of life plenty; yet strangers travel at a great expense. Their post-horses in general are better than I expected, and they have a great number of asses and fine mules: many of the public-houses are good, perhaps in size and convenience nowhere excelled; the beds good and clean, and the provisions generally excellent, but their bills are enormous. Travellers, if they use economy, and are in their own carriage, cannot be accommodated for much less, for three persons, than four guineas a day. As to their religious character, I am at a loss to describe it; no doubt there are many in the higher ranks of life who are Deists; but the great mass of the people, though at present turned out of their old channel, remain attached and riveted to the religion of their education, yet the superstition and extravagance of *that* has received so great a shock, that it is scarcely probable it will ever rise again to the same degree of influence as formerly. There are many pious persons mourning in secret, and desirous of seeing the depraved manners of the people reformed; and I dare not entertain a doubt but He who rules in heaven and in the kingdoms of men, will have a people gathered both from the superstitions and vanities, that have heretofore abounded, who will be a special and spiritual heritage unto himself—may He cut short his work in righteousness and hasten that day! For my own part, weak, feeble, and unworthy as I feel of any employment in His holy hand, I see but little or nothing, towards the promotion of this great work, that has been answered by my being among them; yet, as I came here under a simple apprehension of duty, not to seek mine own things, but the things which belong to Jesus Christ and his kingdom; after all my weak moments, and divers things in the course of this deeply exercising journey, which had better have been omitted, or might have been better performed, I submit all into the hands of my tender and merciful Father, and ask nothing more than that he will spare me from being followed by the arrows of condemnation, and grant me such a portion of peace and assurance in Him, as in the riches of his love, he may see meet, for in my best estate, I am unworthy of the least of all his mercies, and a poor, helpless, unprofitable servant.

"26th. To be obliged to stay here much longer feels unpleasant, but no way yet offers to get to England, the channel of communication being stopped, and we shall have need of patience. Accounts arrived of the preliminaries of peace having been signed, and great rejoicings and an illumination took place, but no insult was offered to our friends, which is very different from England and America, to their great reproach. Friends enjoy more freedom in France than in either of those countries.

"27th. The people are still in a state of rejoicing, full of tumult and confusion; but it appears to me that instead of this vain show, it is matter of reverent thankfulness and secret gladness of heart, to the merciful Author of every good work, that he appears to be disposing the Powers who have stained the earth with so much human blood, to stay their hands. But oh! how can they recompense the thousands of unhappy widows and orphans who are mourning in secret places, their irretrievable loss all over the nations where we have travelled. Oh! when will men be wise — when will they suffer the peaceable kingdom of the Redeemer whom they profess to adore to come on earth as it is in heaven.— How have the great of this world always resisted the coming of that glorious day, for which they pretend to intercede in their prayers!

"First-day, 30th. Had meetings morning and evening; at the latter, through the condescension of the good Shepherd of the sheep, it was a time of refreshment and comfort, I believe, to both the laborers and the auditory: for my own part, having felt for a number of days like a dry and withered branch, I was rejoiced to feel again the circulation of that life and virtue, by which alone all the branches of Christ, the true vine, are nourished and supported to bring forth fruit to his praise. The Truth as it is in Jesus, appeared to rise into dominion—the erroneous and destructive opinions of Deism, which are subtilely making their way into many minds, who will be robbed and spoiled, whether they be of our Society or others that indulge it, of the most inestimable jewel, the most powerful consolation to the soul, both in life and death, that ever a Being, infinite in mercy and boundless in his compassion, conferred on mankind. Oh! that He may protect and preserve our Society from drinking in this deadly poison to the soul — that the watchmen on the walls may be enabled faithfully to sound an alarm to the careless, to whom it may be offered as a gilded bait, and the poor wounded receivers of it, be left to lament their folly in that day when its fatal consequences will be forever irretrievable.

"Fifth month, 1st. This day is foolishly observed in France, and spent in a riotous manner; troops of young women and girls were in different places, dancing under garlands hung in the streets. Feeling no call of duty resting upon my mind, to detain me in this place, the time passes very heavily.

"First-day, 7th. The meeting this morning was attended by about twenty persons, and I hope it was profitable. In the evening about fifty attended, mostly very respectable-looking people, who behaved well, and the opportunity ended in solemn supplication to the Father of mercies. We were refreshed; our hopes of his continued care over us, revived; and we humbly trust it was an edifying season to most present: may the praise of all be rendered unto the Fountain of every blessing, to whom alone it is due.

"9th. The markets here are supplied with plenty of vegetables — sound, good apples, at this season of the year, are sold three for less than a cent; eggs, twelve sous for a quarter of a hundred; butter, about twelve cents a pound; very good beef and veal, about eight cents a pound. As we cannot leave here without our passes but by some deception, which we cannot practise, though many others make use of this means, we have to bear our detention with patience, desiring that after laboring and travelling so much for the promotion of Truth, we may do nothing on leaving the continent, that will bring it into reproach—the eyes of the people being upon us. Oh! that we may be preserved wise and harmless. A proposal being made for our accepting a mode of passing under a deceptive cover, we dare not receive it. May we be kept wise and patient, so that no blemish may be brought upon our holy profession; the snares that are laid for our feet are many, and some very plausible.

"13th. Having endeavored to keep a conscience void of offence, I feel my mind free from condemnation; though I am weak, poor, and liable to err, and may not in some instances have kept in the straight path of duty, yet the Lord speaks peace to my soul."

After waiting in this place, from the 24th of Fourth month, to this day, the mayor and municipality granted them passports.

"First-day, 14th of Fifth month, 1797. The meeting this morning was a solid favored time; the people took leave of us affectionately, and we embarked in the afternoon.

"15th. Being on the English coast, a thick fog obscured the land, and it was thought we might get ashore, and proceed to London by land, without being asked any questions, but we were determined not to be smuggled into England; and having travelled so far without wounding our testimony, we hoped to continue so to the end. A fishing-boat coming alongside, we agreed with them for four guineas, to take us to Dover, about five leagues; there being a penalty upon any captain that lands passengers from an enemy's country, at any port except Dover, Southampton, Gravesend and two others; but being detained by the fog, we concluded to give them three guineas to land us at Margate. When we got to the place, some young Friends came down and wanted us to land, but the officer of the port coming and inquiring whence we came, we honestly told him, from Dunkirk; he said it was not in his power to suffer us to land, and that the fisherman was liable to a fine of two hundred pounds for bringing us, but as we had not landed, the penalty could not be exacted. The officer seemed disposed to be kind, and if we could have assumed the character of alien merchants, we might have had the privilege, but we could not make use of such a plea. Several Friends came, and appeared to regret our not being suffered to come ashore; we however thought it best to push off, and accordingly anchored a quarter of a mile distant. Here several Friends came to us in a boat, and thought no one would molest us if we landed, but we chose to proceed up the Thames to Gravesend; the Friends were very kind, and went on shore and brought us some acceptable refreshments.

"16th. Having got up to Gravesend, the officers came on board, and after making a search, permitted us to land. We went on board a packet-boat for London; there were several respectable people in the vessel, but also some sailors and wicked women, who soon began to be troublesome. An old man checked them for their discourse, at which one of the women pertly said, she hoped we had no Quakers on board. I told her, I had the honor to be a Quaker, and David Sands united in the same acknowledgment: after some time, the passengers mostly collecting in a large room below deck, these women came down also, and David Sands began to speak to them; the people behaved soberly, and the two women became much broken. A young man, a Baptist, seconded him in a feeling manner; and I made some addition. One of the women in particular was bathed in tears, and I cannot but hope it may produce some good effect. When we landed, I went to seek for a coach, and was met by two of my dear friends, making ready to meet us. In London, we met with our dear friend, George Dillwyn, he having got here about eight weeks past.

"17th. I attended week-day meeting, at Gracechurch street, and was permitted to pass it in silence, in thankful remembrance of the Lord's mercies, and secretly to praise his great and worthy name.

"First-day, 21st. Was at the Park-meeting, and in the evening, at Westminster.

"28th. Deborah Darby, Rebecca Young and myself, appointed a meeting at Wandsworth in the evening, which was large, and proved, through renewed mercy, a favored time.

"Sixth month, 1st. The public-meeting began to collect in the women's meeting-house, but Friends apprehending it would not hold the people, the men's house was opened, and it was supposed twelve hundred people assembled in it, and through Divine condescension, was a time of renewed encouragement. Deborah

Darby, Mary Dudley, Samuel Alexander and myself, were engaged in the ministry.

"Sixth month, 6th. We appointed a meeting at Deptford, for this evening, and as the meeting-house was too small, it was held in a part of a maltster's buildings and yard; it was very large, and dear Deborah Darby was singularly favored: we left the people with much sweetness, many of them soliciting another opportunity.

"9th. Had an appointed public-meeting this evening, at Tottenham, in which we were permitted again to rejoice in the Lord, our helper. At the house of a Friend, I found three books said to be sermons preached by me last year; and on looking over them, observed they were full of errors, both in language and doctrine, with which I was greatly exercised, and visited the man who had undertaken to publish them. I found he was a poor shoemaker, who had got some knowledge of short-hand, but was very illiterate, and if he had taken them down correctly, could hardly put them into common sense; the erroneous language and doctrines were such as I never uttered, nor even conceived; and there were, also, many gross absurdities.

"First-day, sixth month, 11th. At six o'clock in the evening, under as much discouragement as ever I remember, attended a meeting appointed for other professors: it was large and crowded; through renewed mercy, I felt my mind much enlarged, and have never felt more sweet peace in my labor, since leaving home. Going out of the meeting-house, a Turk, who had been at a meeting before, waited for me, and said he felt his heart made better; that God was good to all nations, and that those who served him, were the same in Turkey as in England; he took my hands in both his, and pressed them to his breast affectionately. I now felt my mind relieved, and at liberty to leave London shortly.

"17th. Left London, and rode to Portsmouth, and thence proceeded in an open boat, to Newport, on the isle of Wight, and got a person to clean the meeting-house, formerly occupied by Friends.

"First-day, 18th. As we gave no notice of any meeting, the gathering in the morning was small; at the close of it, I felt strength to appoint a public meeting, at six o'clock this evening; which was crowded, and I hope satisfactory; the people behaved becomingly, and appeared glad at our being there.

"19th. The town is full of soldiers, and the pious inhabitants lament the great change taking place, from the simplicity and innocent manners which formerly distinguished the people, to more luxury, dress and licentious conduct. I went to the meeting at six o'clock this evening, though much oppressed with a cold and hoarseness; the house was soon crowded, and the people being still, I was enabled to extend my voice sufficiently to be heard; and Friends thought it a profitable time, for which favor the Lord alone be thanked.

"20th. Went three miles to have a meeting at a farm-house; the man of the house, being necessarily from home, his wife had notified the few scattering neighbors, and about thirty simple-hearted, honest people came, and I thought it was a time of as much love and favor, as I had experienced in England. The young man, the master of the house, arrived just at the breaking up of the meeting, and expressed his sorrow at not being at it.

"21st. A Methodist minister, at the close of their meeting, had given notice of our meeting to be held this evening, at the house of some pious people of the Methodist connection: the woman of the house seemed to be universally esteemed, she held meetings in their cottage and frequently preached to the people. More persons came to our meeting, than the house would hold; and it was owned by our gracious Head and High Priest — the language of encouragement flowed freely to an honest, simple-hearted people, such as I have rarely met with. This woman preaching with such general acceptance, seems to be an advance towards Friends, both in her and others, who approve of her ministry, which is uncommon among people of other societies. I felt easy to appoint a meeting a few miles off, for to-morrow evening. The bishop of Winchester came here to confirm the people of their church, who had not undergone that ceremony: it was said, he had not been to visit this part of his flock for fourteen years. None under the age of fourteen, were admitted, and not then, without a certificate granted by their pastor, certifying that the party had undergone an examination and was approved by him, for confirmation; but it appeared that some had not even seen him on the occasion, and had only sent for their tickets. Our landlady's daughter was much affected when she understood the weakness and absurdity that appeared in this pretence of religion; having never been examined, and knowing little of their confession of faith, she went heavily to the chapel. Some of the clergy have brought themselves into contempt, not only here, but in many parts of the kingdom, by their irregular lives; and my mind was affected on account of the young people who were training up in such formality, and under such miserable shepherds.

"22d. This afternoon, I went to the place where the meeting was to be held in a Methodist meeting-house; which, though it rained much, was filled; the people conducted to our satisfaction, many were humbled into tears, and we parted with their desires for another. May the Lord be praised for his goodness, and we humbled in the dust, for no good thing dwelleth with us, except it be given of God.

"First-day, 25th. The meeting this morning was very large, and remarkably solid and favored; great part of the audience much humbled, and in tears; for which I felt thankful to the Author of all our mercies, to whom alone all praise is due. Feeling comfortably relieved, and at liberty, I took an affectionate leave of them. Had a parting, sitting with the family, who had shown us great kindness, and went to Cowes. The minister, of the dissenting congregation offering his meeting-house, we had a very crowded gathering at six o'clock in the evening; he standing at the door all the time, directing the people to seats, and keeping order. The people were light and gay, and the labor was hard, but towards the close great solemnity appeared, and it ended to much satisfaction, the people acknowledging the truth of what was delivered; and the minister also said, he should pray for me, that the Lord might continue to strengthen me for the work. Several who had attended our meetings accompanied us to the water-edge, and parted in great brokenness, especially our kind hostess. We left, through mercy, an open door for any who may hereafter be sent to this island, where there is a considerable number, almost, if not altogether, convinced of the doctrines of Friends. I had nine meetings among them, and they were made very near to me. We were rowed in an open boat over to Southampton, about thirteen miles, and it was about eleven o'clock at night when we got on shore.

"27th. Appointed a public meeting at Ringwood, for this evening, which was large and satisfactory.

"Seventh month, 1st. Have had satisfactory meetings at Pool, Lymington, and Wareham; went to Weymouth, and thence by the packet, to Guernsey, and had a very trying passage.

"4th. Had an appointed meeting this evening, in the upper part of a spacious store; a large number attended, and through the kindness of our heavenly Shepherd, it was solid; the people expressing their satisfaction, and as we went to our lodgings several inquired of us when there would be another meeting.

"6th. Took passage for the island of Jersey; the wind was so high that we could not make a landing where we intended, but were driven many miles, and there being two ships of war near, they obliged our captain to come on board. The wind continued very boisterous, and the shore all round was rocky. While the captain was absent, our vessel dragged her anchor, and our people became much alarmed, as we must have been driven by the violence of the wind on to the French coast, if we were not permitted to go into harbor, which the captain of the man-of-war gave us liberty to do, but required us to stay on board for the orders of the prince, before we landed. These delays, and the serious danger we were in, were very trying, having taken no refreshment all day. After much toil and difficulty, the wind blowing directly towards the coast of France, we anchored within two hundred yards of land; our letters and my passport were sent on shore to the prince, and after considerable detention, we were permitted to land, and sent under guard five miles to the principal town, St. Helier, where we arrived about eight o'clock in the evening, very weary, and almost sick, for want of proper refreshment. Being taken before several officers and examined, we were told that this island was so circumstanced, that it would be very improper to preach against war at present; the last officer manifested a kind disposition towards us, and we were dismissed. The inn being taken up with guests, chiefly officers, I was taken to the house of two middle-aged women, between eleven and twelve o'clock at night. Looking back on the fatigues and dangers of the day, my soul was made afresh, thankful for the continued mercies of my heavenly Father, and deeply sensible of my own unworthiness to be thus cared for and preserved from one place to another, in a strange land.

"7th. The two women Friends who thus provided me with accommodation, appear to be pious persons; and though separated from the benefits of religious society, they with their niece sit down together on First and other days, in silence, for the performance of Divine worship; they are esteemed by the people as Friends, and well spoken of. They gave me an account of the manner in which Claude Gay, who formerly lived here, was treated by the people, and at length banished the island; whereupon he went and laid his situation before the king, who ordered his officers to receive him again and to treat Friends in a different manner. The father of these Friends had been deceased now for a number of years, and they remained the only professors with us on the island — there were a number of Methodists, but as they could not join in their meetings, they sat down alone. At about eleven o'clock, we sat with them, and after a time of silence and much solemnity, I felt some encouragement to them, and the baptizing power of Truth uniting us, it was a season, I hope, of much comfort to us all. In the evening, they collected a few religious people in the house, and we had a satisfactory meeting. An elderly woman, who speaks at times among the Methodists, said she thought Friends ought not to go from this island so quickly as they had done, none having staid more than two days, and hoped we would stay longer, and she believed the Lord would bless our coming. The Methodists thought we might hold our meetings to-morrow, at a time when those of other societies were not collected, supposing we should have many more persons. This at first appeared plausible, but upon weighing it, I was most easy to propose two meetings; one at ten, and the other at six o'clock. Our friends, with the man of the house, went to seek a proper place, and a suitable room presenting, it was hired for the purpose. Some of our Methodist acquaintances thought we had better publish our meeting through the town, by a public crier, or get hand-bills printed and distributed, to inform the people, neither of which I could be easy to do, but let the notice spread as it might, without taking much pains about it. The place being filled with soldiery and appearances of war, made me feel very low in my mind, with a discouraging prospect of having meetings with them. I feel very much at times for Friends who accompany ministers in these exercising labors among other professors, being well convinced it is often a mortifying business to go from house to house, with invitations to our meetings, and am therefore inclined to lighten their burdens whenever I can, and at this time feel thankful for the company of my kind and suitable companions here.

"First-day, Seventh month 9th. The meeting at ten o'clock, was attended by about two hundred people, and the heavenly Shepherd condescending to grant us his presence, in which only there is life, we had a solid, open, satisfactory meeting in the ball-room, and appointed another to be at six in the evening. Retired to my chamber: it seems to me improper, before these large public-meetings, to continue in company and conversation until they come on — my place at least, appears to be to retire and endeavor to have my mind gathered to the Divine Fountain, where strength and qualification to hold them to the honor of Truth, can alone be found; and after all, I think I always have entered them with fear and trembling, lest the blessed cause should by any means suffer. At six in the evening, many people collected and thronged the house; a rude drunken man coming in, tended to unsettle the meeting; many showed great displeasure at his conduct, and though he was a man of property, the soldiers present attempted to turn him out; all which with the continual thronging of the people, and the room being exceedingly warm, made it trying to us, and the more sober part of the company. My friends and some of the respectable inhabitants, spoke to the people to bring about some order. I stood up, and for a time hoped that stillness might have come over us, but the heat and throng were so great, that I found it best to tell them, I did not conceive the meeting could be held so as to answer my concern, and wished them quietly to withdraw; which but few seemed inclined to do, and said it was very hard they should be deprived of the meeting, by the restless behavior of a few; — however, it still appearing best to Friends, we passed through the crowd, and the rest followed.

We went to the house of our women Friends, where about twenty or thirty serious people following us, we were favored with a precious religious opportunity. One thing which probably added to the unsettlement in the large gathering was, that many of the people did not understand what was said in English, to induce them to more quiet.

"10th. Went to St. Owen's bay, about eight miles from St. Helier, and had a meeting with the people; a large collection of whom attended, but scarcely any understood English; much quiet prevailing, and what I said being interpreted, it was a solid, comfortable meeting, the people being as remarkable for their simple rural manners, as in any place I have been at. Had religious conversation afterwards with a number, gave them some books, and parted in much tenderness. Appointed another meeting in the evening at St. Aubins. A sergeant in one of the regiments sat with us and had some serious conversation; he appeared to be a religious minded man, weary of his situation as a soldier, and said there were a number of religious men in that regiment, and in another then on the island: his situation excited our sympathy. An elderly woman, whose two daughters had been at the meeting at St. Helier, desiring to see us, we went to the house; she said she was grand-daughter to Mary Dyer, who was put to death at Boston, and that there were several other of her descendants on the island. The meeting was not large; for a time it felt very heavy, but at length it proved through renewed mercy, a strengthening time to a number present. After meeting, a pious man, who sometimes exhorts among the Methodists, came and took me in his arms, and was very tender; he was soon to leave the Island, being banished for twelve months for refusing to bear arms, and would have to leave a wife and two children behind, who kept a little shop for their maintenance, which occasioned us to feel much sympathy for him.

"Returned to St. Helier, and on the 11th had a meeting at the Assembly-room, which, through mercy, was satisfactory; but my mind not being yet relieved, I appointed another to be at six o'clock in the evening, which was large, and several of the officers of the regiment came in, one of whom did not seem inclined to behave well, nor to suffer others to be so; but after some time, being more quiet, I was, through Divine assistance, favored to relieve my mind, and take an affectionate leave of the people. Our elderly women Friends, who have so kindly accommodated us, feel their lonely situation as Friends, on this island; but have been mercifully preserved and helped.

"13th. Returned to Guernsey, and attended a meeting there in the evening, which ended to satisfaction; but my mind was not relieved without having a more general public meeting.

"First-day, 16th. The meeting, this forenoon, was to good satisfaction; and in the afternoon, went to one appointed at a place called the Forest; where about one hundred and fifty people attended, and through

Divine help, it was an open time; many of those present were Methodists, and were tender and respectful.

"17th. Having obtained from the trustees and the principal members of the Episcopal place of worship, called Bethel, the liberty of holding a meeting in it this evening, notice was accordingly given; but about the time appointed, the parson sent for the key: the Friend who had it would not give it up. He then met the Friend on the way to the house, and insisted upon our declining holding the meeting, which we were not disposed to do, neither would his own people consent to it, saying, he was only their servant whom they paid, and they would do what they pleased with the house. He then went off, and we entered the house, which was soon filled; many of the audience being the principal people of the island. After some time, they became still, and though it did not appear to be as much favored as some meetings, yet I was helped to open several important doctrines, and passages of Holy Scripture readily and pertinently presented for their support. My mind became relieved, and I hope the cause of Truth lost nothing; the people parted with us respectfully, not at all pleased with the attempt of the parson to prevent the meeting. One of the principal contributors was much displeased with his conduct, and said the doctrine he had heard was true and very liberal.

"18th. A number of the people desired to know when we would have another meeting, but we not inclining to stir up contention between them and their minister, did not think it proper to hold any more in that house. In the afternoon, I went out about five miles, and had a meeting at the house of a person who is a member with the Methodists; at which about eighty of his neighbors attended — an honest, simple-hearted people; it was thought by Friends to be as favored as any we had in Guernsey, for which I was thankful; all praise is due to the heavenly Shepherd. In the evening the meeting-house was full, and it proved, through mercy, a solid, relieving time to my mind; the people took leave of us in much affection. The captain of the packet telling us we must be on board by ten o'clock: on full consideration, I felt now quite easy, and concluded to go — had some disagreeable company on board.

"20th. A French vessel bearing down upon us, our captain hoisted more sail, and getting on faster than the other, though she was within three quarters of a mile of us, we providentially escaped going to France, and arrived at Weymouth in the afternoon. Went to Bristol; and on First-day, the 23d, attended their meeting in the morning, and appointed one for other professors in the evening. The meeting-house is said to contain fourteen hundred persons, but it was not sufficient for the people that came. I was, through renewed mercy, favored to relieve my mind, and we separated in a tender frame.

"26th. Got to Ackworth; attended the meeting with the children, which, through Divine condescension, proved a solid, satisfactory season. At the close,

I believed it right to appoint a meeting at six o'clock the next evening for the neighbors.

"27th. The meeting was large and solid; to the Lord be the praise and glory of his own works.

"29th. At York; visited several places, and went to the castle where seven Friends are confined for their religious testimony against tithes. The buildings are airy and handsome; those Friends have a large room to themselves in the day-time, where they employ their time in handicraft labor. In a religious opportunity with them, the good Master favored with his presence; they were much tendered, and we parted affectionately. The poor curate, who belonged to the parish they mostly came from, about ten days past came to York to enter a complaint to the archbishop, against the priest who put Friends into prison, because he would not pay him for preaching; he made three visits to those imprisoned Friends, and they said he was more affected at seeing them than any who had visited their apartment since they were confined. The curates, who do the drudgery for the priests for about thirty or forty pounds a-year, in many parts of England, are badly paid by their profligate superiors.

"First-day, 30th. At Ackworth; and notice having been given to the neighbors not professing with us, the meeting was large, and, through the continued mercy of our heavenly Father, was a very contriting season, remarkably so to the dear children. A meeting being appointed at Leeds, for six o'clock in the evening, the house was well filled, and I hope it was a profitable season.

"Eighth month, 2d. Got to Liverpool, and on the 3d appointed a public-meeting for to-morrow evening.

"4th. The meeting was large and satisfactory. Had a meeting at Warrington in the evening of the 6th, which was crowded, and Friends thought Truth rose over all, though to myself it felt more laborious than any I had attended for some time.

"7th. Friends proposed that another might be held this evening, as many of the people were desirous of it, but after weighing the matter, I was most easy to return to Liverpool.

"First-day, 13th. Meeting in the morning at Chester, with the few Friends who live there, and about sixty others; it was a time of much brokenness, and another was appointed for the evening, which was large, and held to good satisfaction; the people expressing their approbation of the doctrines they heard. This city has many marks of great antiquity, and is built on a plan different from any other I have ever seen.—Went back to Liverpool, satisfied with my visit to Chester.

"15th. Was at the Monthly Meeting of Hardshaw, and a number of the neighbors coming in, it was large; my mind more than at any other time in England was exercised for our own professors, and through renewed mercy, I was favored to relieve it to my comfort.

"16th. Was at a marriage; many other professors attended the meeting, and some of considerable note;

one who had written much, and was intimate with the prime minister, Pitt, said after meeting, he did not know how it would be taken by Friends, but he could scarcely refrain from standing up, and enforcing by his testimony, to those of his own profession present, the excellent and charitable doctrines they had heard.

"First-day, 20th of Eighth month. The meeting appointed for this evening was large, several ministers of different congregations attending; my gracious heavenly Helper did not forsake me, and I was favored to relieve my mind and feel more clear of Liverpool than ever before; many came up after meeting, expressing desires for my preservation by sea and by land. My daily feeling of incapacity for any good word or work of myself, through the power of Divine grace, keeps me from any exaltation of spirit: may the Lord be with me and keep me to the end from dishonoring the Truth.

"24th. Having waited a considerable time for a favorable wind, for the packet to go to the Isle of Man —while we were at the week-day meeting, a messenger came and informed us the vessel was about sailing; I therefore took leave of Friends in a few words, and went on board.

"25th. Landed on the island: there being a large shed on the shore, and several people offering their assistance, some of our friends went with a joiner, to fit it up for a meeting on First-day, the 27th. We held a meeting there in the forenoon, attended as was supposed, by about five hundred persons, among whom were several of the most respectable inhabitants; the people behaved well, and the opportunity was to much satisfaction. Appointed another for the evening, and notwithstanding it rained much, the place was filled; it was thought there were about six or seven hundred: this was also a satisfactory time, and ended in prayer. Apprehending I was not yet quite clear, appointed another for to-morrow evening; but after coming out, some of the town's people thought that ten o'clock in the morning would be better; I submitted to their judgment, and they made it known. The next day we went to the meeting-place, but the people being confused about the time, only about one hundred came; it proved, however, through Divine goodness, a refreshing time, both to us and the people. Another was appointed for five o'clock in the evening. While at dinner, a respectable man of the island, brought me a letter from Alexander Shaw, lieutenant-governor, under the duke of Athol, inviting me and my friends to Castletown, where he resided; and offering the use of his chariot and servant while we staid on the island, they being now in Douglas (the town): we accordingly accepted his offer. The inhabitants showed us great respect, and the poor fishermen regretted they could not be at the meeting, as they fish all night, and put out to sea early in the afternoon. Nearly one hundred boats sailed out of this port, and they said the others belonging to the island, which were between four and five hundred in all, would meet them at the fishing-place, for they always fished together, under the direction of an admiral or commander, and had strict rules to prevent one having greater advantages than another. When they were drawn out a little way from the pier into the sea, they all took off their hats and said a short prayer: considering their occupation, they generally appear to be sober, considerate men. In the evening, the meeting assembled; most of the respectable inhabitants came, and in the whole, six or seven hundred; it was the most solid and satisfactory of any we have had here, for which I was truly thankful to the Father of mercies. An officer, who sat by me, kneeled down with me at the time of prayer, and seemed much affected, as was also Major Wallop, brother of the earl of Portsmouth, who had sat by me in every meeting. The people were tender, and hoped we would have more meetings before we left the island. A serious soldier followed me in the street, and expressed with much tenderness, his satisfaction, and told me it was a great grievance to him and several of his comrades, that their captain drew them out on parade, on First-day mornings, and hindered them from attending public worship as they desired. Next day, left Douglas — conveyed to Castletown in the governor's carriage; he was walking on the parade, and invited us to dine with him at three o'clock. We took up our lodgings at the hotel, and in the afternoon went to the governor's, and several of his acquaintance being present, we dined with them in the castle. The room we sat in, had walls nine feet thick, and was a very ancient fabric; the governor and his wife treated us with great friendship, and on our mentioning the desire of having a meeting to-morrow, he proposed twelve o'clock.

"Eighth month, 30th. Held our meeting in the ball-room, which was very much crowded. The governor and family, and most of the principal people of Castletown attended; it was to good satisfaction, and at the close I signified my intention of another at six o'clock in the evening. The governor stood up and told the audience that the church would be opened for the purpose, as it was evident no other place would contain the people; he also sent his servant round the town to give notice. Castletown may contain three or four hundred houses. In the evening, the assembly gathered in the place mentioned, and was supposed to be seven hundred. I felt low and poor at entering it; the people's expectations seemed raised, which always depresses me. I was, however, made truly thankful to the Author of mercies, who condescended to cover the assembly with his presence, and it ended in prayer and praises to him, our heavenly Father. The governor, and a man of high rank in the island, going with us to our lodgings, I showed them my certificate, which they seemed pleased with, and expressed unity with me, &c.

"31st. Took the governor's carriage and servant, and arrived at Peel, another considerable town of about four hundred houses; the majority of the people fishermen. We delivered the governor's letter to the high bailiff, who said he would exert himself to forward our views, and offered a school-house or the guard-house, for a meeting.

"Ninth month, 1st. At meeting in the guard-room, the soldiers having seated it with planks. The high bailiff, and several others who had interested themselves for us, attended. After I had been on my feet about half an hour, the people crowded the house and round it so, those without striving to get in, and it raining, that I perceived it would not do to continue the meeting. The high bailiff remonstrated with them, and I sat down a few minutes, but the throng was too great to hold the meeting through, in that solemnity which had at first attended; not that the people were inclined to be rude, but quite otherwise; yet so many being anxious to get in and hear, kept the meeting in an uneasy state; so after sitting a short time, we broke up, the people regretting it. We told them if we could have a more convenient place, we inclined to hold another meeting at five o'clock, and left it to them to provide for us. In about a quarter of an hour, a person came to tell us that the Methodists would be obliged to us if we would accept their meeting-house, which we accordingly did. It was near the sea-side, and the weather very stormy with hard rain, yet as many came as filled the house, being about five hundred; and a good meeting it was: thanks be to Him, who is ever worthy. After the meeting was over, the fishermen who had been out to sea, finding the storm increasing, were returning into harbor, but through the violence of the tempest, several of their boats were dashed to pieces on the rocks, but no lives lost. This disaster, added to their continued disappointment of catching fish this season, made the people seem much distressed. Having a sum of money from a benevolent Friend for the poor, I distributed some of it among them, for which they were thankful; they generally appear to be a very civil, quiet people, and religious in their way, live poor, and are now much discouraged.

"Ninth month, 2d. Proceeded to Ramsey, eighteen miles from Peel. This island being exposed to high winds from the sea, trees do not thrive in it, yet in some spots they do better. A person who had lived in Philadelphia came to see us, and also the curate, who kindly offered us a large school-house for a meeting, which we accepted; — the judge, and high bailiff, also offered their service.

"First-day, 3d of Ninth month. At meeting this morning, two priests and the curate attended; the house held about three hundred, but it was thought many more were crowded into it, and many others could not get in; it was a satisfactory season, and another was appointed at five o'clock this evening, in the same place; the garden was also opened, and many stood there: it was estimated that, inside and out, there were more than five hundred persons; a great number for so small a town. It felt to me as much owned, and as great solemnity prevailed, as at any we had on the island, and concluded with much brokenness among the people; thanks be to Him that is forever worthy, and nothing to us but abasement. The people pressed for another meeting to-morrow, and the judge thought if I would submit to have another, as many as could afford it, would be there, and inclined to make a very handsome collection, and as he knew I would not receive it, he was sure it would be a gratification to me, to see it distributed among the poor who were distressed by the failure of the fishery. I assured him I could never admit of anything of that kind, but was willing to subscribe myself to their necessities, out of meeting; he heard my reasons and was satisfied. Went on second-day to Kirkmichael, and found that a meeting would be agreeable, but the landlord undertaking to give notice, and making it to be in the afternoon, and we having fixed to be at Peel, at a meeting at five o'clock, we could not stay their time, at which some of the people were sorry and blamed him: I left the place rather heavy at the disappointment. Had a meeting at Peel at the time mentioned; the house was filled, and it proved a solid, relieving time: thanks to the Author of all good.

"Ninth month, 5th. Went to Douglas, twelve miles; and it being a stormy evening, and the fishermen not disposed to go out, I appointed a meeting principally on their account. About three hundred of them attended, and many of the other inhabitants, and through mercy, it was a solid, favored opportunity: I was then easy to leave the island. We were informed the governor had expressed his sorrow that we should be at any expense on the island, saying it was a reproach to the Isle of Man, to let us be at expense, while we were engaged for the people's good. Major Wallop came and took a kind leave of us; and all things being ready for leaving in the morning, I wrote a letter to the governor in acknowledgment of his kindness, and retired to rest under a thankful sense of the manifold mercies of my heavenly Father, who had condescended to conduct me peacefully through my concern for this island; which, and all his kindness to me, ought ever to be remembered with gratitude. 'The Lord is good unto all; his mercies are over all his works—his works shall praise him, and all his saints shall bless him; they shall speak of the greatness of his power, they shall talk of his kingdom, for his kingdom is an everlasting kingdom, and his dominion throughout all generations.'

"Ninth month, 7th. Arrived at Whitehaven in the afternoon, and went to the widow Jane Pearson's, who took us in kindly; most of the ground on which the town stands, is on rent payable to lord Lonsdale.

"First-day, 10th. The meeting was large and to good satisfaction; the evening meeting was soon exceedingly crowded, and great numbers out of doors, supposed in the whole to be one thousand people; the house having small windows, was so warm and oppressive, that it was very trying and exhausted me much. I did not think it as open a time as in the morning, but it closed well; and I proposed another for to-morrow evening, not feeling easy to leave the place without it.

"11th. The meeting this evening, appeared to be solid from the first sitting down, and was, through renewed condescension, a precious relieving time to me: on retiring to bed and looking back upon the day, I felt as much sweet peace as I remember to have experienced for a long time past: thanks be to Him who is ever worthy. Some time back I had a desire to get home this autumn, but my prospect of Ireland and Scotland not admitting of it, I was now favored with a good degree of resignation to bear the disappointment.

"13th. Attended the week-day meeting at Swarthmore, one mile from Ulverstone, where the members of society chiefly reside; about forty Friends came to it, and perhaps twelve of other societies; and it was held in comfortable and refreshing silence. I mentioned my prospect of a meeting with the inhabitants at five o'clock in the evening, and a Methodist minister who was present, stood up and offered their meeting-house, which he thought would suit us better, as it was in the town: Friends acknowledged his kindness, but after he and the others were gone, they seemed to have some strait about it, and at length concluded that it should be at Swarthmore; thinking the people would come out, which I doubted, and had no scruple of accepting the offer. The meeting-house at Swarthmore, is now in good repair, and may hold when the chamber and back part is open, about five hundred persons; at the entrance next the moor, is a covered door-way of stone, with an inscription, signifying the time of its building, and G. F. at the end of it; there are also two large arm-chairs very heavily made, altogether of wood, and carved on the back; one was for George Fox, and the other for his wife, to sit in: there is also an ebony bedstead, which George Fox left for Friends who were travelling, to lodge on. The meeting-house stands high, and commands a beautiful prospect of the country and town of Ulverstone. Swarthmore Hall is a large pile of antique building, with an avenue into the yard, where Margaret Fox's carriage used to enter by a gateway of rough stone arched on the top. The house, as well as the farm, is at present the property of some person not a Friend, and rented: the rooms are large, particularly that where the meeting used to be held: it is paved with stone down stairs; up stairs, the wainscoting round the room is carved,* as well as the wood-work over the chimnies, with some representations of Scripture passages. Margaret Fox lies buried about a mile from thence, where Friends buried their dead at that time. We walked to town by the paved way on which the family used to walk, which is mostly shaded with trees. There are about twelve families of Friends, who keep up the meeting. Going over these grounds caused me to feel serious, but not superstitious. At Elijah Salthouse's, he showed me their ancient Monthly Meeting book in the days of George Fox, which was curious; and also an old folio bible printed in 1541, in old English text, with rough plates; it has a chain and small padlock to it, by which it was formerly chained to the wall in the meeting-house; it is in pretty good keeping for its age. The reason alleged for its being chained in the meeting-house is, that in that day, cavil-

* This ornamental work was no doubt performed in judge Fell's time.

lers at the doctrine delivered were sometimes present, and Friends referred to the text to satisfy them, and also to show to the world that the calumny thrown on Friends of rejecting the bible, was false. It was likewise made use of by poor Friends who came from a distance to meeting, and would be there before the time, who employed themselves in reading it; — a far more consistent and becoming employment than many now are in the practice of before meetings begin, such as conversing about news, trade, politics, &c. The weather being stormy, and the meeting so far from Ulverstone, only about two hundred attended; many of whom being religious people, it was held to satisfaction, yet I did not feel myself relieved.

"14th. The minister of the Independent congregation, sent to know if we inclined to accept of their house this evening, which he should cheerfully make ready for us if we thought proper. Believing I should not feel clear without his offer was accepted, we did so, and the meeting was large; the people conducted well, and through the condescension of our heavenly Father, it was a refreshing time to me, believing that Truth was much in dominion; and I retired to rest, easy to proceed in the morning.

"15th. Got to Kendall, to George Stewardson's; was much oppressed with a cold:—the weather so wet; they said there had not been a dry day for a month past, which had much injured the harvest, the wheat growing in the shock, and a great deal of hay being nearly rotten.

"First-day, 17th. The meeting was larger than any I have seen, except London and Bristol; and an appointed one this evening was very large and crowded; it was supposed there were fourteen hundred persons within doors, and many out; the Author of all good was mercifully pleased to be with us, and it concluded in thanksgiving.

"19th. Attended their week-day meeting, wherein I was silent: appointed one to be held at six o'clock this evening, for all who inclined to attend; which, though it rained very hard, was large, consisting of about one thousand people, who behaved becomingly. My cold and hoarseness made it trying to me to speak, yet it closed comfortably: the minister of a dissenting congregation was much affected, and took leave of me with expressions of unity, and prayers for my preservation and return to my friends in peace. A number of our female ministers are travelling in Scotland, and these northern parts of England; but no man Friend, except Thomas Scattergood and myself; David Sands is in Wales. What hath or doth hinder them, but the too great attachment to the pursuits of this world? O! what a pity, in such an abundant field of labor as this country affords! Lord, loosen our Society more and more, that they may be ready to enter the field thou art opening in Europe.

"21st. At Cockermouth, where there are about twenty families of Friends, who keep up the meeting. The wages of laboring people here are very low; men twenty-one pence per day, and find themselves; most of the people, men, women, and children, wear clogs, made of leather above, and wood and iron for the soles, which seems to be general in the north of England, except for such as are of considerable property.

"22d. Appointed a meeting for six o'clock this evening; a number of Friends came in from the country, among whom was John Hall, of Broughton, a minister; the meeting was large and satisfactory.

"First-day, 24th. Attended their forenoon meeting at Wigton, at which were Mary Watson and Mary Sterry; the former had good service. I did not think myself authorized to appear by way of ministry, as indeed I seldom do among Friends. The members of society in Cumberland and Westmoreland, appear to be a plain, honest people. Arrived at Carlisle in the evening, and a meeting being appointed at six o'clock, it was large; several of the clergy attended; and through the condescension of our heavenly Father, it was a solid, satisfactory time. Appointed another meeting for to-morrow evening. There are about thirty-two families of Friends here, and there may be fifteen thousand inhabitants in this city. Many Friends came in from the country to the meeting; and also some people of note in the town, and some of the clergy: the people were remarkably still, and the Lord favored us with a truly consolating meeting; my mind felt quite relieved, and I had an affectionate parting with many of the people.

"27th. Lodged at Hawick, forty-four miles from Carlisle. The laborers on their farms live generally in a cluster of twenty or thirty houses; are meanly accommodated in small mud cottages, with thatched roofs, almost like stables; the children, and most of the women, without shoes—turf is the common firing, and their bread of oatmeal. Arrived at Kelso a little past eleven o'clock, and finding that the widow Margaret Anderson and two daughters were gone to meeting, we went and sat down with them; they and one man, not an acknowledged member, composed the whole meeting; some others who are descendants of Friends join them on First-days. Their lonely situation affected me, and I could not but reflect on my dear native city and the meetings there, where there are so many to encourage and strengthen one another. Oh! what advantages do Friends in such places enjoy, and how thankful ought they to be! May the sight of many poor and solitary ones be remembered by me, if the Lord spare me to get home, and be a perpetual incitement to walk worthy of his manifold mercies. There was something solid and precious attended us, and we were glad we had sat with them. I proposed a meeting for the people of the place; but it being thought the notice would be too short for this evening, it was appointed for ten o'clock to-morrow forenoon. The lands being farmed out in large tracts, the poor can get none; and the farmers who employ them, feed them with skim, or as they call it, blue milk and oatmeal, made into crouder or hasty-pudding, potatoes, turnips, kale, &c., but very little meat. The river is well stored with salmon, but none are suffered to take them, but such as purchase that privilege of the Duke of Roxborough. Notwithstanding their plenty, they are six-pence sterling per pound, so the poor must taste them but seldom.

"29th. Very little notice being given, the meeting was small; at the close of which I appointed another at six o'clock in the evening. I felt much discouraged at having a meeting here; the minds of the people not appearing open towards Friends; but about two hundred attended. I thought Truth did not reign, and to me it was a low, and I feared a fruitless season; yet the people said they hoped we would stay over First-day; it was however still and quiet throughout.

"30th. Went on — passed through a large town called Dalkeith, and arrived at Edinburgh in the evening.

"First-day, Tenth month 1st. Friends have built a new meeting-house in a retired place, which will contain about five hundred persons. There are about twelve families of respectable Friends residing here; and we went to the meeting, in expectation of seeing our members alone; but the people came in until there were three hundred, who appeared becomingly, and it was on the whole to satisfaction. Appointed another meeting at six o'clock in the evening, at which about five hundred attended, among whom were many high professors, who behaved well; it was thought to be a favored meeting, and I left it peaceful and easy, and appointed another for Third-day evening. This city is said to contain one hundred thousand inhabitants, though it does not cover a great deal of ground. The houses are in general higher than in any city in Europe, from five to ten stories; the ground being very costly, it is almost covered with building, and scarcely any yards. In the new city, the houses are large, plain and substantial—they generally have stone stair-cases in one quarter of the building, which ascend to the top of the house; and frequently the several stories are occupied by different families, and have from four to eight chambers each: these families may be from six to eight or more in one house, mostly unacquainted with each other. The space between the joists and ceilings and floors, is filled with a composition of saw-dust, &c., which prevents the communication of sound, and the families are more conveniently accommodated than might be expected. At present there are no American students north of Virginia at the college. Our friends say, they do not desire to see Friends' children sent here from America, it being generally destructive of their morals and religious principles.

"Tenth month, 3d. The meeting this evening was large and comfortable; a number of men of science attended, and it closed in reverent thankfulness to the Author of all our mercies. Yesterday evening our friend Phœbe Speakman, with her companions Ann Crowley and J. Birkbeck, came in from their journey to the north.

"5th. At the week-day meeting this forenoon, about forty Friends and a few others attended. Phœbe Speakman had good service, to the comfort of all; her call seems altogether to our own members. At the close of the meeting, finding my mind not yet relieved, I proposed a public meeting at six o'clock. Our Friends here set a good example, by shutting up their shops while they go to meeting. The meeting in the evening was very large and crowded, many men of letters attending, and I entered it in fear and trembling for the precious cause, which is often my case. I think I can say, I seek not mine own honor, but above all, the exaltation of Truth and its testimony. The people behaved in a solid manner from the beginning, and it proved, through Divine condescension, a relieving meeting, and I took leave of the people with much tenderness. After meeting, some pious persons expressed themselves in an affectionate manner. I hope the kind expressions of some after meetings will only have a tendency to make me more humble and sensible that to me belongs nothing, but all to Him, whose is the kingdom, the power, and the glory, and all the praise of his own works for ever: our rejoicing is the testimony of our consciences, not the well-done of the people.

"7th. Rode to Leith, and took passage in a pinnace across the water to Kinghorn; then taking post-chaise, we passed through the town of Kircaldy and several lesser towns, and got to Dundee in the morning of the 8th. Two respectable men, Alexander Webster and William Smith, visited us, who appear to be convinced of our principles and very friendly. Some notice having been given, and a large hall well seated, we went to the meeting with expectation of seeing very few, as it was the time that all the different places of worship began, and the people are very exact in this country in attending their places of worship, and keeping the First-day religiously in their way. However, about four hundred came, mostly men, and after a few minutes, behaved well. It was thought to be a comfortable meeting, and I appointed another at six o'clock in the evening. Having at the meeting in the morning used some expressions, inviting such as were not satisfied with the doctrine, to call on me and express their minds, three respectable citizens of the place, but of Deistical principles, joined our friends in the street, professing a desire for an interview with me, which I thought had best be deferred until after our meeting in the evening. The convenience of the hall being enlarged by a different arrangement of the seats, and opening two rooms adjoining, the whole were so closely stowed that I had very little expectation we should be able to hold the meeting to satisfaction, and expressed my fears to the people. They endeavored, however, to be still, became very solid and attentive, and I saw scarcely any uneasiness. The meeting closed solemnly in prayer, after which it was some time before we could get the people to move, so that we could get through, and numbers followed us to the inn door. It was thought there were one thousand or more assembled; and it was said many hundreds went away who could not get in. The three men aforementioned came to the inn; we found them strong in their opinions;

one seemed to be what is termed a Fatalist, and thought that Judas could not have done anything but what he did, nor any man else from the beginning of the world. They appeared to be men of good education, and the points were argued with coolness, and they parted in a very friendly disposition. We don't know that much was gained; but we all concluded nothing was lost, as they were driven to their shifts, and willing to drop the argument, and said they wished there was a body of Friends settled at Dundee. I retired to rest, thankful for the merciful preservation and help through the day.

"9th. The town of Dundee stands on the river Tay, about eight miles from the sea; and as well as almost every village and town in England and Scotland, has many soldiers in it. Dined at our friend Alexander Webster's, who is under convincement; his wife, who continues with the Baptists, was pleased with our visit to Dundee, was very kind, and I hope preparing to be of one mind with her husband. Another meeting being appointed for this evening, the people hired a man, as they did yesterday, to preserve order and keep the rude boys out of the house. Although we went before six o'clock, the house was nearly full and became very crowded. I was led to speak plainly against the doctrine of Deism — the people behaved quietly and some were much tendered; and though I did not think Truth triumphed so much as last evening, yet it was a relieving time to me, and the meeting broke up in solemnity. William Smith's wife was at it, with which he was rejoiced, and she confessed feelingly to the truths she heard.

"10th. Parted affectionately with William Smith and Alexander Webster, who said they were strengthened by our visit; but a young woman, who is also under convincement, and lives with a rigid aunt, was not suffered to come to any of our meetings, nor to see us; which was a grief to those two men, and to her also. They meet together at times like Friends, and I cannot but hope Truth will one day be more prosperous in Dundee than it is at present, though the absurd doctrine of unconditional election and reprobation, so rigidly held by many, must first be renounced. Our landlord acknowledged he was much edified by our meetings, and parted with us with many good wishes. Rode through a fine grain country, pretty much in sight of the sea, and got to Montrose, and visited a widow Milne and daughter, the only Friends at that town, and had a religious opportunity with them to our satisfaction.

"11th. Went to Urie, the place of Robert Barclay's birth and death. The present possessor is lately come to the estate: he is a young man of eighteen, named Robert, and was out hunting;—the likeness of Friends seems quite extinguished; the father of this young man retained a regard for our profession in the early part of his life, but went off, got to be a member of parliament, and died about two years past. The young man's preceptor told us, he knew Mr. Barclay would have been glad to see us; and asked us to stay until he returned from hunting, and to dine there about four o'clock, which we declined, having determined to be at Aberdeen in the evening. The library room, which is small, is the place where Robert Barclay is said to have written his works; — there are a great many ancient Friends' books, all Robert Barclay's writings, and nearly all the pieces in opposition to him, and many other books of more modern date on different subjects. The meeting-house, which has not been made use of for a number of years, stands within a few yards of the dwelling — the ministers' gallery and some other seats remaining; but it now appears to be a place for broken furniture and lumber. The preceptor took us about half a mile from the dwelling, to the top of a little mount, the highest land in the neighborhood, which was the burying-place of Friends; the family are buried together, and now inclosed by a house built over them, at the expense of David Barclay of London; they consist of seven graves: it is probable that several of the family died in other places. We left the former residence of the excellent apologist and defender of our faith, with heaviness of mind, and with reflections upon the impossibility of the best of men conferring grace and virtue upon their descendants. The country from Urie to Aberdeen was very poor; the distance about fourteen miles.

"12th. Passing through a poor country and with hard riding we got to Old Meldrum — some of the Friends had gone to their meeting; but our friend John Elmslie meeting us in the street, took us to his house; and after a little refreshment, we also went to meeting, where there were only two men and eight women — it was held in silence; and at the close I appointed one for the people of the town, at six o'clock in the evening; which, though not large was thought satisfactory. The town is small, and the people generally in low circumstances.

"13th. Went on to our ancient friend George Cruikshank's, who lives with his son John, who married a daughter of John Wigham's. This family appear exemplary in their house and manner of living, and may be gifted for service in the church. Our friend George Cruikshank's daughter was very ill; she bears her lingering painful disorder with great patience and resignation, and we had a comfortable religious opportunity in her room. At six o clock went to a meeting appointed at Inverary, a village about two miles off; the house held about three hundred people, was well filled, the people quiet in the time of silence, serious, tender and attentive. I thought them more like thirsty ground than in any other place we had been at in Scotland, and the Lord favored us with a memorable time, to our great comfort; the praise of all was rendered to Him, whose due it is: the people were very thankful, and expressed much desire for another meeting. O! my dear friends of Philadelphia — how gladly would these, and many more in desolate places as to vital religion, receive the crumbs that fall from your spiritual tables almost untasted.

"14th. Our ancient Friend went with us to Kinmuck, four miles, to the family of John Wigham, who are settled on land which they have improved, being managed by his eldest son, a hopeful young man. The village of Kinmuck is about half a mile distant, quite small, but has several families of Friends and a meeting-house. Rode to Aberdeen about fourteen miles. A letter being received from Philadelphia, mentioning that symtoms of the yellow fever had again appeared there, it was affecting to me; but having left all in obedience to my apprehended duty, I commit all to Him whose power is sufficient to control and stay the hand of disease, when and where he pleases.

"First-day, 15th. Notice having been given to other professors, the meeting was held in Friends' meeting-house, which was comfortably filled: there are but six families of Friends belonging to it. After a little time the people behaved orderly and were very attentive; it grew more and more solid, and ended to satisfaction. Appointed another for six o'clock to-morrow evening. This town stands upon the river Dee; the land round it is not rich, and the people are employed in knitting worsted, wollen, cotton and raw silk stockings; also spinning the yarn for them and for linens: there are many rows of good houses, the streets well paved, and in general more cleanly than the other towns we have passed through in Scotland; the city is supposed to contain twenty-five thousand inhabitants.

"16th. The meeting this evening was very crowded; it was thought that four hundred got in, and a vast many went away for want of room — all the avenues for air being stopped, it became very warm and trying.

Although many had to stand, they presently got quiet, and a solemnity prevailing, the people continued attentive, and were tendered. We believed it was a season not soon to be forgotten; the Lord's good presence having been thankfully witnessed, all the praise was rendered to him, who is now and for ever worthy. After meeting, a sensible man came to our lodgings, and told us he had, for several years, been a seeker after Truth—was thankful for what he had now heard, and wished us to stay longer in Aberdeen, having no doubt he could obtain a place for a meeting that would hold one thousand or fifteen hundred people, who, he thought, would come if we had another; but feeling my mind clear, I did not think it laid upon me. Agreed to breakfast with this man to-morrow, and I retired to bed, thankful for the help and preservation through the day.

"17th. Went accordingly to see John Melles and his wife and children; who appeared to be people of good circumstances, and were very open and friendly. They said many people marvelled that I spoke as I did last night, without notes, as all the preachers in Scotland use them, and supposed I had been bred to the ministry, &c.; so little idea have many in the present day, of the nature of our ministry. We left Aberdeen, and after passing through much poor country, chiefly in oats, arrived at a village called Lawrence Kirk in the evening.

"18th. Rainy and cold; instead of proceeding direct for Glasgow, as I was in hopes of doing, I found my mind turned to go by Dundee again. We were well accommodated at the inn, and had good wheat bread on the table, as well as oat cakes; but the latter is the bread of the poor. The people in the country appear to be poor, many of the women and children were without shoe or stocking, though it was quite cold, and the highland mountains on our right covered with snow on the tops. Considerable oats and barley yet to cut, and much more to get in and stack. They have little fuel, and the bleakness and exposure of the country to cold winds, require a hardy race of people to endure; which they certainly are. My two travelling companions, George Miller and William Farrer, made some remarks on Americans using the word 'thee' instead of 'thou,' where the latter would be most proper; they were of the mind that it was a departure from our testimony, and had crept in from a desire of pleasing others by a soft accommodating form of speech, and was inconsistent with the practice of our ancient Friends. I never thought it proceeded from a desire to evade our testimony, but through custom had prevailed in many from ignorance of grammar rules; we are, however, recommended by an apostle, to hold fast the form of sound words. Arrived at Dundee in the evening. Our two convinced friends, Alexander Webster and William Smith, called upon us, and appear to have gained strength to avow the principles of Friends more openly than heretofore, and to sit down together on First-days in silence, with such who incline to sit with them. The accounts they gave us, and the comfortable feeling of our minds, induced us to believe we had been rightly directed to visit this town again

"19th. The Tradesmen's Hall was again seated, though not so conveniently as before, we being placed in the middle, and the people not inclining to go to the far end, they blocked up the door-way, and prevented many from getting in; had it been otherwise arranged, we believed it would have been filled. About five hundred attended, chiefly of the most respectable inhabitants. My mind was in a remarkable manner tenderly affected towards them, and through the gracious condescension of our heavenly Father, the opportunity was to our great comfort and thankfulness. After meeting, two religious men and a woman who had an uncommon knowledge in the Scriptures, and were of a tender spirit, visited us. They expressed their convictions in all the foregoing meetings, as well as this, though they had never heard a Friend before, and were united with the doctrines they had heard, and were only come to have further information as to some points in which they still had doubts, particularly whether water baptism and the sacrament so called, were not enjoined for Christians to observe as a standing ordinance of Christ. We had much freedom in exchanging sentiments with these tender people, who had read some parts of Barclay's Apology, lent to them by Alexander Webster since we were first there; they said they had never heard those matters so clearly stated as in this opportunity, and could say they now thought there was not anything essential in them: we parted in much affection. A man also came into our room while we were thus conversing, and opened his mind to us: he said he had been at all our meetings, and ever since the first, was under strong convictions for his past bad conduct, but was comforted in hope, by the doctrines we held, of the universal grace and free pardoning mercy of the Almighty to returning and repenting sinners, which was very contrary to what he had been used to hear, of absolute and unconditional election and reprobation. He appeared like a prodigal son returning to the arms of the Father of mercies—was much broken, and thought that through Divine grace he should renounce all his former evil practices: I endeavored to encourage and strengthen him in his good resolutions, and he left us in tears; his state affected me much, and remained on my mind, with strong desire for his preservation. Retired to rest with a comfortable evidence of being in our places — the Lord be praised.

"20th. Our two friends, Alexander Webster and William Smith, with several others, were disappointed and affected on hearing we proposed leaving them without another meeting; the people appeared to draw hard to detain us longer, but feeling that things were comfortably left, and the minds of many stirred up to further inquiry, we concluded to send them some books from Edinburgh; and the two Friends crossing the river with us, we had a tender parting from them, and rode on to the county town (Cooper), where we lodged

"21st. Set off in the rain and cold, rode through

the towns of Kircaldy, Kinghorn, &c. and arrived at the ferry opposite Leith: it blew very hard, yet thirty of us passengers went in a sloop, and had a rough, wet time, and poor accommodations, but arrived safely. A young man under convincement, and Anthony Wigham, were waiting for us on the quay; we took a seat in the coach which goes every half-hour for Edinburgh, and soon got to George Miller's, where we were kindly received.

"First-day, 22d. The meeting-house was nearly filled in the morning, and the people solid and attentive. At six o'clock in the evening it was much crowded, and the Lord was rich in mercy to us; the people parted in a kind and tender frame, and I was in hopes I might now pass away from this city, so famous for its learning and science, that it is said there are seldom fewer than one thousand young men attending the University from England, Ireland and foreign parts; more than forty Americans being here at present.

"24th. A young man who was at some of our meetings on the Isle of Man, being now here attending the medical lectures, frequently visited us, and expressed a fear lest while endeavoring to obtain worldly knowledge, he should unhappily lose rather than gain in the knowledge of God and of our Lord Jesus Christ, which he was convinced many of his fellow students had done; and feelingly expressed his desire to keep, through God's grace, free from the pollution of sentiments and manners so unhappily prevalent among the professors and pupils in this place.

"25th. Attended their week-day meeting, and appointed one for six o'clock this evening, requesting that the notice might be particularly communicated to such who were considered seeking, religious people. The evening was remarkable for storm and rain, so that even some women Friends who attempted it, thought they were obliged to give out and return home; yet from two hundred and fifty to three hundred came, nearly one half of whom were women, supposed to be such as I most wanted to see: it was the most confirming and solid meeting of any we attended in Edinburgh; and after taking an affectionate leave of them, I felt perfectly clear and easy to leave the city. On the next day we parted with several Friends, and also with our kind, hospitable landlady, Ann Miller and family, with much tender feeling. Passed through a pretty country, surrounded with high hills, and having several handsome seats of noblemen in sight of the road; arrived at Glasgow in the evening, and put up at one of the largest inns I have seen in Europe, having about one hundred rooms.

"27th. Breakfasted and dined with a worthy man and his wife, who are convinced of our religious principles; they, with two or three other sober persons, sit down and hold meetings for worship in the manner of Friends. Appointed a meeting to be held at six o'clock this evening; when about four hundred attended, and behaved well. I then appointed another at the same hour to-morrow evening, and lodged at the house of a young Friend from Manchester. Glasgow is well laid out and built; contains many large and handsome public buildings, and the private houses are not inferior to any place I have seen — the streets wide, straight, well lighted by lamps, and has excellent foot-ways, superior to most we have passed through in Europe. The city and adjacent villages are extensively in the manufacture of fine cotton stuffs, muslins, fine linen, &c., and is said to contain sixty thousand inhabitants. The meeting in the evening was attended by about the same number as the one last night, did not hold so long as common, feeling that those I most wanted to see were not present, and I marvelled that there were no more than we had before; but was informed that the Presbyterians and the seceders from them, accounted the most rigid to their faith of any in Scotland, had no unity with the Methodists, and our having the meeting in their house, kept many away. I appointed the meeting for to-morrow forenoon at the Tradesmen's Hall.

"29th. The meeting in the Hall was comfortably filled with many people of the first rank, and was satisfactory; appointed another at six o'clock this evening, which was crowded, as well inside as round the door, and on the stairs. Through Divine favor, a solemnity soon spread over us; and though I seldom have entered, or stood up in, these great meetings with more fear, and even trembling, than in this, yet the good Shepherd and everlasting Helper of those who put their trust in him, was mercifully pleased to bear me through, beyond anything I had experienced in

Scotland, and indeed to my own reverent humiliation. The pernicious doctrine of Deism, and the pharisaical righteousness of some professors of Christianity, were principally what I had to open to the audience, who were so still, that some afterwards said, they heard distinctly outside the Hall; and I have seen but few in all my travels equal to it—it closed in humble thankfulness to the Author of every mercy: after which I took leave of the people, apprehending I might now be at liberty to leave them; many came up very tenderly and respectfully, and hoped we would not go away without another meeting, which I told them I would consider, as well as I was capable of. We endeavored to get out, but the audience seemed not inclined to move until we went foremost, through an opening they made for us; several asking for another meeting, and many followed us almost to our quarters. I can scarcely express the thankfulness I feel to the Author of all our mercies, who has been pleased to carry me so peacefully through my visit to Scotland.

"30th. Notwithstanding the importunity of the people, I did not feel the propriety of another public meeting at the Hall, having reason to hope, as it closed well last night, the way will be open for future fellow-travellers; yet weighing what was best to be done, was easy to propose a meeting in the house of John Robertson, at six o'clock, for those who appeared most inclined to Friends' meetings; and such being accordingly invited, about sixty came. The time of silence was solemn, and proved a prelude to the continuance of Divine favor throughout. Several were much humbled, particularly two gay young women, sisters, who had been at all the meetings, and were of considerable rank in the world; they staid with us after meeting, and one of them acknowledged she had never received so much benefit as in the meetings of Friends. We told them of the few who sat down together on First and Fifth days at John Robertson's house, where they hoped they should be strengthened to attend.

"31st. Put forward on our journey through a country the soil of which is naturally poor, but being manured with lime, sea-weed, &c., is made to produce good crops of oats and barley: passed through several towns, and for a number of miles in sight of the sea; and at night, Eleventh month 1st, arrived at Port Patrick, and with difficulty procured lodging at a private house, the inns being crowded. The wind blowing hard and directly ahead, we were obliged to stay here. There are abundance of poor-looking people almost naked, who come here from Ireland to beg. The town contains about two hundred huts and houses, surrounded by high barren mountains, and not above four houses in the place that can be called tolerably good; the women, lads and girls go barefoot, and some of them were sliding so on the ice. Mutton costs here four pence, and beef six pence per pound, and much of it very poor.

"4th. The wind coming out more fair, we went on board the packet and arrived at Donagadee, in Ireland, in the evening.

"First-day, 5th. Sat down with the family and a

few others who commonly attend with them, and at the close of the sitting I proposed a meeting at Newton this evening, of which our friend T. Bradshaw gave notice in the town. At six o'clock, though very wet and discouraging, yet about four hundred came together and behaved well, and through renewed mercy it proved an open time.— Appointed another for to-morrow evening.

"6th. Went to Newton Ards, where a number of officers and soldiers attended the meeting; but I thought it not so open and satisfactory as the last.

"8th. Was at Belfast; the streets of which are very dirty, the poor people very much so, and without shoes or stockings; the women and children go through the mud, now in the Eleventh month. Went on to Antrim, and were kindly received by the family of Gervas Johnson, who is now on a religious visit to Friends in America. An appointed meeting at six o'clock in the evening, was solid and satisfactory, as was another at the same hour next evening—the house was filled, and the Presbyterian minister attended both this and the last; it was quiet and ended to our satisfaction.

"11th. Took a post-chaise for Lisburn, accompanied by several Friends, and passed through a fertile country, but the huts of the poor peasants were miserable: the town we passed through to-day had been much injured a few days before by some rioters, and the windows and some doors broken; the sufferers were such as are called *United Irishmen.* This part of Ireland has been long famous for rioting. With the help of lanterns we walked out to the boarding-school of Friends, for the province of Ulster, which consisted of about fifty scholars, boys and girls; their supper was potatoes and milk — they looked healthy and were decently dressed; having some little religious communication, many of them were tendered, and I was glad we were there.

"First-day, 12th. Attended their meeting. The custom of Friends in this town, is to have a second meeting after the rising of the first, and not to dine until after the last; but feeling a concern to have a meeting for the people at large in the evening, the afternoon meeting was put off. The public meeting at six o'clock was large, and except some interruption from rude boys, was held in much quiet. Although the people behaved well in general, I did not think it so open as many others.* Some appeared much affected, and an elderly man reached out his hand, and said it was the Gospel that had been preached, and he wished me well.

"13th. Visited the boarding-school again; the situation is fine, and commands a beautiful prospect. Large additions have been made to it since the decease of John Gough, who formerly kept it: it has forty acres

* It is not strange that our dear friend found so little openness, as he had to treat upon that divinely authorized passage of the apostle, "This is a faithful saying and worthy of all acceptation, that Jesus Christ came into the world to save sinners," &c.; for it is well known, that through the subtlety of the serpent, Deism and a disregard of the Holy Scriptures had gained considerable hold in many parts of that country.

of land on a long lease. The National Meeting subscribed four thousand pounds, and the province of Ulster raises annually about three hundred pounds for its support; this with some little income beside. enables the institution to board, educate and clothe fifty-six children, from eight to fifteen years of age. at three pounds per annum; they bringing with them one good suit, and also a common one: — the whole expense for one scholar, is about thirteen pounds Irish, per annum. Went to Hillsborough and had a meeting in the evening, which was quiet and satisfactory; then accompanied Louisa Conran, wife of John Conran a minister, to their house about two miles; he was out from home on religious service. The poor people in this part of the country, are busily engaged in sowing wheat, digging potatoes, &c.; the women and children everywhere without shoes and stockings. Potatoes, with a little oatmeal, sometimes milk, and now and then a bit of meat, make up their principal food. I visited a number of the poor in their cottages, the women spin and the men weave linen, muslin, &c., but are very poorly clad, indeed almost naked; their houses very cold, with little light but what comes in at the door; the walls of mud and straw, roofs thatched, floors of earth, and small fires of turf, for which they pay dear to the landholders; a straw bed or two, with some stools, a table, a few bowls, &c. make up their furniture. How would a sight of these poor oppressed people, make many, even of the poor in Pennsylvania, thankful for their blessings!

We distributed a little money among them, and they returned many blessings.

"15th. Attended the week-day meeting at Ballindery, the roads were bad; met by the way with a blind man, who had his mother, aged eighty-six, on his back in a sack, led by a faithful dog. Post-chaise one shilling per Irish mile.

"16th. Attended the Monthly Meeting at Lisburn: unexpectedly to myself, and contrary to my usual lot in Friends' meetings, there was a necessity laid upon me to appear in the ministry—the labor proved hard, and more laborious than among other people; after which I felt peaceful and easy. There was much consistency in their appearance as to our profession, but more weight in answering their queries, and conducting their business, would have been proper.

"17th. Went with our friend Louisa Conran two miles to dine, after which proceeded to Lurgan, about eight Irish miles, through a populous country; the people on the way-side dwell in wretched hovels of mud and straw, many children almost naked, and this in the midst of a fertile country, abounding in the produce of the earth; but the poor live very poorly indeed, perhaps in every way more distressed than in any country I have seen; and the rich lamentably oppressive. It being market-day when we arrived, the market-people were packing up their stockings, linen, yarn, &c.; many of whom were intoxicated with strong drink, which is said to be a common case on market days. The houses are all white, being overcast with lime, which is much the case in this country.

"First-day, 19th. Though unwell I went to meeting at Moyallen, and through Infinite condescension it was thought to be a favored time. Attended the evening meeting at Lurgan, though quite poorly with the cold I had taken—the house was supposed to contain seven hundred persons, and was filled: it appeared as open a time as I have had in Ireland.

"21st. Was at William Pike's, with whom we went to Dungannon, a considerable town, and visited T. Greer's, jr., and his family. About eighteen months past they removed to this town, having before lived at a beautiful farm some miles off, but were obliged to leave it, in consequence of being in much danger from rioters. One evening, seven persons came with their faces blacked and otherwise disguised, armed with pistols, &c., under pretence of searching for guns, but abused the family, robbed them of two watches and above one hundred guineas; which had such an effect on his wife, that she has not yet got over it. Had a public meeting, at which, though a wet evening, there were about seven hundred present, and it proved a favored season — many soldiers and officers attended, several of whom were much affected.

"24th. Attended a public meeting at Rich-hill, the house pretty full; I thought it a laborious time. A drunken priest who attended was held up to the people in such a manner, that they thought he could not have been so described if I had not received some previous information; but they were satisfied their conjecture was wrong, and were glad he had been so handled. I knew not that there was any in his station present until after meeting.

"Appointed a meeting to be on First-day morning, the 26th, at Newry. The Methodists offering their house, and we not seeing any better, accepted it: they took much pains to accommodate the people, and though the house contained about seven hundred, it was too small; yet the meeting was very quiet, and through renewed mercy a favored opportunity. We had a public meeting in the Presbyterian meeting-house at six o'clock in the evening; the house was large, yet it was much crowded, and many did not get in. It was said that fifteen hundred persons were present: the meeting concluded in prayer and praises to our heavenly Helper, who had been mercifully with us through the day. The minister of the congregation said at the close, that we might have the house again whenever we saw fit to use it, and thanked us for our service.

"27th. We left the town, but had not gone far before we saw about one hundred and fifty persons kneeling on the wet ground, both men and women — found it was a Romish funeral; the priest dressed in his white robes, and a corpse in the middle, over which he was making prayers, and performing some ceremonies. We stopped, and had an opportunity of seeing some of their gross superstitious ceremonies, and the making a bowl of holy water, which he did by muttering over it a few Latin prayers, and putting in a handful of salt; he then sprinkled the coffin; the people arose, and were likewise sprinkled, which the poor women seemed eager to catch, and returned him a courtesy.

"28th. Reached Dublin, and on the 30th went with two Friends to visit the poor, principally in those parts called the Liberties, where the most distressing scenes of human misery presented themselves in abundance, such as my eyes had never seen before, neither is it in my power fully to describe. We went through the different apartments of fifty or sixty houses, with scarcely any glass in the windows, the ground floors of earth, and everywhere filled with almost all kinds of filth; — in some rooms two, three, to nine or ten women and children, and some men, many of them sick and with very few rags to cover them, sitting round two or three little pieces of turf, and many without any fire at all, lying about on a little dirty straw in the corners of the room — they had no bed-clothes, and were almost perished; complaining of having nothing to do and nothing to eat, some for twenty-four hours or more. The dampness and dirtiness of their houses, and the filthiness of their persons, must remain undescribed:— they greedily seized sixpences and shillings, as if their miserable existence depended on them, and returned us many blessings, some in very singular language. A large number surrounding us in the street, we went to a baker's shop and distributed among them fifty loaves of bread. Dined by candle-light, wet and weary, at R. Clibborn's.

"Twelfth month, 1st. Visited a charity school, of which Friends had been considerable promoters; it consisted of about eighty boys and girls; they appeared ragged, and many without shoes or stockings, yet kept in pretty good order. The institution is supported by subscriptions made annually. At six o'clock attended an appointed meeting for the people generally: although the evening was very wet, yet the house was nearly filled, and the people were quiet; but not feeling my mind relieved, I appointed another at Sycamore alley, on First-day evening. Spent much of the 2nd in visiting the poor near Summer Hill, particularly at a spot called Mud Island, where there may be one hundred poor houses, many of which are of mud, and many miserable inhabitants, some without any fire, the day cold and damp, and the floors of earth quite wet; they appeared to have no other beds than straw, and were miserably provided with that. I distributed a number of guineas among these almost naked people, and visited about one hundred families. In returning to our friends we purchased about one hundred loaves of bread, for which we soon had numerous customers, giving only one to each person.

"First-day, 3d. Attended the meeting in the forenoon at Meath street, which was large. I had a heavy cold by going so much among the poor in the wet. Went to the appointed evening meeting, which was exceedingly crowded, and it was said that many hundreds went away; the meeting was quiet and ended well. Appointed another in the same house to be on

Third-day evening: truly these engagements are not desirable to the flesh. I long for a release in the Lord's time; may I be enabled to keep the word of his patience.

"On the 4th, went with two young men on another visit to the poor, and relieved many miserable human beings. The memory of these visits cannot soon be effaced from my mind. May they teach me to be humble and thankful for the blessings I enjoy. O my dear country folks! could many of you who live in ease and abundance, far removed from these affecting scenes of wretchedness, behold them, profitable impressions might be made for life. To see a mother and daughter, the youngest of them sixty years, almost naked, without fire, on a damp earthen floor, lying upon a little straw, only a few tattered rags for covering, and very little to eat, how must every feeling heart be touched! In another place there were two widows with seven children, two of them blind and nearly naked, and one of the mothers racked with rheumatic pains; they had no fire, and not two ounces of bread in the house. They have no laws here to oblige the parishes to take care of the poor, and more than twenty thousand in Dublin are in deep distress, many through their own folly and wickedness, but not a few for want of employ. Walked a mile and a half to a Friend's house through the wet, (for it rains every day,) where we received shocking accounts of the murders and plunder of the United Irishmen in the south, within a few days past.

"5th. Went with Deborah Darby and Rebecca Young to the public meeting this evening: it was a very respectable congregation, one Romish and several other priests present, and I thought it the most open and favored opportunity I had been at in Ireland; the people behaved well, and at the close were very inquisitive when there was to be another meeting. I was thankful for the renewed mercies of the day.

"7th. Visited a blind boy about eleven years old, who appears to be a prodigy, and has a memory so tenacious that he can retain almost all he hears, and repeat a large portion of several books, &c.; it is so surprising, that all who have seen him acknowledge it to be an extraordinary gift.

"9th. A number of invitations were sent to me by Friends. but it was not possible for all to be complied with; indeed, I desire to have much more retirement than I can obtain. Friends do not enough consider poor travellers who stop among them, or probably they would not crowd upon them so much as they do; they mean it as a kindness, but it often amounts to oppression.

"First-day, 10th. It was concluded to open both meeting-houses, neither being capable of containing the people that would probably come. I attended at Sycamore alley, and they were both thought to be favored. In the evening the public meeting at that place was soon filled; the mayor of the city and some principal persons came, among whom there were eight or nine priests of different congregations, and many officers. My mind was opened in an unusual manner, and after speaking some time, some pieces of coal were thrown in at the end windows, which alarmed the women, and many of them rose: two of the officers of the army immediately went out to find the disturbers, and drew their swords. I sat down for three or four minutes, when they returned, and the people becoming quiet, I rose and proceeded, and it proved to be a truly comforting, tendering time; thanks be unto Him who is ever worthy of all praise: — the meeting ending in awful prayer and praises — the people parted from us in much love, and I felt my mind relieved of public meetings in Dublin.

"11th. Spent the forenoon in visiting the poor, and distributed about eight guineas that were put under my care, to a very wretched company."

CHAPTER VI.

Dublin — Poverty and wretchedness — Limerick — Fertile land — Cork — Foundlings — Clonmel — Rich Friends — St. Patrick's Well — Affecting partings — Widow Usher and daughters — Abraham Shackleton and his notions — Arrival in Wales — Manners and habits — Bristol — Bath — Hannah More — William Wilberforce — London—Norwich—Newspaper commendations—Benjamin West —Visit to the King, Queen, and Princesses — Meetings in London —War Taxes—Mary Fletcher — Shrewsbury —Wrexham — Opposition and meeting at Ormskirk — Liverpool — Re-enters Wales — Large meetings — Sails for Ireland — Dublin Yearly Meeting — Defection in fundamental principles — Violations of the testimony against war — Arduous labor to counteract unsound doctrine — Return to England — Birmingham — Soup-houses — London Yearly Meeting — Long walks to Yearly Meeting — Interviews at Newgate — Difficulty of obtaining a passage home — Murders by the Catholics in Ireland — Embarks at Bristol for America — Detention at Cork — Notes of the voyage—Arrival at home — Sickness and death.

"Dublin is certainly a very fine city; many of the streets are wide and elegantly built, perhaps Sackville street is not excelled by many, if any, in Europe; it is one hundred and twenty feet wide — that and some others have lamps before every door; indeed, it is the best lighted city I have seen. Many of the houses are four or five stories high, of pretty good brick — the best streets uniform and straight, with good flagged foot-ways. The public buildings are grand, exceeding those of London, especially the custom-house, college, parliament-house, exchange, &c.

"The trade to Dublin is not great for its size; perhaps one hundred vessels are in port, the greater part of which are colliers. The city may contain two hundred and fifty thousand inhabitants, many of whom roll in luxury; but there is no comparison that I have seen in Europe for wretched habitations in the alleys and back streets, which are filled with human beings, who, in their present filthy mode of living, nakedness, depravity and morals, are really the most affecting sight to a humane, feeling mind, that perhaps any city in the world can exhibit: many of them are exceedingly hurt by drinking the pernicious spirits made of malt, rye, &c., called whiskey, of which an immense quantity is distilled in Ireland. Another source of misery is, the numerous lottery offices in the city, which make a splendid appearance after candle-light; in some streets there are many whose doors are continually surrounded by poor, half-naked people, who lay out their little all, which, perhaps, they have begged, in the hope of gaining by their chance; but the keepers of these offices have made such nice calculations upon chances, that *they* are sure to gain. This is noted as being a great source of misery to thousands of poor, even such as swarm about the streets begging, who are induced to venture their small pittances, in hopes of obtaining more, in which they are often greatly deceived; and if one in a great many should gain something, it serves to keep up the delusion. In the present state of things, it does not appear probable but that Dublin will continue to harbor from twenty to forty thousand miserable beings as it now does, until some employment can be found for them, and they, by some means, be brought to labor for their own support. Indeed, in all parts of the kingdom, this class more or less abounds.

"12th. Being the Monthly Meeting, we produced our certificates; and Friends thinking it would be a satisfaction to the women's meeting to hear them, William Farrer and myself, with Thomas Fayle, went in, and through renewed mercy had a tendering time among them. On lying down to rest, it was clear in my mind, that now it would be right to leave Dublin.

"13th. Arrived at Rathangan in the afternoon, and found Joshua Wilson's carriage waiting for us at the side of the canal; we went to his house, about a mile from Rathangan.

"14th. Breakfasted with our friend Jane Watson, and went to their meeting, where a number of people attended, and it was thought to be a solid, good meeting; Jane said it was a comfort to her.

"15th. Set off for Mountmellick, the weather being wet and stormy; before we got to Portarlington, a town of some note, principally inhabited by the descendants of the French Hugenots, who were banished out of the kingdom, one of the felloes of a wheel of our chaise broke; we walked into the town and hired a post-chaise, but before we got a mile from thence our post-chaise broke down in a very dirty place, Jane Watson, William Farrer, and myself, in it. It rained very fast, and being invited, we went into a miserable cabin with little fire, where lived two wretched families, with several children, to whom we gave some money, and they poured forth a profusion of blessings, as usual. Most of the poor being Roman Catholics, their benedictions are often very singular. We had to stay a considerable time before another chaise could be procured, and were very cold, though well clad; yet most of the family were without shoes or stockings: I thought we ought not to complain, but be thankful. When we entered our third chaise, it still raining hard, and the waters much raised, we were in some danger; but by going one mile round, we arrived safely in the evening, and were kindly received by J. Pim and wife. Mary Ridgway being there waiting for us, we were mutually glad to see each other.

"16th. Visited the provincial school for the province of Leinster, consisting of about fifty scholars, healthy and very decent; we had a tendering time with them and their tutors; and also visited the boarding-school for girls, wherein they were much broken into tears. The town of Mountmellick is not large, consisting of only one street about half a mile long.

"First-day, 17th. Attended their meeting, consisting only of Friends; had a few words to say at the close, which being of a very singular kind, I was glad that Mary Ridgway and Jane Watson could acknowledge their great satisfaction and unity with it,* my mind having been much exercised during the meeting. The afternoon meeting was also a trying, painful time to me, though quite silent. Friends having heard of my general line of service among other people, marvelled that I did not appoint a meeting of that kind for the

---

*It is cause of admiration and humbling acknowledgment, that Divine influence, the only real qualification for Gospel ministry, should thus preserve and guide the messengers of the Lord's love and mercy to the people, as that they should in their labors be led in the same line, and give them to feel and expose defection, however secretly held or glossed over with very plausible pretences, even in some of the foremost rank. Our friend Nicholas Waln, when on a visit to this nation, in the year 1795, without any previous information, opened in the Province Meeting at this place, an intimation which had impressed his mind with great exercise and painful concern; showing, that however disguised and hidden, there was a spirit at work that would divide and scatter, and draw off many that were then in high stations, into self-sufficiency and disbelief of the truths of the Gospel. This was such a surprise to some, that they were for passing a censure upon him; but a few deeply experienced minds fully united with and encouraged him. Now, when our friend William Savery was here, this rending, disorganizing spirit was again impressively felt and detected; soon afterwards it showed itself by a false profession of more enlightened and liberal views of the Christian character, setting little value on the Holy Scriptures, and endeavoring to destroy the faith in the eternal divinity of our Lord and Saviour Jesus Christ; treating his atonement and propitiation as a fabulous scheme, invented to impose upon the credulous, and not worthy of the enlarged ideas of philosophic minds; which caused great distress, and almost broke up the meetings in several parts of the nation.

evening; but all seemed closed, and I could not attempt it. After tea, finding a freedom to propose a meeting of the scholars of both the schools, and the children of Friends in town, in which my two friends Mary Ridgway and Jane Watson united, we met with them in the provincial school — about one hundred children in all, their master, mistresses, and thirty or forty other Friends. My mind, which had been so exercised all day, presently after sitting down, felt sweetly opened to them; they were soon broken into tears, and a more precious opportunity I never remember with children. They took leave of us in tears, and I felt much refreshed and comforted, and have reason daily to acknowledge, that it is the Lord who opens and none can shut, and shuts and none can open.

"20th. Being at Limerick, I appointed a meeting this evening; the house was filled — three priests of different congregations sat with us, and it was thought to be an open, satisfactory time.

"The new part of this town is regular and well built; it is on the Shannon, fifty miles from the sea. Pork here is bought at twenty-two shillings per one hundred and twelve pounds, but much inferior to American; — beef excellent, and much of both are salted and shipped. Some of the poor in this neighborhood give six guineas, and some more, a year, for an acre of potato ground, when manured by the landlord. To earn this six guineas takes a great deal of the year in labor for their landlord, at six-pence or eight-pence per day and food; so that the state of the poor is indeed a very hopeless one in this country. It takes them considerable time to cut and dry their turf, and in some places they now pay high for the privilege of getting it from the bogs, and many of the poor have no way of getting it home, but as the women carry it a long distance on their backs.

"22nd. Went to their week-day meeting, where many other professors came, also two ministers of the church of England; and through the merciful condescension of our heavenly Father, it appeared to be a good meeting; after which William Farrer and myself went off in a post-chaise for Cork. Passed through a fine country of rich land. It being near the time called Christmas, the people everywhere seemed preparing for it; most of the poor get some meat or poultry, and were bringing home on their backs plenty of broom, furze, turf, &c., to keep better fires than usual: most of the women and children were without stockings or shoes, and also many of the men at this cold season of the year, the air being very chilling and wet. The verdure of the fields and meadows, and their prolific appearance is such as I have never seen in any country. The lands in the counties of Limerick, Cork and Tipperary, are so rich naturally, that much of it wants but little manure. Got to Cork this evening, the cost of the carriage, turnpike, &c. for sixty-three English miles, was about four guineas.

"First-day, 24th. The meeting held in silence; but near the close I believed it right to propose an evening meeting with other professors. Dined in company with

Mary Dudley, &c. The meeting in the evening was very crowded — David Sands, who had been confined here with indisposition for several weeks, attended; also Mary Dudley — the people were quiet and attentive, and the opportunity ended in solemn prayer. Appointed another for Third-day evening.

"On the 25th, after dinner, observing a large gate near the house with an inscription, informing that the walls enclosed a foundling hospital, I felt an inclination to go over and see the children. The masters and mistresses soon collected the children, about two hundred and twenty boys and girls, from five to fourteen years old, tolerably clothed, though mostly without shoes or stockings. After a little time in silence, David Sands, Mary Dudley and myself, had something to offer to the company: many of the children were attentive and some in tears: the masters and superintendents expressed their satisfaction. The institution is principally supported by a tax on coals, and the children, when about the age of fourteen, are bound out apprentices to such business as they incline to. The city of Cork is large, and many streets wide, handsome and well built; yet a more dirty, disagreeable city to walk in, I have scarcely seen; it is built on both sides of the river Lee, and may contain one hundred thousand inhabitants.

"Third-day. The common meeting was pretty well attended; Mary Dudley was large and instructive in her testimony, and it ended in prayer. Went to the appointed meeting in the evening, and found the house well filled: the knowledge of God and of Jesus Christ his Son, was shown to be of more value than all other science. Many people of the first rank were present, some priests, &c. David Sands had a good testimony and closed the meeting in prayer. I believe that through mercy the Truth was in dominion; the people were very quiet and attentive, said to be the most so ever remembered in Cork at those promiscuous meetings. I felt my mind much relieved, and though greatly unexpected, concluded to leave Cork in the morning.

"27th. Took leave of several Friends who were very affectionately attached, and I do not remember ever having left a city with so general an expression against my hasty departure; but I believe all is right. Passed through a pretty village where Samuel Neale formerly lived, and got to Youghall in the evening.

"28th. Attended their week-day meeting, which was silent; and proposed a public meeting for six o'clock in the evening. The house was nearly filled—several officers and soldiers attended: it seemed, for some time, to be laborious, but the people being still, and towards the latter part tender, we separated in much solemnity.

"29th. Accompanied by several Friends, we proceeded on our journey; but having taken a cold, so that I could neither stoop nor draw my breath without pain and difficulty, and the road being rough, I rode in great pain. The country is more beautifully green at this season than any I know of in America in any season. Got to Robert and Mary Dudley's, at Clonmel, in the evening.

"First-day, 31st. Was at their forenoon meeting, after which I mentioned my prospect of having an opportunity with other professors at six o'clock in the evening: the meeting-house, which was large, was soon filled, and it was said that several hundreds were out of doors. The crowded situation of the people kept them uneasy for a little time, but afterwards it became more quiet: the people outside being very desirous of seeing and hearing, they talked much; but were at length induced to be still, and we had a solid, favored conclusion, through condescending mercy, in solemn prayer and praises. The officers and soldiers behaved well, and my mind was filled with thankfulness.

"Second-day, 1st of First month, 1798. Attended an appointed meeting in the forenoon, which was not so large as last evening. It was not my judgment to have it at this time of day, but it seemed necessary to condescend to the sentiments of some Friends, who afterwards believed that the evening would have been better; I however was enabled to get through to my own satisfaction, in exposing the pernicious doctrine of Deism; and the opportunity was owned by the Divine presence and power; and it afterwards appeared that there were three professed Deists present.

"Friends in Ireland seem to live like princes of the earth, more than in any country I have seen — their gardens, horses, carriages and various conveniences, with the abundance of their tables, appeared to me to call for much more gratitude and humility, than in some instances, it is to be feared, is the case. The easy situation of some has been an injury to them and their families: many have been much shaken, seriously tried and afflicted; and may all work together for their good! This town of Clonmel is larger and better built than Youghall; it may contain twenty thousand inhabitants, is situated on the banks of a little river called Suir, on which they carry their produce in flat boats to Waterford. I had some serious conversation with dear Mary Dudley, on divers matters that had taken my attention in Ireland. In the evening it being the usual time when the scholars at the school, instituted by Sarah Grubb, sit down in the manner of a meeting; we had the children of Friends of the town added to them, and it was a comfortable opportunity; about eighty children being present, Mary Dudley was favored in her testimony and the children much affected.

"First month, 3d. At a Friend's house about three miles from town, a very sumptuous establishment indeed, which I did not omit to tell him was quite too much so. On this place is a large run of water, called St. Patrick's Well, to which the poor Roman Catholics resort on St. Patrick's day, and wade in the water till they are very cold; and at other times of the year many come from a distance, some sent by the priests to do penance, who thereby suppose they wash away their sins: it is kept almost constantly muddy by the people so frequently going into it. Three fourths of the people in Dublin, and southward in Ireland, are supposed to be Roman

Catholics; and some say seven eighths. They are an oppressed people, and it is thought that two out of three do not get meat six times in the year. They have but little milk, and indeed scarcely anything but potatoes and salt. At present they are very uneasy, commit many riots, robberies and murders; refuse to pay tithes of the few potatoes, &c., which they raise, and seem to be almost lawless.

"I visited a public charity school, principally attended by Ann Grubb; and if it was not for the care and support given by Friends, it is supposed it must have dropped; it is held in the old meeting-house of Friends; one hundred and fifty poor ragged children, boys and girls, are taught reading, writing, knitting and sewing — the boys nearly all without shoes or stockings, and also the greater part of the girls.

"4th. Attended the Monthly Meeting, the fore part of which was held in silence. I went into the women's meeting, and through renewed favor it was a solid, satisfactory time. Elizabeth Pim, a minister, was acceptably engaged in prayer. Appointed a public meeting to be at six o'clock this evening, which was large, solid and relieving to me. Mary Dudley was drawn forth in prayer and praises at the close, to our refreshment and comfort.

"5th. Went to the widow Grubb's, at Anner Mills, and after breakfast proceeded to Carrick, a considerable town, where almost all the inhabitants are Roman Catholics. Our dear friends Deborah Darby and Rebecca Young having appointed a meeting here, we attended it; about three hundred persons were present, and Deborah Darby had an open time, and it closed with solemnity; though the Catholics are so walled round that it is hard to penetrate them. After dinner, being about to separate, I felt heavy, thinking it might be a final parting between dear Deborah Darby, Rebecca Young and myself: retiring into silence, some few expressions were uttered, and Deborah Darby was preciously drawn to supplicate the Father of mercies for preservation, especially of us who had been united in his love by sea and by land; most of the Friends present were much broken into tears; and thus we solemnly took leave of each other. It was also a very tender parting between us, who were going for Waterford, and our kind hostess, Mary Dudley and her daughter. William Farrer and myself went with our friend Ann Fayle, in her carriage to a Friend's house about nine miles from Waterford, at which place we arrived on the 6th.

"A great trade is carried on here in provisions, as pork, beef, butter, &c. Notwithstanding the great abundance of provisions that appear everywhere, this place, like most others in Ireland, abounds in poor and beggars; and all the suburbs for a great distance are made up of poor thatched cabins.

"First-day, 7th. Attended their morning meeting, which was large for this country: at the close I proposed a meeting for the town's people this evening, which was very large and crowded; it was thought there were one thousand persons present, and yet many went away. Great stillness prevailed, and the people were very attentive; through renewed mercy it broke up in a solid, tender frame, and I appointed another for Third-day evening.

"8th. Went to see the place intended for a boarding-school, which is a fine, healthy spot; from thence we visited the widow Usher, a valuable woman of excellent understanding, who has been received among Friends within a year past; since which she has lost two excellent daughters in consumption, a third is now near her end, and a fourth evidently going the same way. She has been supported in her affliction marvellously, and her daughters have made a precious end, as the one now going will also soon do. She was sensible, and looked on us with a sweet countenance — all felt like peace around her bed, and I was comforted in being with the family.

"At my lodgings in the evening came Robert Greer and Abraham Shackleton, the latter from Ballitore, who had come forty-two miles in order to see me. He holds opinions of a singular nature; objects 'to the five first books of Moses in particular, but in general to the accounts of the Jews in the Old Testament, and various parts of the New Testament; professes to think there is little if any need of books of any kind on religious subjects; that they only darken the mind and keep it from turning itself wholly unto God, the fountain of all light and life. But of all books of a religious kind, he especially dislikes Friends' Journals, and has but a slight opinion of ministry and discipline, and all secondary helps in general; but is for having all people turned to the Divine Light in themselves alone. Christ, he says, was a good man, the leader of the people, because he was wholly obedient to this light, which he was in an especial manner filled with. He thinks the Evangelists are poor historians, that Paul brought much of his epistles from the feet of Gamaliel, and many parts of them are therefore rabbinical stuff,— Christianity was the same to those who were obedient to the anointing, before the coming of Christ in the flesh, as since,' &c. 'I perceived all this was accompanied with a pretended looking towards a greater state of perfection and redemption, than our Society has yet arrived at. For my part, I could not see as he did, nor unite with him in his erroneous expressions and opinions, and I feel a fear they will produce much hurt, if he and others in this nation are not brought into deep abasement; his talents and morality making error in his hands more dangerous. We separated without much satisfaction, at least on my side.*

---

* We have here a further disclosure of some of the deleterious principles of the deceitful, subtle spirit, which worked under the specious garb of outside morality and great professions of universal benevolence, and carried away many unsuspecting souls into the vortex of Deism, and at length into Atheism. It is very remarkable, that a great withering and falling away overtook nearly all of them, and upon some of the principal promulgators of those unrighteous doctrines, an awful blast was evidently brought. This same insidious spirit having since got into America, lamentable desolation of a considerable number of meetings of Friends in different parts ensued; and it is

"After retiring to rest, I could get but little sleep for some hours — Satan is indeed full of subtleties — who can discover them, but He who dwelleth in and covereth himself with unapproachable light? I thought or dreamed, that I saw a man in a field, who appeared to be attempting to pluck a few tares that were growing among choice wheat, but he pulled up more wheat than tares, and trod down abundance more with his feet; and I thought he had far better let them alone until the harvest.

"First month, 9th. Attended the week-day meeting: my mind was much exercised and heavy, but near the close was drawn forth in prayer, and afterwards felt peaceful. Went with Abraham Shackleton to a Friend's house, and opened to him more of my disapprobation than I had before. Attended the public meeting in the evening, which was large; much solemnity and quiet prevailed, and it ended in praises.

"10th. Stayed much at my lodgings, writing; and received a letter from Abraham Shackleton, in which he *appears* lovingly disposed towards me, but evidently wrong, so far as I am able to judge, in many of his opinions — took leave of him, and had much concern on his account, and in that state went to bed. Fifth-day, seeing ten miserable beggars sitting round a Friend's

---

to be feared that numerous individuals, who at first had no idea of its destructive nature, have been plunged into complete infidelity, and entire repugnance to the doctrines of the Gospel, and the unspeakable benefits conferred upon man, through the propitiatory sacrifice of the Lord Jesus.

door, I sent for ten loaves of bread, but before they were distributed thirty others appeared, and each had the same quantity. This is the way in Ireland, and there is no coming to an end of the business. Another letter came from Abraham Shackleton who has gone for his home, and I am not sorry for his leaving us; he has given me much exercise.

"11th. Dined in company with several Friends, one of whom belonging to Enniscorthy, appeared much concerned at the new opinions that had been manifested in their quarter. My mind was exercised with much thought, whether it might not be proper for me to go to Ross, about ten miles off, where a person of some note had been convinced and come amongst Friends, though I cannot but desire, as a man, to get through my engagements as soon as possible in this land. Lord! strengthen me to say, 'thy will be done,' for in this only there is peace.

"12th. Visited Elizabeth Usher, and found her in much Christian resignation to the will of the Lord, though her third lovely daughter was to be buried to-day; having lost two others in a consumption, and a son in another way, within a twelvemonth; her father at this time lying a corpse, and her fourth and last daughter likely very soon to follow her sisters in the same disease. Her state of mind, as well as that of her dear remaining daughter, was truly instructive to me. Her son, who had not professed with Friends, came a few hours before Judith's death, to take leave of her; she looked at him with much serenity of countenance, bid him farewell, and said with a voice louder than she had for some time, 'All is peace, sweet peace,' and so departed, praising God in joyful hope of a blessed change approaching. Her corpse was carried to the meeting-house, but not brought in where the meeting was held, but left in the women's meeting-room, which is their custom; for as they are surrounded by Roman Catholics, they might take up the opinion that Friends brought the corpse into the meeting, with the idea that it would be profitable to the departed spirit to pray over it. Through the renewed mercy of our heavenly Father, it was a precious parting meeting; many of the dear youth were much affected, as also others. The corpse being put in a plain oak coffin and placed upon a hearse, was led slowly through the streets to the burying-ground; friends, relations, &c. following promiscuously: — all business seemed to cease as we passed along, and much stillness appeared among the people, many of whom knew the family, they being of high rank; the grandfather who lay a corpse, was the eldest alderman of the city. At the graveyard, a multitude were collected, both Friends and others, high and low, and I believed it my duty to say a few words, and rehearse the comforting expressions of the deceased; after which there was a further communication from another Friend, and many not of our Society were much broken. The Lord be praised for his goodness.

"Feeling my mind much comforted and relieved of going to Ross, or anywhere else in Ireland, I took an affectionate leave of many Friends in the graveyard, at which divers expressed their surprise, and wishes to detain me over First-day; but believing it was a good time to leave them, I got into a post-chaise and went about seven English miles, where the packets for Wales lay. After dinner we sailed, there being no cabin passengers but William Farrer and myself; we passed down the river Suir, and were out at sea soon after the light appeared at the light-house.

"13th. Arriving at Milford in Wales, we set off for Haverfordwest; the road and country very hilly, yet exhibiting some pleasant prospects of well-cultivated farms, but the soil much inferior to that we had left in Ireland.

"First-day, 14th. The meeting at Haverfordwest consisted of about sixty persons, and was a solid, tendering time to myself and others: there are about five families of those professing with us at this place. Had an appointed meeting in the evening, but the house was not half filled, owing as was believed to the person who undertook to give the notice being in low repute, and had done the business very imperfectly. The people in the street hearing my voice, kept coming in, which rather unsettled the meeting; but near the close we had a little quiet, and it ended quite as well as I expected.

"15th. Proceeded through a hilly country as before, the valleys pleasant and fertile, though the land is generally poor, except where it is made otherwise by lime and other manure. Pembrokeshire exhibits a pleasant picture; the houses of the farmers, scattered among the hills, appear neat and comfortable, the people warmly clad, and few barefoot or ragged, as we have lately been accustomed to see in Ireland; — the houses are mostly thatched, and all are white-washed outside, which gives them an agreeable appearance at a distance. The women all wear hats, like men — we met many of the farmers' daughters, well mounted on horseback, with great-coats and hats on; — riding on horseback is preferred in this hilly country. Much simplicity of manners was obvious in the people of our inn, and they accommodated us with kindness and good lodging.

"16th. Got to breakfast at Carmarthen, which is a decent town, perhaps ten thousand inhabitants, beautifully situated on the side of a small river, which empties into the Bristol channel; it is surrounded with high hills, well improved and cultivated to the tops; the country much more fertile than that we passed through yesterday; the valleys and hills covered with beautiful verdure, look as green as ours in the fourth month. The weather is more serene and clear than in Ireland, and the people very respectful, industrious, and not fond of show and finery — they work hard for a little money; a woman with one or two pack-horses or asses, will travel on foot eight or nine miles, with about one and a half bushels of oats, which brings them about fourteen pence more than they cost; and in summer not more than nine pence. Laborers have six pence a day and their provision.

"17th. Had a meeting appointed at Swansea, which was pretty well attended; the people were quiet and attentive; I thought it was, through Divine mercy, a good meeting, and I left it peacefully.

"19th. In passing through the country, I saw several large ancient castles, the parks and fields beautifully green, surrounded with hills; and hundreds of sheep, deer, goats, and cattle feeding — an attractive spot of earth indeed. Got on to Marlborough: the inn we stopped at had formerly been a seat of the Duke of Marlborough; it was the largest and most splendidly furnished I have seen in England; the gardens, park, forest, &c., make it a great resort of gentry to spend a few days. Arrived at Bristol in the evening, and on the 20th visited a number of Friends, and had some thought of moving on in the morning; but upon considering it more fully, I concluded to stay at Bristol.

"First-day, 21st. The meeting was large, many not professing with us coming in. Some of our Society here make an appearance unbecoming our religious profession. Through heavenly goodness a solemnity soon spread over us, and it was a satisfactory meeting, for which I felt thankful. That held in the evening was very crowded, but still and orderly; there were several ministers of other societies present, and the opportunity appeared to be favored with the presence of the great and good Master of assemblies, and ended in thankfulness to Him for this additional mercy.

"22d. My good friend and companion, William Farrer, having received a letter from home, informing of the illness of his nephew and partner, thought it his place to return there, which was some trial to me, having travelled in true fellowship on the continent and on these islands ten months together; and we parted in the same, both being affected at the separation. Several Friends accompanied me to Bath, at which we arrived before noon. The public meeting this evening was large, a considerable number of other professors attended, and many could not get in; they behaved with great propriety, and I felt my mind relieved to my own satisfaction. Very few of the members of our Society here have the appearance of Friends, and some said they were sorry they could not attend, but they were engaged on parties at that hour. Having paid a visit in the forenoon to the famous Hannah More and her four sisters, some of them being present at the meeting, came and invited us to their house again; there came also a middle-aged, well-dressed woman, who shook hands with me, and asked when it would suit me to receive a visit, as she wanted to have some conversation with me. I told her this evening, and while at supper she came; she stayed about half an hour, appeared to be a singular and extraordinary character, had been bred a Roman Catholic in London, but growing uneasy with the practices of that people, she went off to Rome, expecting her mind would be relieved at that fountain-head of religion, but was greatly deceived; and after residing there three years, protesting against their errors, for which she had several times been likely to lose her life, she returned through France. Not finding true religion there, she had come to Bath about nine months since, disgusted with all professions and separated from them, yet seeking the Truth; she was overjoyed at being at the meeting, having never thought of inquiring among Friends for religion: after expressing a little to her, we parted.

"23d. This being the season for drinking the waters, the town is crowded with gentry, who make a splendid appearance, and live in great dissipation, to the disgrace of religion and morality — it is said that one thousand persons attended the concert last night. Believing it right to have another meeting, one was accordingly appointed at a meeting-house of the dissenters, which was thought would hold twelve hundred persons or more; and it was presently filled, and proved, through the adorable mercy of our heavenly Father, to whom be all the praise, a precious season, ending in solemn prayer and praises. Hannah More having desired a Friend to bring me to their house again, I there found the celebrated William Wilberforce, who had been at the meeting, which I knew not of; but it was somewhat remarkable and unusual, that I should be led to touch upon the enormity of the slave trade; we soon became quite familiar, and he asked me many questions about the state of religion in the different parts of the continent where I had been, and appeared much pleased that I had had an interview with Thomas Paine. Hannah More and her sisters are all unmarried, live in good style, and do a great deal of good — they have written and compiled many excellent works, some for the use of charity schools, &c. They are a band of sisters, desirous of employing their time in doing what may be beneficial in the world, and avoid all the gay and dissipating amusements of Bath. We did not retire to bed till near twelve o'clock, and after the fatigues of the day, I was favored to lie down rejoicing in the goodness and mercy of God.

"24th. On leaving Bath, I was persuaded, that notwithstanding the great dissipation abounding in the place, the Lord hath a considerable number of sincere hearted, seeking children there, though our Society is indeed at a very low ebb. Looking back at my visit among the people, thankfulness covered my mind, that the Lord had preserved me, as I humbly hope, from wounding the blessed cause of Truth, which is at times above all things dear to me. I had dreaded going there, but was convinced that the Lord is sufficient for his own work. Got on to Melksham, and had a meeting in the evening; the house was not large enough to hold the people, but though crowded, they soon became quiet and solid, and it appeared to me to be an open, tendering time, ending with much solemnity—praised be the great name of Him, whose is the power and the glory. Passed on to Devizes, but felt no necessity to make much stay there: walking through the market, I took notice of a monument in the middle of the street, erected to commemorate the sudden death of a woman, who told a *deliberate lie*, in order to defraud. The inscription is a solemn warning, to deter people from frauds and lies in making bargains.

"26th. Went through Windsor, where the royal family were: the enormous pile of buildings, called Windsor Castle, is near a mile in circumference, standing on very high ground, and commanding an extensive view. As we rode through the forest, I saw many servants, and some of the nobility, who were attending on a hunting excursion. At Staines, I thought it right to appoint a meeting for this evening, and Friends being active in giving notice, though it was now late in the afternoon, the meeting-house was soon filled—many stood, and some could not get in; the people were still and attentive. I believed there were many religious persons present, but also some Deists; many were much tendered, and through renewed mercy it was a time of favor.

"27th. Got to London, and was kindly received by my beloved friends J. Savory and others, after a separation of near eight months.

"28th. Attended two meetings, and two burials. Had an appointed meeting in the evening, which was much crowded with people of other religious professions; my mind was solemnly covered, and I was favored with much openness, to the praise of Him, who is the Author of all good, and to my own abasement, as unworthy of so great and repeated mercy: dear George Dillwyn made a solid and pertinent addition, and the meeting closed in prayer and praises—returned to my lodgings wearied, but comforted in looking back on the labors of the day.

"Second month. 3d. Went in a post-chaise for

Norwich, and reached a Friend's house about half a mile out of the town.

"First-day, 4th of the month. Attended their meeting; some not members stepped in, and there were about two hundred under our name; very few middle-aged, or young persons, who had a consistent appearance in their dress; indeed, I thought it the gayest meeting of Friends I ever sat in, and was grieved to see it. I expected to pass the meeting in silent suffering, but at length believed it most for my peace to express a little, and through gracious condescension was favored to relieve my mind, and many were tendered. Had a meeting in the evening, in a large meeting-house in another part of the town: there seems to be but few upright standard-bearers left among the members in this place, yet they are not entirely removed.—Attended the public meeting, and the house, though very large, could not contain the people by several hundreds; but considering their crowded situation, many being obliged to stand, they soon became settled, and through mercy it proved a remarkably open, satisfactory meeting, ending in prayer and praise to the Author of every blessing. The marks of wealth and grandeur are too obvious in several families of Friends in this place, which made me sorrowful, yet saw but little opening to relieve my mind; several of the younger branches, though they are enabled, through Divine grace, to see what the Truth leads to, yet it is uncertain whether, with all the alluring things of this world around them, they will choose the simple, safe path of self-denial. This city is supposed to contain about sixty thousand inhabitants, which, perhaps, is too high an estimate: it is pleasantly situated, but has many poor, and numerous beggars in the streets.

"6th. Attended the Monthly Meeting at Ipswich, in which they read my certificate, and in the women's meeting I had a little to communicate: in the evening had an appointed meeting for other professors, which appeared to be heavy; yet I believe, that through the preservation of the heavenly Shepherd, there was nothing lost.

"8th. Was at Bury: this town is not large, but bears the marks of great antiquity—has many singular ruins in and about it, and is considered one of the handsomest small towns in England. King Edmund is said to have died, and been buried here. The public meeting, this evening, was crowded, but still, and through the regard of our heavenly Father, a good opportunity.

"11th. At meeting at Hitchen; and visited the boarding-school, where my mind was drawn towards the children in much affection, and they were all broken into tears; it was, indeed, a time of special favor. The appointed public meeting, this evening, was large, many went away for want of room, and many stood outside, in the yard, all the time; and through infinite mercy it proved a favored time—closing in prayer and praises to God.

"12th. Visited several elderly Friends, and then

went to Hartford, which is a large county town; and not feeling easy to pass it without a meeting with the inhabitants, one was accordingly appointed for this evening;—the house was not quite filled, and for some time the meeting seemed rather heavy; but through the condescension of our heavenly Father, it proved at length a good and comfortable season.

"13th. Passed on through many villages, and arrived at my usual lodgings in London before noon. In this last turn was out eleven days, and felt peace and quietness to attend me in the close.

"Second month, 14th. A publication appeared in one of the public papers approving of what was delivered at Norwich and Bath; but I thank my God, who has yet preserved me from being elated or much depressed, by the well or ill-done of the world. If I can but obtain the answer of a conscience void of offence to God and man, that is the great object of my concern and will be enough.

"After having visited a number of Friends, and attended several meetings, I went to Horselydown on First-day, the 18th; was at their meeting, and appointed a public meeting for the evening, which was very crowded; some of the most respectable people being present — a great solemnity seemed to spread over us in the time of silence, and though I felt remarkably poor and tried at entering it, yet through the gracious condescension of our heavenly Father, it was one of the most comfortable meetings to myself, I remember to have sat in London: praises to the Author of every blessing.

"First-day, 25th. Visited a number of Friends last week; to-day attended the meetings at Westminster, and appointed one for other people this evening, which proved a good meeting, to the praise of Him, whose is the power and the glory of all.

"27th. From a particular impression on my mind, I visited a man in prison, who was under sentence of death. His cell being small, damp and dark, the gaoler invited us, with the criminal, into a better room. He was about fifty years of age, and his wife was staying with him to see his end. After his condemnation, he was at first much distressed on account of his condition, but having been favored to find a place of repentance, he had hope in the mercy of God and was not afraid to die: — he seemed in a calm, quiet state of mind, but not boasting. Some advice was communicated to him, and we left him thankful for our visit.

"Third month, 5th. Visited the soup-house which is principally under the care of Friends; there are several of these charities in and about London. The soup is made very good and nourishing, and the poor give a penny a quart for it; this one is in Brick-lane, and makes about fifteen hundred quarts a day—it is a great relief to the poor, for which they express many blessings to Friends as they pass through the streets.

"7th. Having appointed a public meeting, I went to it this evening in much fear: it soon became exceedingly crowded, and the passages being filled, some hundreds stood round the doors; many respectable people attended, and much solemnity prevailed in the time of silence. I was led to speak of the awful signs of the times, and on some passages in the Revelations; the Lord was good to us, and the way was opened in a remarkable manner to declare the truth; and He condescended to tender my own heart, and also most of the congregation, for which there was an offering of thanksgiving to Him; after which I was much humbled, saw and felt myself unworthy of his many mercies, and retired to rest with much thankfulness.

"10th. Dined at Benjamin West's, in company with George Dillwyn; and he having concerted the necessary measures preparatory to a visit to the royal family, George Dillwyn, Mary Knowles and myself, went with him in his carriage to Buckingham-house, where we arrived about six o'clock. The queen ordered the pages to show us into one of the apartments, where we waited about five minutes, when one of the lords came to conduct us to the drawing-room. The king, queen and three of the princesses, with prince Ernest Augustus, met us with pleasant countenances. Being informed of my late journey on the continent, the prince asked me many questions, but with rather too much rapidity. He particularly wished to be informed of the present state of Lyons, which gave me an opportunity of expressing my feelings on the horrors and miseries of war, and that it must be devoutly wished by every good Christian, that a total cessation of that dreadful practice should take place; and which every one, according to his rank and station in the world, ought to labor to promote: to this the queen and princesses, who stood close round us in a group, gave an emphatic assent. The king and queen asked questions on several subjects, to which I gave answers as I was qualified. The king engaging in conversation with George Dillwyn, I turned to the queen and princesses, who all appeared highly pleased with the interview. She gave me the names of the children and their ages, and told Mary to bring her sister Amelia, who was unwell, but she came in;— she is a tall girl of fourteen. We conversed with the king, queen and children, like old acquaintances; and I told them I was grateful for their condescension in receiving us in this social manner — for there was not a single person with us in the room all the time. The king asking me about the situation of things between France and America, I told him I seldom meddled at all with politics, as it was not my business. No, no, no, said he, I understand; but as a people you can never form so natural an attachment with any nation of Europe as England; we are united by religion, relationship, commerce, disposition, &c. I replied, that I valued the connection, and hoped the family compact would never be broken; — and the queen, who had caught a part of the conversation, desired I would repeat it; was much pleased with the idea, and spoke of it to her daughters with satisfaction. The king spoke of the Theophilanthropists in France, but had not a right idea of them. I told him I desired to embrace the good as my brethren, under every different modification of outward form and profession in the world; —to which he and the queen replied, 'A good Christian must do so, for he has the same regard for good people of different professions.' After much free conversation, I could hardly take leave of them without tears. Benjamin West made a motion; the king and queen, with the children, drew a little back, and with gestures of respect, bid us a 'good evening.' I said a few words at parting; George Dillwyn also expressed a little. After we retired, Benjamin West staying a little, heard the king say to the queen, 'Charlotte, how satisfactory this has been.'

"First-day, 11th. Attended meetings at Ratcliff and appointed one for this evening, which was held in a malt store — above one thousand people attended; and though all could not get seats, they behaved remarkably well. It was thought to be a solid, favored time, but my mind was very much stripped at the close; surely the Lord is good to sustain and support so poor a creature as I am, under these weighty engagements.

"16th. Concluded to hold a meeting this evening with the people, in the king's dock-yards, at Chatham. I admired the quiet and order of the workmen, a great number of whom are Methodists; the meeting was full, mostly from the dock-yard, and it appeared to be a solid comfortable season.

"18th. At London, and attended their meeting at Gracechurch street. A public meeting being appointed for this evening, great numbers came together — many of the gay families in and round London were present, with a multitude of other professions, supposed to be upwards of two thousand; yet they were very quiet and attentive, and the Lord was pleased to be with me, so that I rejoiced in a hope, that Truth had risen as high as in any of the public meetings I had had about London; it ended in thanksgiving, and I took leave of the people, not doubting I should now depart from this city soon.

"19th. I mentioned my prospect of appointing a meeting for Friends only; and though I felt weak and fearful about it, yet was most easy to appoint one for to-morrow evening. Walked to the soup-house in Spittal fields, where a few Friends were busily employed in distributing about fourteen hundred quarts of soup, which they do in about two hours — the poor people bless the Quakers and seem very grateful for this relief.

"20th. Attended the appointed meeting, which was large; a great many had to stand all the time — a solemnity prevailed; and it was made, through the heavenly Father's love, a season long to be remembered; the light and airy, as well as the formal and precise professors, were tenderly spoken to; and the humble, upright-hearted among the youth and others, comforted. It was such a time of cementing union and love with my brethren and sisters in Society, as I never experienced in England before. At the close George Dillwyn kneeled down, and in a lively manner gave God the glory, which was and ever will be his due. A considerable number expressed a hope they should see me again in London, and my own mind was doubtful whether it was a final parting; however, I believed it a right time to leave the city at present, and commit the future to the direction of Him, who hath been pleased to be mercifully with me, far beyond my deserts: — many were in tears, and it was after nine o'clock before I could get out of the meeting-house. I retired to rest relieved of London, and with much thankfulness of heart to the Father of mercies.

"23d. After having visited several Friends, went on to Shipstone; and being informed of the burial of a young woman at Chipping Norton, I felt most easy to attend it, though several miles off. A large company were present, so that the meeting-house was much too small for them. I had some remarks to communicate, and it appeared to be a favored, contriting season. The grave was walled up about one foot and a half high, with brick, and floored with the same, laid in mortar; the coffin was let down and covered with flat stones, laid on the brick wall in mortar. Went on through a part of Oxfordshire to Evesham, a large market-town in Worcestershire, where there are a few Friends and a meeting. Friends here were under a good deal of concern, as I have found in many other places, about paying taxes declared to be for the express purpose of carrying on the war. I think our peaceable testimony is so much concerned in it, that many Friends will find it the way to peace, to suffer, rather than actively comply: it will no doubt be a trying time to many, through which I hope the standard will be held up a little higher against the horrid practice of war, than has yet been the case in England.

"24th. Passed through a good country to Bridgenorth, on the head of the Severn: most of the town stands on a high rocky hill; the lower town in the vale. The rock is so soft that many of the poor live in chambers cut out of it; some families one story above another. Great simplicity prevails among the country people; their language partaking a little of Welch, and differing from any I have heard in England. We rode over very high and uneven ground, the Severn flowing below us, and passed through the town of Brosely, among the iron works and over the iron bridge. This valley, for a mile or more, is filled with iron works; the hills are steep and rugged, yet covered with houses, gardens, &c.; for the people are dependent on the works. It has a very dark appearance, even the trees and bushes are quite blackened with the smoke; and in the night the fires have a terrific appearance. We arrived at Sunny-side, and were received at Sarah Darby's with much kindness. Dear Deborah Darby resides here, and Rebecca Young was here also.

"First-day, 25th. Visited our ancient, honorable Friend, Ann Summerland, a minister beloved, and now in her eighty-ninth year — she leaned on my arm to the meeting-house: many not professing with us came into the meeting, and at the close I appointed a public meeting for the people generally. The meeting in the evening was large for the place, and appeared to be a solid time throughout. Mary Fletcher, widow of the late John Fletcher, of this parish, having had a numerous meeting in the Dale this afternoon, occasioned more people to be at ours; she preaches much in various places round this neighborhood; bears an excellent character for piety, both from Friends and others, and is certainly an extraordinary woman.

"26th. Went on to Shrewsbury, where Rebecca Young lives, and had an appointed meeting this evening. As it was the time of the assizes, many came in, so that the house was too small for the company; yet the people were very quiet and attentive, and through the goodness of our heavenly Shepherd, it closed to our comfort, in praises to his great and ever worthy name. A messenger being sent on, a meeting was appointed at Elsemere, on the borders of Wales, sixteen miles from Shrewsbury, which we attended the 27th. The people not being accustomed to see Friends often, were somewhat uncivil as we passed through the street. The room held about three hundred, but more were outside and thronging to get in. On explaining to them our reasons for appointing such meetings and the necessity laid upon us both to labor and to suffer reproach, if the Lord permitted it, for his name sake, they became quiet, and though impatient to get in were serious and still. Deborah Darby had a favored time, and I made some addition, and Rebecca Young closed the meeting in prayer; so through the mercy and goodness of the Lord our helper, Truth came into dominion, and at parting with the people, they thanked us for our visit. An ancient woman seemed very loving, and told Deborah Darby there had never been a meeting of Friends in the town since her remembrance, and that she was thankful for this.

"Went to Wrexham on the 28th, and held an appointed meeting at eleven o'clock; and it being fair-time, which continues a week, the inn and streets were crowded: the manufacturers from Manchester and Birmingham, were here to get orders for goods, and the Irish traders with linen, so that it looked like an unfavorable time for a meeting: about one hundred and fifty came in, but seemed rather restless; and the waiter of the inn frequently called one or other out to some who had business. Deborah Darby spoke, and for a time they were pretty still, yet several were moving out and in; a considerable part of the company being such who had come out of the country to the fair, and probably had never seen a Friends' meeting before. I having something to offer, and speaking pretty loud, many came up from below stairs; and though there was still much unsettlement, yet a number were solid and quiet to the end; it closed in prayer, and on parting with the more serious class, they lamented that the meeting had not been at another time, when we should have had a large company, and the people more settled. Went on for Liverpool, and travelled through a pretty country to Chester, where we arrived after much detention, about nine o'clock at night.

"29th. Attended their meeting — my mind to-day much exercised about right direction, when and how to move towards my dear home, desiring to be released as soon as the Lord may please to make way for it in peace.

"Fourth month, 1st. Went out to Bickerstaff, which had once been as large as most country meetings; but for seven years past no members have resided there, except two old people; the house is the most antique and simple of any I have seen, and was nearly filled with plain, honest looking country people, chiefly farmers and laborers from the neighborhood, who were still; many were tender, especially some of the most aged, and I trust the good Shepherd was with us. Friends having obtained leave for a meeting at three o'clock in the Town Hall of Ormskirk, we proceeded thither; but found that some prejudiced people had been influencing the magistrate who gave leave, to countermand it. He said, that upon consideration, he did not think such meetings ought to be encouraged, especially on the sabbath day, when every person ought to be at their own place of worship; and he therefore ordered the constable to stand at the door and suffer no one to go in. The place had been seated, and the notices spread in the town. I felt calm, expecting the people would not all be pleased with the order. It appeared that a person, by the initials supposed to be one of the new lights from Ireland, had been there some weeks past, and said something that offended the minds of many, and the people behaved rudely. I was concerned how it might end; thinking if any prejudices had got in, and we were obstinately refused a meeting, I must endeavor to vindicate our principles and testimony, either out of the windows of the inn, or in the market-place. I ate but little at dinner, and before three o'clock a servant came to inform us from the constable, we might hold our meeting at four o'clock, when the public worship would be over. Some of the young men stood at the Hall door, and also pasted up a paper, informing that the meeting was postponed till four o'clock; at which time we went—the constable having just opened the door, vast numbers were crowding up stairs, and they came in, until no more could either stand or sit: it was supposed about five hundred persons were there, some of them the most respectable people of the town, who sat near us; but it was very evident they came with prejudiced minds in a general way, and expected to have something to ridicule. It is certainly a very important engagement, and fraught with serious consequences, to attempt to hold such meetings, and to leave them so as to shut up the way of those who may come after; which, indeed, is injuring the cause we profess to promote. Believing it right to stand up and express a text of Scripture, many began to smile, and I had not been in such a meeting for a long time; yet feeling my strength increase as I proceeded, and the heavenly Shepherd near, the people dropped their countenances, and became serious — many at length were much affected; and towards the close, which was under a feeling of reverent thankfulness to the Lord our helper, an evidence was granted, that the holy Truth was as able as formerly to chain down light spirits and put to silence the scorner. Returned to Liverpool. Several vessels going for America, I am tried with daily anxiety about home, in a manner I have not experienced since I left it, and my mind much exercised that I might know the will of God and do it, whether to go from England at present or tarry a little longer.

"First-day, Fourth month, 8th. At meeting, my mind was opened in an unusual manner, and I felt comforted in believing the gracious Helper of the poor was near and his presence with us. Appointed a public meeting for this evening, which was large, their commodious house being filled, and it was said that many of the first rank in the town were present. The call of the Lord's people out of Babylon was opened; showing that Babylon signifies confusion, and that all priestcraft and false foundations, laid by human wisdom and authority, in establishing systems and modes of worship, not proceeding from Divine wisdom, were in the confusion, as well as the civil policy that involved nations in cruel and destructive wars, and permitted men to ravage foreign countries, and carry their inhabitants into the most inhuman hands of slave-masters. The meeting was still and attentive, and much solemnity reigned, for which, impressed with a sense of the mercy and goodness of God in thus favoring us, the meeting closed in prayer and praises —retired to bed with thankfulness to the Author of every blessing for support through the day.

"10th. Having attended Hardshaw Monthly Meeting, in which the business appeared to be well conducted, I returned to Liverpool. The roads were dusty, and the people diverting themselves in the fields with dancing and other sports, which they call 'folly fair,' a proper name for such vanity. Low in mind, not seeing how to move for the best as respects my leaving this country. My natural feelings are strongly drawn towards home, but no light seems to shine upon it; and I never had more need to ask for patience than at present.

"14th. Went for Lancaster: the land through this part of the country appears to be but an indifferent soil; the farms, hedges, &c., not in that neatness which is apparent in many other places in England.

"First-day, 15th. Attended their meeting, and appointed one for other professors in the evening, which was crowded. I was considerably enlarged in communication, respecting the righteous of former ages, both under the law and the Gospel, and the manner in which they obtained confidence in God; and that the same means would produce the like effect now, both to individuals and nations: the people were quiet, remarkably attentive, and through holy condescension it was a favored opportunity — the praise of all was solemnly rendered unto Him who is for ever worthy.

"16th. Got on to Liverpool, and on the 17th was at the meeting of ministers and elders, and it appeared to be a profitable season. At the Quarterly Meeting for Discipline, the subject of paying taxes for the support of war was considered, and it appeared that many

Friends were much straitened in their minds about the practice, in most of the Quarters in the nation.

"18th. The meeting this afternoon was large; it was thought there were two thousand people present: some doctrinal subjects were opened by William Jephson, in a remarkably clear and convincing manner, and it was a favored time; ending in prayer and praises unto God, who helped and strengthened us. Many of the people expected another meeting, and seemed loth to depart.

"20th. A ship is to sail in two days for Philadelphia, and my mind is much exercised, not feeling liberty to return to America. A public meeting this evening was large, at which were Deborah Darby, Rebecca Young, and Charity Cook: the Lord in great mercy owned us, and favored with a renewed eating and drinking together as in his presence, where his banner over us was love; in which I believe many not professing with us partook, and parted in great sweetness.

"21st. Went on for Chester, and on First-day, the 22nd, had a public meeting there — the house filled — Deborah Darby had an open favored time; the people were solid and a number expressed their thankfulness, wishing for another meeting; but one having been appointed at Wrexham, twelve miles off in Wales, for this evening, we left Chester; passed through a pleasant, well-cultivated country to that town. Held the meeting in a large room, supposed to contain six hundred, but it was much too small; and that and a room adjoining were crowded to such a degree, that it became very warm, so that some were ready to faint; yet the people seemed inclined to be still. After speaking some time, numbers pushing to get in caused uneasiness and unsettlement, and I then proposed, that if another place could be immediately obtained, we had better proceed thither. A respectable looking man said, the Independent meeting was at our service, if we chose to go there; but dear Deborah Darby not being willing to go into a place of worship of another society, stood up and spoke to the people, which had a good effect. The crowd however was too great to continue, and we broke up the meeting, and appointed another at ten o'clock in the forenoon, at the same place. The people seemed sorry it could not be continued, as many of them were poor and could not well attend on a working day.

"23d. The meeting being accordingly held, about eight hundred attended, and it proved a satisfactory time, to the refreshment and comfort of many; much tenderness being apparent, the people were full of expressions of their satisfaction, and many asked for books, which we had not to give them, but promised to send them some. Wrexham is one of the largest towns in Wales, and may contain eight or ten thousand inhabitants.

"Proceeded to Oswestry, a considerable town, about sixteen miles distant; and passed through many pleasant vales, &c. A large room being prepared for a meeting, it was supposed seven hundred persons were present; and after considerable communication we parted with the people in much tenderness—many acknowledging the Truth and asking for books.

"24th. Going towards Welchpool, we found the roads very much cut and hilly; the valleys were beautiful, and many barren mountains were in view—the farm-houses generally small, and the dress of the people rather mean. Several Friends from Colebrookdale having joined us, we held a meeting in the evening at our inn; but it was an hour before more than forty persons came—two Friends spoke; after which, feeling an engagement to speak, and my voice being heard at a distance, the people crowded up stairs and filled both rooms; they were quiet and attentive—a few persons who had been drinking too freely were unsettled, yet the meeting ended well, and we appointed another for to-morrow evening.

"25th. Attended the meeting of ministers and elders this morning, which was small but solid; the poor Welch Friends were much affected with the smallness of their number and with their weakness. The meeting for Discipline, which is held only twice a year in Wales, and is similar to a Quarterly Meeting, consisted of about thirty-two men of their own members, sixteen of them Welch, and as many from Shropshire. I felt very low about the meeting to be held this evening, Friends saying the people have never been very free in coming to them. Deborah Darby and Rebecca Young being much wearied, excused themselves from attending. The Town-house had been obtained, and it was soon filled, and a large number stood in the street, but so situated as to be able to hear; they were still both within doors and without, and many were much tendered: the opportunity ended in prayer, and Friends thought that, through Divine favor, it was the most solid meeting they had known in that town.

"26th. Attended the meeting for Discipline, and went into the women's meeting with my certificates, where I had an open, tendering time, and dear Deborah Darby appeared in prayer in a solemn and comforting manner. A person who lived at Montgomeryshire, eight miles off, requesting Friends to hold a meeting there, and Deborah Darby and Rebecca Young having wished to have one there a few months back, which the parson prevented, they now thought it right to go; and believing it required of me to go another way, though much in the cross, I took an affectionate leave of them, in order to proceed to Dublin Yearly Meeting. Passed through a mountainous country, having very little appearance of wealth or luxury; the inhabitants spoke little else among themselves but Welch, and many of them speak English with difficulty; they look like a healthy, hardy race — the women almost universally wear hats like men, and work much in the fields and barn. The inhabitants seemed to live in humble style, and to be much unacquainted with the fashionable world. Giving our coachmen, at different stages, a little extra pay to get us on as fast as they could, to Holyhead, we arrived there the 27th at night, and found a packet just hoisting sail and the passengers going on board. They allowed us a quarter of an hour to procure provisions for the voyage; so that if we had been half an hour later, we should have missed our passage. There were only three passengers besides ourselves, and a good sloop, in which we were well accommodated. On the morning of the 28th, we plainly discovered the mountains of Wicklow — and the captain, A. Savory and myself, being the only persons who had lain in provisions, it was all brought upon deck, the others joined in our repast, and we all eat very heartily.

"29th. When about two miles from the Dublin lighthouse, a boat came to take the passengers on shore; at such ports many are seeking to empty the pockets of travellers. We breakfasted at a miserably dirty, though large hotel, showing us at once that we were out of England. Went to Meath street meeting-house, where Friends were assembled — the widow Usher of Waterford, spoke a few words in prayer, and Friends seemed glad to see me come into the meeting. Appointed a public meeting at six o'clock in the evening, which was, through the renewing of our heavenly Master's favor, an open, satisfactory time, and the praise was returned to Him who alone is worthy.

"30th. Second-day; the Meeting for Discipline was held, and much solemnity was apparent at the opening. Leinster province meeting contains almost as many Friends as Ulster and Munster, and there is only one small meeting in Connaught. In considering the reports from the different meetings, the subject of reading the Scriptures took up the attention of Friends.

Some of the accounts being deficient, Friends could not easily get over it, but were not sufficiently clear and explicit in mentioning their painful apprehensions, and were about to pass it by. I pressed their closer attention to it, but some were for going on, though many minds were oppressed, knowing the pernicious sentiments that had obtained, even among some members in high stations. I now saw in part what brought me to Ireland again. I urged it again, when Friends spoke their minds freely, and it appeared that a number in different parts of the nation were in a disposition to lay waste in great measure the Holy Scriptures, disputed the Divinity of Christ, and were not united with the present ministry or discipline of our religious Society, but yet professed to exalt the Divine Light and immediate revelation very highly. After several hours spent on the subject, a large committee was appointed to take the matter into consideration, and join with the women Friends in bringing in a report. David Sands and myself were requested to sit with them. Went to my lodgings fatigued, but convinced that it was my duty to attend this meeting.

"Fifth month, 1st. The meeting of ministers and elders was exercised on the same painful subject as the Meeting for Discipline; some of the disaffected were present; several active members, and one elder of Dublin, sat with their hats on while David Sands was in supplication.

"2d. The committee of men and women Friends, respecting the Scriptures of Truth, met, and also a number of concerned Friends, both men and women: several Friends said they knew members, who not only openly allowed their disbelief and disregard of a great part of the Holy Scriptures, but who also denied the Divinity of Christ, and many things recorded concerning him—and pretended that they were so illuminated as to have no occasion for books or outward helps—some of these they believed had come into the committee, who might speak for themselves. I urged such who were dissatisfied with the doctrines of Friends in these respects, to be candid and open, that we might discover what their sentiments were, observing that no honest man ought to hold sentiments he was ashamed of. I told them it was well to take one thing at a time, and to read the head of the chapter on the Holy Scriptures in Robert Barclay, and if Abraham Shackleton or any other, who I supposed to be the cause of uneasiness, had anything to object, I hoped they would stand forth. On its being read, J. B——y said he agreed to the proposition that Barclay had laid down, but there were several parts of the Scriptures he could neither call holy nor require his children to read—he would not go so far as to deny the authenticity of them in general. Abraham Shackleton agreed in words at least, but was for mutilating the Scriptures, saying that many parts were unprofitable, and some things derogatory to the Divine Being—there were five books, he observed, between Genesis and Job, but did not say which, that he could very well spare, and some other parts of both the Old and New Testaments — he did not deny that Jesus Christ was a Divine person, but it was not clear what his ideas of the Divinity were. After we had sat about three hours, those who were not of the committee withdrew, and Friends then spending another hour in considering the subjects, appointed three men to bring in a report. On attending the committee in the afternoon, a report was brought in, but before there was time to go through it, adjourned until to-morrow.

"Fifth month, 3d. The committee on the Holy Scriptures and on the unsound doctrines held by some members of Society, having met, a report drawn up by the sub-committee to be presented to the Yearly Meeting, was read, setting forth that there was reason to believe, that some members of Society held the Scriptures, particularly some parts of them, in very light estimation, and were also tinctured with unsound doctrines, and proposing it to be recommended, that such should be tenderly treated with by the Monthly Meetings, and if they could not be brought to condemn their errors, the Monthly Meetings should request the assistance of the Quarters to labor further with them, and if they still persisted to hold those pernicious opinions, Friends were then to declare their disunity with them.* The meeting again assembling at five o'clock, the report of the committee, with some small

* Most of the persons who had unhappily imbibed these unsound and pernicious opinions, which were the cause of so much sorrow and concern to the Society, soon after relinquished their membership or were disowned.

alteration, was adopted and sent into the women's meeting. Some Friends having obtained the freedom of cities, by taking an affirmation to keep a gun and bayonet in their houses, and a few others being at present contractors for the army, this very serious subject took up much time at this sitting of the meeting, and it was ordered that a minute should be brought to the next sitting, directing Monthly Meetings to deal with such delinquents. The first is a practice of many years' standing, and but lately taken notice of in a Society capacity. Some who were so circumstanced, sent to the corporations a resignation of their freedoms.

"4th. Attended the meeting at Sycamore alley, and had to mention the expressions 'the memory of the just is blessed,' bringing to the remembrance of the company present, the worthies of our Society who had been formerly raised up in Ireland; the youth were tendered, and through Divine mercy and favor, it appeared to be a profitable, good meeting. In one hour after this, the meeting of ministers and elders met again, when my certificates being read, some Friends were appointed to draw a returning one from this meeting. J. B—— sent in a note, desiring to be admitted into the meeting to relieve his mind; Friends sent out a committee to hear him, but did not admit him — he was one of those persons who thought lightly of some part of the Scriptures. Attended the Meeting for Discipline, which recommended its representatives not to urge in the Yearly Meeting of London, the request for a distinct Yearly Meeting in Ireland; all who spoke to the business, thought it was no time to break up the connection, in which I much united.

"5th. The meeting was brought under the consideration of appointing a committee to visit Quarterly and Monthly Meetings in this nation, as it appeared to be a trying time to Friends, from circumstances both within and without the Society, which subject I had felt impressed on my mind for several sittings. Three or four of those members who had given the meeting much exercise and trouble, opposed the motion, but a solemn calm coming over the meeting, many Friends expressed their unity with the concern, and six men Friends were appointed. The meeting adjourned until afternoon, when it sat till eight o'clock at night, and closed in a solid and comfortable manner. Though it had been a painful, exercising week to many, it was thought to be as profitable a meeting as had been held for a number of years.

"First-day, 6th of the month. Attended their meetings for worship and appointed a public meeting for the evening, which was very large, more than the house would hold; there were many people of high rank, some officers, and several of those called clergymen present. I was led to combat the Deistical opinions, and through the continued mercy of our heavenly Father, it was one of the most solid, satisfactory meetings I ever sat in Dublin.

"7th. Meeting of ministers and elders: a lively zeal was manifest to stir up Friends to attend to their several gifts, and to be watchful in keeping down those who may attempt to introduce unsound doctrines among Friends. Our certificates were signed by all except three members who are leaning, it is to be feared, to the new opinions — the meeting concluded in a serious, satisfactory manner, after having agreed to print Robert Barclay's chapter on the Scriptures.

"8th. At meeting at Meath street, I mentioned the passage in which it is said, that our Lord passed through certain cities without doing many miracles, because of their unbelief. Mary Ridgway then took up the subject, and had a lively testimony; David Sands closed the service on the same, and it was thought to be a profitable meeting — Friends took leave of each other in much tenderness. In the afternoon there being many Friends at the house where I was, I took an affectionate leave of them all, several expressing they believed I was right in coming again to Dublin, for which I was thankful and felt encouraged.

"9th. Went on board the packet with a number of Friends who are going with us to England. Arrived in the evening at Holyhead, and our baggage being taken to the Custom-house, I searched in vain for my trunk, which could not be found, and was very uneasy at the loss, as many valuable articles were in it. I determined to stay at Holyhead until I could learn something about my trunk; it was rather a dreary time to my cousin A. Savory and myself. The town is small, and a dull place, except when the packets are either going out or arriving from Ireland; there are perhaps about one hundred houses in it, and as to trade it seems very dead.

"12th. Early in the morning the bar-keeper came into my room and said, your portmanteau is in my possession. It had been found after we sailed from Dublin, and sent on by my friend Joseph Wilson. Rode to Bangor ferry — most of the towns in Wales are very dull, both as to navigation and inland trade. Got to Aberconway, one of the most ancient little cities I have seen, particularly its walls and towers: being a thoroughfare from Dublin to London, draws travellers to it, and the money thus disbursed, furnishes the inhabitants with their principal support. Rode in sight of the Irish channel, and crossed several mountains, one very high, the road being cut into the side of it with the sea almost perpendicularly under it. From this height there is a very agreeable view of the ships sailing in the channel; of the verdant, beautiful valleys, and humble cottages, with their inhabitants, between the mountains; the horses, cattle, ploughs and people, so far below us, that they appeared very diminutive. Men and women seemed to take an equal share of labor in the fields. Got to St. Asaph, which is but a small town, having rode sixty miles to-day.

"First-day, 13th. Passed through a well-cultivated country, and one of the finest valleys in Great Britain, the fields and meadows luxuriant, timber trees in the hedges, etc.; much rural simplicity prevails. Arrived at Wrexham. Several hundreds of soldiers having come into the town on their way to Ireland, the people seemed in a bustle and no probability of a meeting among them to advantage, so we sat down quietly to our bibles. In the evening it plainly appeared. that a meeting could not have been held to satisfaction, as the people began to be very noisy, and much taken up with the soldiery.

"14th. Put on through Elsemere and Shrewsbury, to Shefnal: saw a great number of furnaces and forges at Ketly, which, with the coal-pits and smoke from numerous steam-engines, made the country appear black for many miles, covering the trees, shrubs, houses, etc., and with the blackness of the people and many fires burning, formed altogether an extraordinary scene. With much diligence we got to Birmingham and staid a little while among our Friends. Went to a house where they were delivering a quart of soup and a half-penny worth of bread to each poor person, for a penny. Friends are the chief supporters of this benevolent institution, from which the London associations took their rise; they brought each of us a little of the soup, which was well relished and good. They serve about one thousand per day: the applicants looked poor but far removed from the filthy, degraded and wretched condition of the poor in Ireland; it did my heart good to see this mode of relief promoted and patronized by Friends. They sell the soup very low, rather than give it, which in great measure prevents those from partaking of it, who would sell it if given gratis, and apply the money to get strong drink. I had a public meeting in the evening, which was very large, the crowd and heat being great, several young women fainted, which occasioned some disturbance. Afterwards the people sat in great quietness, and Friends hoped that the testimony of Truth was owned by many in the meeting not of our religious profession. After meeting, one of the ordained ministers, a man of pious character, endeavored to encourage me, apparently with much sincerity.

"16th. Went through a fertile country, abounding in rich pastures, fine sheep, large cows, etc. Got to Coventry, and it being their meeting-day, we went to it: the house was nearly full, and it appeared to end with solidity. In company with Friends going to the Yearly Meeting, went to Towcester. My mind very low about entering London again, which I had left comfortably, with a hope that it would not be my lot to see it again in this visit, yet could see no other way for me. My friends endeavored to cheer me, as some of them thought when I left it I should not get away peacefully without attending the Yearly Meeting; and I endeavored after resignation. The people knowing it is the time of the Yearly Meeting, look pleasantly on Friends as they pass along the roads, especially the inn-keepers, as Friends have to stop at their houses — they were very obliging, but were hard set to provide all with post-horses.

"18th. Attended the usual morning meeting preceding the Yearly Meeting. Thomas Scattergood appeared in prayer, and also Elizabeth Usher from Ireland; Friends kept their seats a considerable time after she kneeled, not knowing her, for which I was sorry. I stood up, and Friends followed my example; much solemnity appeared to cover the meeting, and it so ended. Dear Deborah Darby, Rebecca Young and myself, agreed to be at the meeting at Wandsworth on First-day, the 20th, and to have an evening meeting at Stockwell.

"20th. The meeting at Wandsworth was large, many of the rich gentry having seats thereabouts were present, and several Friends from London. Deborah Darby and Rebecca Young were favored with living testimonies, and through renewed mercy we were comforted in believing it was a good meeting. The meeting at Stockwell was held in a corn store, which being large and well seated, it was thought that five hundred persons were present, yet great numbers did not get in. The people were quiet, but the ceiling being low and the windows and doors much stopped up by the crowd, it became very warm, yet the company kept very still. After I had relieved my mind, Deborah Darby had a powerful testimony, and the opportunity ended in prayer; the people withdrew in an orderly manner, desiring another meeting." These complimentary notices had little or no weight with him, having in himself the indubitable sense and feeling, that if any good was done it was of the Lord's mercy, to whom alone all praise is due.

"21st. In the meeting for business, much was said by several Friends to keep the members to plainness and simplicity without formality, there being much room for better example in the families of some in high stations.

"23d. A Friend of Lancashire spoke a few words in the ministry, with which I had unity. He was formerly sailing-master of a frigate, in the time of the American war, but was now an acknowledged minister, keeps a school for a livelihood, and he and his wife walked up to the Yearly Meeting, nearly three hundred miles, as did also another minister of Cumberland, who is in the station of a servant — several others walked from fifty to one hundred and fifty miles.

"24th. I thought it my place to go into the women's meeting, which being united with, I was favored to relieve my mind respecting the departures from Gospel simplicity in some of the rich and great. Deborah Darby in much sweetness offered up a solemn prayer. With the great wealth that is among Friends, there are many generous hearts who are disposed to apply it for approved and religious purposes.

"First-day, 27th. Attended an appointed meeting this evening at Islington, which was held in Friends' school and work-house, called Clerkenwell; it was much crowded and oppressively warm, and many out in the yard — the people still and attentive. Deborah Darby was preciously drawn forth in prayer and praises, and through renewed mercy we parted solemnly. Lodged at a Friend's house at Hampstead; the grounds, garden, &c. were in high style, I thought much beyond true simplicity. Being on one side of Hampstead heath, it is a fine, open situation, and seems to combine almost everything this world could afford; and the owner gives a welcome reception to Friends; but more conformity to the simplicity and ways of Truth would have made it still pleasanter to me—his taxes, charities and other expenses, amount to near four thousand pounds sterling, per annum.

"30th. The Yearly Meeting closed, having held thirteen days.

"Sixth month, 1st. Was at the Meeting for Sufferings, wherein Friends were encouraged to keep in remembrance the professors with us in Germany and France. Attended a public meeting at Westminster this evening, in which Deborah Darby was largely engaged, and Rebecca Young also lively and pertinent, and it ended in thanks to Him who is ever worthy.

"First-day, 3d. Was at a public meeting this evening held at the Park meeting-house, which was so crowded that the young people of our Society were requested to go out to give room for others, which many of them did and staid in the yard. Through Divine favor and mercy I was enabled to relieve my mind far beyond my expectation, for I entered the house in great fear. This is often my situation before these large, important meetings, and the prayer of my heart in secret is, 'Lord preserve me from wounding thy holy cause;' and blessed be his name, He has often manifested himself to be strength in weakness and a present helper in the needful time; for which, under a present sense of my own great unworthiness, I desire in the depth of humility to render unto him the praise of his own works.

"4th. For several days past my mind has been much turned to think of the poor prisoners in Newgate; four men and one woman were executed last week, and several more intended for this week. It is truly an afflicting circumstance, that numbers are continually sent out of the world in that way, in this country; many for small crimes. The woman now under sentence, had passed a bank-note of only twenty shillings value, knowing it to be counterfeit; her master gave her an excellent character, except in that one instance, yet no pardon could be obtained. Believing it right to make the attempt, though it was very trying to me again to enter those dismal abodes of the wretched, and having the company of a few Friends, we were readily admitted. Had an interview with a young man of a respectable family, condemned for a species of forgery, though it was believed, by most people, that no fraud was designed. We had a humbling time—such another baptizing season I never remember on a like occasion; he was greatly contrited, and bathed in tears, and his wife being present, was very thankful, and it was with difficulty we retired from this most extraordinary, affecting scene, which I have no language to describe, but trust I shall never forget it: in the midst of judgment, the Lord eminently remembered mercy. The poor man continued calm, and died in reverent hope in the mercy of God through Christ Jesus. Much interest had been made for him, but to no purpose, so sanguinary are the laws of this country. Visited two others, and had a quiet, solid time with them. Oh, when will these legal murders cease? We went out of these abodes of human wretchedness, thankful to our ever gracious Helper, and peaceful in having submitted to such a trying service.

"Sixth month, 6th. Went on board several American ships, but could determine upon nothing respecting taking passage; most of them have guns, or go under protection of armed vessels. The thought of being detained here as a prisoner after my business is over, and the difficulty of procuring a passage, sunk me very low.

"13th. Went to meet with the captain of the William Penn, and to my great disappointment, found all his berths for cabin passengers were engaged, though he had not yet taken in a bale of goods — having set my mind much on going in this ship, I became quite discouraged.

"16th. Was again on board the William Penn, her cabin berths being all engaged, I looked at the steerage, and thought it might be worthy of consideration, whether I should go in that, but determined upon nothing; returned to my lodgings in much heaviness, on account of the difficulties that seem to attend an attempt to return to my beloved home.

"17th. At Devonshire-house meeting, which was large; Christiana Hustler, though very weak in body, had a lively testimony. I proposed a public meeting there at six o'clock in the evening, which I went to in much fear; the people collecting in multitudes, several of high rank, and conducted with stillness and much solidity. I thought it a more laborious meeting than some I had been at in that house, yet it closed with much comfort to my mind in prayer and praises.

"18th. Went again on board the William Penn, and found the captain; there being still room in the steerage, concluded to keep it under consideration. By a letter from Ross, in Ireland, we were informed that all the Friends in that town, of which there are about six families, were preserved from injury in person or property, during the great slaughter and burning lately perpetrated there: the Friend writes, that he could count two hundred and fifty dead bodies at once in the streets, from his own window. It is a special mercy from the Lord, that Friends have been so preserved.

"First-day, 24th. Was at Devonshire-house meeting this afternoon; my mind was led into sympathy with some not of our Society, who were looking for some great thing to be done to convince them of our faith; and I was led forth much more largely into labor than I expected, and hope the Lord was pleased to favor with his help and presence — the opportunity closed solemnly.

"27th. Went in company with three Friends to visit William Wilberforce, to lay before him the distressed state of the people in Ireland, as we had been informed of it by a recent letter from a Friend there. We had a private interview with him, and freely expressed our sentiments, which seemed to give him much satisfaction; then returned to London, having reason to believe our visit would not be wholly lost.

"29th. Visited the school and work-house at Clerkenwell; most Friends speak of the comfort and sweetness they find in attending this institution, which has been abundantly blessed; several who have been educated there have become valuable ministers, and also many are useful and promising young people in Friends' families. On my return to my lodgings, observed a man, who, I believe, was first awakened to religious concern in a meeting at Horsleydown, about a year past, preaching to a great crowd of people in Moorfields: his expression and looks betrayed much wildness, and I was afraid the ardor of his mind would land him in insanity: the people were generally civil. I had much conversation with him; his weakness is an apprehension of great and extraordinary revelations. At first his state of mind was calm and quiet, but by associating with some men of warm imaginations and high opinions of themselves, he seemed now likely to lose even his understanding.

"First-day, Seventh month, 1st. Went to Staines to attend a burial — many people came to the meeting, the greater part of whom were not members of our Society; some of the young people were much affected, and it proved a solid opportunity. Appointed an evening meeting for people of other societies, which was very large, it being thought that as many stood out of the house as were in it. I arose with a concern which the apostle had clearly expressed for me, and I think it best in a general way for ministers to make use of Scripture expressions in their testimonies: the words were these, 'Take heed, brethren, lest there be in any of you an evil heart of unbelief in departing from the living God;' and I was led to speak on the danger of an unbelieving heart. The fore part of the time seemed very laborious, but afterwards, as the Lord opened the way for it, I had to address a different class, and through great condescension it was a season of much brokenness and favor, and the meeting ended in thanksgiving to the everlasting Fountain of all spiritual help. I was afterwards informed there were some at the meeting who held Deistical opinions."

Seventh month, 7th. Being detained by not finding a suitable vessel to take his passage for America, he spent the time in attending meetings and visiting the sick, aged and infirm, yet under much depression at being so long prevented from returning home.

"First-day, 8th. Went to Deptford, where some of the most sober of the people attended the meeting; and though not so large as was expected, it was through mercy a comfortable season. Dined at a young woman's named Jane Jefferys, in company with several Friends. She was convinced of our religious principles about two years since, received into membership and sometimes speaks a few words acceptably in meetings. Her parents being displeased at her change, turned her out of doors; she commenced a little mercer's shop and mending of umbrellas — her business is now increased, and she appears to be blessed for her integrity. A person who had been at our meeting here last year and then accommodated us, sent to know if he should fit up a place for a public meeting in the evening, which being my prospect, he took much pains in putting the place in order. It was a large hop and malt house, and notice being given, though a wet evening, it was supposed that seven or eight hundred attended; were very quiet and well behaved, and through Divine mercy and goodness it proved a tendering, favored opportunity, ending in praises to our ever gracious Helper and Preserver; many appeared thankful for it, and one well-dressed woman with tears, expressed her gladness at having been present.

"10th. Set off for Bristol to seek for a passage, and arrived there about half-past ten o'clock at night, it being one hundred and sixteen miles.

"11th. Went on board a vessel which was small and her accommodations but poor — then to another, but it being uncertain when she would be ready, and also taking guns on board for defence, I could not agree to take passage in her. Visited several Friends, and in the evening had another interview with the man who is before noticed as speaking in Moorfields: he had been convinced in Guernsey, was filled with an opinion that he was called to some great work in this nation, and abounded in visions and revelations. I retired to rest with deep inquiry on my mind, 'Lord, what wouldst thou have me to do in my present situation?' not yet seeing with clearness the ship to return in. Affecting accounts are received from Ireland of the ruin and devastation there, so that it is said many Protestants have abjured their religion to save their lives. Friends have also been required to embrace the Romish religion in some instances, as the insurgents have said there should be but one religion in the country, yet no violence was offered to any member on that account. Two young men, who had latterly appeared under convincement and attended Friends' meetings at times, declaring they could neither take an oath nor deny their faith, suffered death. One who was a member having departed from the testimony of Truth, and associated with others to oppose the insurgents, was killed with all his party, about twenty in number. One innocent young man was shot at behind his master's counter in mistake, being taken for another person. The Quarterly Meeting being held at Enniscorthy the next day but one after the great slaughter and burning of that town, Friends had to remove the dead bodies out of the way of the carriage wheels. The meeting was small but solid, and Friends met with no interruption, which was a great favor from the good hand of Providence, worthy of grateful thanksgiving.

"13th. Attended the week-day meeting at Bristol, which I hope was an instructive one: the expectations of both Friends and others being for a public meeting in the evening, they requested to know if one should be appointed, but I felt nothing sufficient to authorise it. In company with several Friends, I had another opportunity with the man mentioned before, who thinks his call is to all people — refuses to work at his trade, &c.: much tender advice was given to him, but it had little or no effect upon him. Such is the state of those who are so unhappy as to exalt their own imaginations into the seat of revelation, be they ever so inconsistent with Scripture and reason, concluding they are the command of God to them. On this score our Society and others have suffered much.

"14th. Set off to reach London if possible to-night, and with great diligence arrived there about nine o'clock in the evening, said to be on this route one hundred and eighteen or one hundred and twenty miles.

"First-day, 15th. Attended Grace-church street meeting, and at the close believed it my place to appoint an evening meeting, which was much crowded, the people remarkably still, and it was satisfactory; our gracious and heavenly Shepherd, notwithstanding our unworthiness and manifold infirmities, continues to be a present help to those who call upon Him.

"20th. Concluded to take passage in a vessel I had before been on board of at Bristol, though she was not likely to afford such comfortable accommodation as some others which had guns for defence. The kind expressions of care and love for me from my friends, humbled me into tears of gratitude before the Author of every mercy, who had graciously preserved me in unity with my brethren.

"First-day, 22d. Had an appointed meeting at the

Peel, the house became so crowded that the young people were desired to give way to strangers, which they generally did, yet it was said that some hundreds went away for want of room. My mind was much humbled: the people, though greatly crowded, were still, and a solemnity prevailed that made us joyful in the house of prayer and praise, with which the meeting ended, and Friends said they did not remember so orderly a public meeting in that house."

After this he had several religious opportunities both at meetings and in families, there being much unity and attachment manifested by Friends towards him. He took coach on the 26th for Bristol, being accompanied by several of his particular friends, but did not get there until half-past eleven o'clock at night.

"First-day, 29th. My kind friends have manifested great attention and benevolence towards me in several respects. Attended their meeting this forenoon, where I was favored to relieve my mind comfortably, and the meeting appeared to end well. Was at an appointed meeting in the evening which was very large, and I felt my mind strengthened under an apprehension of duty, to show that as God is love, there was an obligation on us as Christians, to endeavor to live in Him, that we might also manifest a living in love with each other. The meeting ended in prayer and praises to the Author of every mercy, for this renewed favor. I was comforted in spirit for the Lord's goodness in granting relief to my mind, as ever since leaving Bristol last, I believed it would be my duty to attempt another meeting of this kind: no doubt with me the Lord hath many sheep in this city, not yet nominally of our fold.

"31st. While in meeting a messenger came in and beckoned me to come out, informing that my passport was come from the duke of Portland, and desired I would immediately go with him to the custom-house, as the controller was waiting beyond his usual hour to grant me liberty to sail for America. My mind not being quite relieved of the meeting, I desired of him a little delay, and returned to the women's meeting, where I had an open, tender parting. Then went to the custom-house and was soon cleared. Many Friends came to my lodgings in the evening, and it pleased our good Master to grant us his presence.

"Eighth month 1st. A number of Friends accompanying, we went to a place about two miles from where the vessel lay, and in an upper room of the inn had a comfortable, religious opportunity. I had in much brokenness to express my thankfulness to my blessed and good Shepherd, who had carried me through a great journey and voyage, and notwithstanding my many infirmities, had granted me now in the close a portion of sweet peace, which was not of merit but of his own mere mercy; and it closed in prayer and praises to Him who is ever worthy: we then parted with many tears.

"Getting on board we soon set sail, but our captain

not liking to go to sea that night, we dropped anchor under the shore of Wales.

"6th. After a rough passage, got into the cove of Cork, and dropped anchor; I took boat and went on shore, then in a post-chaise to Cork, and next day attended their usual week-day meeting.

"8th. Returned to the vessel. Cove* is a poor, dirty town, and may contain three hundred houses, the greater part of which are very mean; the inhabitants depend upon the shipping for a livelihood, and provisions are very low, except when the fleet comes in; butcher's meat from three to four pence per pound; poultry, fish, potatoes, &c., in like proportion.

"12th. Went to Passage in our boat, then took horse and got to Cork to their meeting, which was pretty large, and I hope a profitable one.

"14th. Was at their usual meeting, and after dinner took boat for the vessel, it not being prudent to stay long on shore, as the sailing of the fleet was daily expected. In our passage in the boat it rained much, and night coming on it was very dark and boisterous; we searched long from one vessel to another, but could not find ours, and being as wet as we could be, determined to go to land, as it was dangerous staying on the water much longer. This was a miserable alternative to go to a town with so little hope of getting a lodging, but we providentially landed safely, though not without danger, and the lads belonging to the boat, after much inquiry found me a bed, the people lent me a few dry clothes while mine were put to dry, and with a little refreshment I went to sleep, and on the 15th got on board the ship again.

"First-day, 19th. Went on shore again and attended their afternoon meeting, and also a burial, at which was a great concourse of people, and I had some religious service, which appeared to be a time of favor and comfort to the relatives of the deceased.

"First-day, 26th. Went to Cork, attended their meeting, and appointed a public meeting for the evening, it having been on my mind since my first landing; it was large, and several Friends with myself thought the Lord favored us with his presence.

"27th. Was very desirous to get to the ship, and procured a horse and proceeded to Cove, but no boatman would go to the vessel, as the wind was high and it rained very hard: I was therefore obliged to stay at an uncomfortable house that night.

"Eighth month, 30th. Very uneasy at our detention; went to Cork, and attended the meeting, which was chiefly in silence, but a time of comfort.

"31st. The ship of war fired a gun about six o'clock in the morning to put to sea. Our captain being on shore, we were among the hindermost in getting off; and coming on board in great haste, brought no fresh provisions except a few pounds of beef. About ten o'clock all the ships were under sail, said to be ninety-six. Several Friends came off in a boat and brought us a number of fine vegetables, &c. We had a religious sitting together and parted most affectionately, not expecting to meet again on these shores. The wind becoming unfavorable we had to return, which damped our spirits much, but there seemed no other alternative than to anchor again at Cove, yet under this great disappointment we endeavored to encourage each other in resignation.

"First-day, Ninth month 2nd. Held a meeting in the cabin, the captain and passengers were present, and we were favored with a solid, comforting season.

"8th. A signal being given for the fleet to get under weigh, all the harbor seemed to resound with acclamations of joy, and by the middle of the afternoon we were in the centre of the fleet off the old head of Kinsale, and next morning out of sight of land.

"12th. The sea and wind having for two days been very high, the waves frequently dashing over the vessel and pouring down the cabin stairs, our dead-lights were put in, the cabin-doors closed, and our situation became truly gloomy — a great part of our live stock was destroyed. Our captain and mate are very vigilant and proved themselves masters in the science of navigation. The helm being lashed we lay to for some hours, and such an awful scene I had never before been in at sea; the fleet was so scattered we could see but eight or ten ships. I kept my berth the greater part of the day — our situation called for resignation and confidence in Him whom the winds and sea obey, and I was thankful for the portion that was mercifully granted me, yet was desirous, if consistent with his will, to see my beloved connexions and friends at home.

"13th. The storm had considerably abated, the sea gradually subsided, and the wind though light was fair; we passed the day in some degree of ease and went to bed in thankful acknowledgment, that 'the winds which blew at heaven's command, at heaven's command were still.' Found we had for two or three days been off the bay of Biscay, a place of much danger with respect to the French.

"15th. Saw no vessels and supposed we were separated from the fleet, but in the afternoon some of them came in sight. I was only desirous of having company on account of our vessel being leaky, and by no means fit to put to sea alone, and also an apprehension that we should be short of provisions and water if the passage proved tedious. I never wished to have any other protection from an enemy than the arm of a gracious Providence.

"First-day, 16th. The weather being fine, the captain, all the passengers and some of the crew, sat down with us at meeting in the cabin, which proved a time of profitable reflection on the Lord's goodness in preserving us through the late storm. We were for some time made uneasy by an apprehension that our captain had an intention of leaving the fleet, and considering the state of our vessel were obliged to remonstrate with him, and though he assured us he would find the fleet, yet we were not without suspicions that he did not desire to join it.

"22nd. Had entirely lost sight of it. After seeking it for two days past, a general dissatisfaction appeared both among the seamen and passengers, several of the former having been prisoners with the French; for my own part, the only desire I had of continuing with the fleet, arose from an apprehension of more safety as respected our continual leaking.

"First-day, 23d. Held our meeting as usual, and had cause to believe we were owned by the holy Head of the church.

"27th. Early in the morning the captain came to my room and informed me there was a ship in sight, but he could not yet discover whether it was an enemy or not: as she was bearing towards us the passengers and seamen were in alarm, some securing their most valuable things, putting on their best clothes, &c.: the captain also endeavoring to appear to the best advantage. I sat down quietly waiting the issue; the prevalent opinion among our people was, that she was a Frenchman, and our seamen seemed confident that she was. This suspense and fear lasted more than an hour: I was preserved from fear or disturbance, and said I was under no great apprehension of danger. When they came up they ordered us to lay to till they came on board, which they did, being armed, no hats but handkerchiefs tied round their heads, with strong appearances of being neither Americans nor Englishmen; all our people seemed in consternation and dismay, but when their captain boarded us and shook hands with ours, all countenances brightened again, yet with a mixture of fear and doubt. The captain of the stranger said he knew me, had seen me in France, and was pleased to meet me again as a friend — they spent an hour with us in a social manner, informed us that the ship was the Camilla, a letter of marque from Boston for Malaga, had fourteen guns and thirty-five men; and ordering his men into the shrouds, they gave us three cheers, fired a gun and parted from us. By the papers they left us, I found that the yellow fever was prevailing in several towns and cities, and that the deaths in my dear native city had amounted to between thirty and forty per day, for three days the week previous, which depressed my spirits much. O Philadelphia! Philadelphia! thou whom the Lord has known and favored above all the cities I have ever seen, is there not a cause why thou shouldst so repeatedly be made to read the roll written within and without, with mourning, lamentation and woe? Doubtless there is, or thy God would still have preserved the walls of salvation around thee, and thy gates would have resounded with anthems of praise.

"My companions in the ship seemed unusually happy all day after our escape, but the situation of my dear and tender connexions and friends at home, now in distress, lay so near my heart, that I retired to my room very heavy.

"First-day, 30th. Held meeting as usual, and was sensible of the necessity of rendering praise unto God for the favors received, and endeavoring to walk more worthy of them, lest He should withdraw them from us; his mercies are indeed new every morning.

"Tenth month, 1st. High wind and rain, the cabin

close shut up, and the passengers in the steerage were kept down all day.

"4th. Being on the banks of Newfoundland, we took plenty of fine fish, to the joy of the ship's company.

"First-day, 7th. The wind being high, the ship rolling and tossing so much, and several of the passengers not well, it did not appear practicable to hold a meeting, but we got the children and lads to read each a chapter in the Bible.

"First-day, 14th. Held our meeting, and being now in sight of land, the people on board were not so settled as could be wished, but it ended better than I expected. Our leak, which was the cause of so much serious uneasiness, was not so now, and the consideration of again beholding my native land, frequently filled my heart with gratitude, gladness and thankfulness to the Author of every mercy. But alas! how short-lived are our times of rejoicing in this ever-changing scene. A pilot came on board and informed that the yellow fever was raging in New York, and with still greater violence in my endeared Philadelphia, which struck me with sadness. It being almost a perfect calm, we made very little way for several days — found that several vessels of the fleet that sailed when we did, had arrived at New York about a week since.

"18th. Were near the desired port."

Note.— On p. 233, William Savery mentions, that while he and his companions were at Berlin, they were visited several times by a Major Marconnay, who had been an officer of some distinction under the king of Prussia; and appeared to be con-

He landed at New York, soon proceeded towards Philadelphia, and finding his wife and family had retired a few miles out of the city, on account of the

vinced of the truths of the Gospel, promulgated by those disinterested and faithful ministers of Christ. On page 243, under date of Tenth month, 30th, 1796, he alludes to a letter which they received at Pyrmont, written by this person, expressive of his satisfaction with their visit to Berlin. Since the Journal was in type the Editors have obtained a copy of this letter, and apprehending it will be acceptable to their readers, they have inserted it below. It furnishes evidence of a mind, in which the work of regeneration was carrying on, struggling under religious concern, and longing for a more full participation of that glorious liberty which is the privilege of the sons of God. It is delightful to observe how congenial minds, under the forming power of Divine grace, harmonize with each other in the unity of the one spirit wherever they meet, or however previously unknown. Outward distinctions, whether of station, country, or profession, seem to melt away and become lost, in the aboundings of that love which flows in their hearts as children of one heavenly Father, and objects of the compassion and mercy of the same Redeemer and Saviour. It is no less remarkable, that in proportion as the heart-changing power of the Spirit of Truth is submitted to, and the blessed realities of religion experienced, the soul becomes increasingly sensible of the emptiness and unsatisfying nature of outward forms and ceremonies, and longs to partake more largely of the living substance. The letter also serves to show the feelings of affection and fellowship, excited in the minds of some they met with, in the course of their laborious and painful journey; and that though their speech and their preaching was not in the words which man's wisdom teacheth, yet under the powerful influence of the Holy Spirit which accompanied, it was instrumental in awakening not a few to a serious consideration of the things which belong to their soul's peace.

awful prevalence of the pestilential disease which then had become very mortal, he got to them as early as practicable. When the sickness and mortality had

---

A Translated Copy of a Letter from Major Marconnay to William Savery, David Sands, &c.

"My last words to you, dear brethren, were 'God be with you'—words that came from the fulness of my heart. I love you with my soul. I was never so soon inclined to unite with any men as I was to unite with you; and never felt so soon a constraint to open my mind to any as I did to you. I have opened this heart of mine into your loving souls; but yet you are not wholly acquainted with my tried situation; for there are feelings which cannot be expressed in words—I seem as if I was forsaken of God, and yet I abhor this thought. I have no desire to live or to die—for the pleasures of the world, let them be what they may, I have neither taste, sense, nor feeling; but who will believe, that notwithstanding this disgust of the world, my heart remains shut up from higher and heavenly enjoyments. The precious sense of the sonship with God; the assurance of faith, and the consolations of the word; of all that I formerly enjoyed, tasted and felt of these gracious gifts, I have now scarcely a remembrance.—My prayers are weak and powerless, as if I cried unto God from afar, so that he cannot hear me. This is also a thought I abhor. Such, my dear brethren, is nearly the circumstances of my soul: let your hearts now feel with painful compassion, how it is with me; and fall down on your faces before the throne of the great and merciful Being, and pray for your poor weak and wounded brother, that Jesus Christ may again be formed in my heart, and that I may again rightly fix my eyes upon him;—then shall I be able to stand in this heavy exercise.—I shall then take from his hand the bitter cup and not murmur, but wait for his help—then I shall be enabled in the end to exclaim, 'Lord, Lord God, gracious and merciful, thou art great in thy kind-

subsided he returned to Philadelphia, and as usual was industriously engaged in his mechanical business, as well as in visiting the sick and infirm, and in the dili-

---

ness and faithfulness; —who was ever confounded that put his trust and hope in thee?'

"Yesterday, the minister, Howick, sent for me, and said he had just received a letter from the king, who was very willing and ready to give you an audience; and oh! how gladly could I have called you back, as I wished most heartily an interview between you and our good king. I told the minister, it was possible you might have staid over yesterday, the 21st, at Potsdam; on which he immediately despatched a chasseur to the General Bishosswerd, notifying him that you might probably still be there; whether the chasseur has met with you, I know not; but if it be according to my wishes, you will have an audience with the king to-morrow at nine o'clock. And in this case, I desire you to give me as soon as possible, a circumstantial information of your conference; for be persuaded, I thall not make any bad use of what you may intrust me with. Your letter to the king, the minister sent to him yesterday; but the books, which the messenger could not take, were sent to the monarch to-day.

"Now for the conclusion: 'God be with you'— his light be your guide; his love and grace, in and through Jesus Christ, your protection and defence in all danger: be of good comfort, and filled with joyful hope.— He that is with you, is stronger than he that is against you.

"Never shall your memory be effaced from my soul: I shall not cease to love you; it will be a comfort to my weary soul, if sometimes you will make me joyful by imparting a few lines of love, and nothing but death will be able to prevent my answering your letters. In love I embrace you in my heart, as your ever-loving brother,

"Marconnay.

"*Berlin, 22nd October,* 1796."

gent attendance of religious meetings. His tender, sympathizing mind, not being easy without endeavoring as far as in his power, to alleviate the afflictions of his fellow-citizens, occasioned him to be frequently in the abodes of suffering and misery. As the yellow fever had for several years visited the city, and he was much within the sphere of its virulence, he thought it most prudent to be very sparing in the use of animal food, and almost totally abstained from it, which some of his friends believed tended to weaken his frame, and rendered the system more accessible to other disorders.

From an apprehension of religious duty, he attended the Yearly Meeting of New York in the year 1800, having the full concurrence of his Monthly Meeting in the service, and on his return home produced a minute expressive of the satisfaction of Friends with his company and Gospel services among them. In the Ninth month, 1801, under similar feelings and with the unity of his brethren, he attended the Yearly Meeting in Baltimore, where his labors of love appear to have been cordial and encouraging to Friends.

Excepting these engagements, it does not appear that he travelled much after his return from Europe, but was diligent in the discharge of his weighty trust as a minister of the Gospel of Christ.

His constitution having become much impaired, indications of dropsical disease appeared; he however continued to attend meetings, and to visit the sick and afflicted.

In the Third month, 1804, he was confined to the house, except occasionally riding for the benefit of exercise and change of air. During the course of his sickness he was supported in resignation to the Divine will, and notwithstanding his abundant labors in the service of his Lord and Master, was led to take a very humbling view of himself, as an unprofitable servant, having nothing to depend on but the long suffering and goodness of God — observing, "I thought I was once strong for the work, but now I am a child brought back to my hornbook, and have nothing to trust to but the mercy of God through Christ my Saviour." He had been remarkable for his firm and unshaken belief in the divinity of our Lord and Saviour, Jesus Christ, in his propitiatory sacrifice for the sins of the world, and in all his glorious offices for the salvation of mankind, being often fervently engaged in setting forth these blessed Gospel doctrines and enforcing them on his hearers; and in the solemn moments of disease and death, his reverent dependence and hope in his Saviour did not fail him, but proved as an anchor to his soul. And a short time before his death, under a sense and feeling immediately imparted, he expressed "glory to God," and continued in great composure of mind, until the 19th day of the Sixth month, 1804, when he calmly resigned his spirit into the hands of Him who gave it.

INDEX.

A.

B.

C.

D.

I.

J.

K.

L.

M.

N.

O.

P.

Q.

R.

S.

41

W.

THE END.

www.ingramcontent.com/pod-product-compliance
Lightning Source LLC
LaVergne TN
LVHW020922110826
845150LV00004B/743

* 9 7 8 1 4 2 5 5 5 5 3 1 3 *